MW00324431

Give Him Time

Charles G. Fuller

CROSS BOOKS

CrossBooks™
1663 Liberty Drive
Bloomington, IN 47403
www.crossbooks.com
Phone: 1-866-879-0502

First published by CrossBooks 11/30/2009

ISBN: 978-1-6150-7081-7

Library Congress of Control Number: 2009942389

Printed in the United States of America
Bloomington, Indiana

This book is printed on acid-free paper.

Acknowledgements

To my sister in Christ, Nancy Prillaman who manages the broadcast and reproduction ministries of God's Time, Inc., and who has encouraged me to extend my calling beyond the days of my pastorate.

To my wife, Carol, who has made this book a reality through her devotion to the project, researching and compiling hundreds of scripts written for broadcasts years ago and giving them new life in book form today.

To the thousands of listeners and viewers of "God's Minute" who for nearly 30 years were a daily congregation and multiplication for this pastor's outreach with the Gospel.

CGF

Happy New Life

❧

Have you noticed how difficult it is to always remember we are in a new year during its first week or so? Time and again our wastebaskets testify to the number of occasions we misdate letters, checks and memoranda during early January. A year's habit is stubborn to acknowledge that a change has taken place. Stubborn acknowledgement notwithstanding, the change is real... nothing can alter the fact that the old has been done away! The spiritual parallel is so obvious. I hesitate to say more, but it may be profitable for me to "write aloud" what we already know to be so. When Christ took up His residence in us, at our conversion, something factually exciting took place. "Therefore if any man be in Christ, he is a new creature; old things are passed away; behold all things are become new." (II Corinthians 5:17) There it is... a statement of fact... We have a new nature. It is not enough however, to remain in eternal status. We are to live in the appropriation of this sacred fact. There is real Christian pragmatism in the recognition that we do no have to serve sin any longer, for we now have the nature to fulfill the Desires of God. "Likewise reckon ye also yourselves to be dead indeed unto sin, but alive unto God through Jesus Christ our Lord. Let not sin therefore reign in your mortal body, that ye should obey it in the lusts thereof. Neither yield ye your members as instruments of unrighteousness unto sin: but yield yourselves unto God, as those that are alive from the dead and your members as instruments of righteousness unto God." (Romans 6: 11 – 13) Happy New Life, Christian!

Read II Corinthians 6: 1 - 10

More than a year is new, we are new with Jesus as our Savior. Thank you Eternal Father for giving us eternal life, to be lived here and now.

❧

I once attended a meeting in a seacoast city and stayed in a motel located on the beach. There is something fascinating about watching the ocean and there is something appealing about going to sleep while listening to the sounds of the surf. One night during my stay at the seaside motel, I fell asleep to the rhythmic sounds of the sea. When I awakened the next morning, the first sound I heard was the ocean crashing its waves against the beach. I thought, "You know, that ocean has been running all night!" Some things are always constant. They never cease. They will be there whenever and wherever you are. God is like that. He is everlasting and His Son is changeless too. The Bible speaks of "Jesus Christ, the same yesterday, today and forever". In a changing world, we need a changeless God at the controls of life. Does He control yours?

Read: Psalm 90

"Heavenly Father, thank you for being who you are and all you are, all of the time. Stabilize me today with your reliability."

A group of Brownie Scouts was meeting with their scout leader who asked what they had done the previous week to be a help in their homes. One said she had helped make beds, another that she had dried the dished each evening after supper and another said she had run some errands. But one young Brownie had an unusual report about the help she had been at home. She said, "I did just like Mother and Dad told me.... I stayed out of their way!" Well, needless to say, the little girl slightly misunderstood her parents' instruction, but her idea prompts the realization that Jesus has given us exactly the opposite instruction. He said, "I am the way the truth and the life; no man comes to the Father but by me." (John 14:6) He <u>wants</u> us in His way!

Read: Matthew 7: 13 - 27

Thank you, Oh God, for making a way for us to come to you. Keep me mindful that the way we come to you is always the same, whether it be for salvation, for forgiveness, for prayer, or for assurance; it's the Jesus way.

One of the great devotional book writers was an Englishman by the name of Oswald Chambers. Speaking of her husband, Mrs., Chambers said that people were constantly seeking opportunities for conferences with her husband in order to pour out their troubles and secure valuable advice. Mrs. Chambers remembered a woman who cornered Dr. Chambers following a service where he had been preaching. Mrs. Chambers said she just resigned herself to a long wait until the conference was over, but to her amazement, her husband finished his conference in short order. When asked how he did it, Dr. Chambers told his wife, "I just asked the lady if she had ever told God about her problems. When she said she had not, I told her to go home and do that first and that she probably would not need to see me at all." Are you troubled and heavy-hearted? Consider the Lord's words, "… Let not your heart be troubled neither let it be afraid." (John 14:27) Then tell Him what is on your mind.

Read: Philippians 4: 4 - 7

Heavenly Father, today I want to take you at your word and I want to take your word seriously. You have provided a peace which exceeds explanation so I want to leave my concerns in your hands in exchange for peace from your hands.

Complaints

A pastor who is well known among many Christian people used to have a unique way of handling complaints and gossip among those who came to him bearing such tales. He would take out what he called his "complaint book", tell the complainant to slowly make his criticism while he wrote it all down. Then after the pastor had written down the choice morsel of criticism he would turn the book around toward the complainant and say, "Now you sign this and as soon as I have time, I will discuss these matters with the person involved!" The pastor said in 40 years had had made hundreds of entries in his book but he had never had anyone sign a complaint. That is why the Bible says, "If a man be overtaken in a fault, restore him, you who are spiritual restore such a one in the spirit of meekness; considering yourself, lest you also be tempted." (Galatians 6:1)

Read: Galatians 6: 2 - 10

Lord, thank you for your patience with me and for your forgiveness of my failures. I am all too ready to find fault in others when I so easily serve my own sinful nature. Deliver me, I pray from my readiness to be more a critic than a healer.

Years ago, the comedian Dick Van Dyke, wrote a book called, <u>Hope and Hilarity</u>. In the book he relates some of the innocent but penetrating things children say about God. He tells of a mother trying to comfort her little girl whose pet had been run over. The mother said, "Just think dear, our little pet is in heaven with God." The child, seemingly much more ready to deal with reality than her mother said, "But Mommy, what does God want with a dead cat? How ready to deal with reality are you today? Is your life really a happy one? And when life is over for you, what then? The Bible says that Jesus came centuries ago to give people both everlasting and abundant life. Do you have that kind of life? It is available from the only one who can give it to you. If you have Jesus in your heart you have the resource for abundance! We really are facing reality when we live like someone surrounded with eternal abundance.

Read: Philippians 4: 12 - 19

Lord, forgive me for my selfishness. I so often mistake my wants for my needs. You know exactly what I need and I trust you to supply it.

❧

Do you have the same problem I do during the first few days of a new year? Time and again, I will date checks and letters, automatically, just as I have for the better part of the twelve preceding months. I will catch myself, in this force of habit, and think, "But it just doesn't feel like a new year". Whether it seems like one or not, the year is a new one. Sometimes, Christians have to be reminded of a similar truth about themselves. Because Jesus Christ has been invited into our lives, we are new persons.... new born.... living in the privilege of a newness of life. Of course, we do not always feel like new people, but we are new creations in Christ Jesus, whether we feel like it or not. Perhaps this is a good time to underscore some truths about the nature of our salvation: Salvation is predicated upon what God has accomplished, not upon how we feel at a given moment. Salvation is not fully realized in our daily living until it is lived out on a daily basis. Salvation can become increasingly fresh or increasingly commonplace according to how significant our relationship to Christ is day by day. But in time, they will have no more newness than that which we claim from it, living one new day at a time. I suppose that truth is what gives real dimensions to Biblical admonitions like: "This is the day the Lord has made, we will rejoice and be glad in it." (Psalm 118:24)

Read: Romans 6: 3 - 6

Father God, I can't really trust my feelings, but I can trust your Word. You tell me with Jesus as my Savior I don't have to feel new only realize I am new. Help me to live "new" today.

Be All You Can Be

❧

Recently, I was in an air terminal, waiting to make a flight connection, so I did as many air travelers, I picked up a newspaper to read. Being a daily newspaper for a huge city, it had page after page of want ads. One such want ad captured my attention. Its caption read: "Be All You Can Be." The advertisement went on then to assure the reader he would be all that he could be by simply coming to work for the firm doing the advertising. God sent Jesus to the world to make it possible for people to be all they could be. The Bible says plainly the reason Jesus came was that we might have eternal life in heaven and abundant life on earth. For all of our own effort, we can ever become all that Christ can make us if we will let Him. Let Christ make you all you can be and let Him do it...today.

Read: Jeremiah 29: 11 - 13

Gracious Lord, you have already done more for me than I could possibly realize. And to think you have still more in mind for me defies imagination. I don't want to settle for less than what you have in store. Lord, increase my faith.

Tuning The Keys

❧

I am no musician, but I understand that a piano gets out of tune by hard use, among other things. The constant striking of the keys, which in turn, strike the strings, causes the loosening of those strings. So from time to time, the strings need adjusting if they are to produce good sounds. By the same token, common everyday experiences have a way of pounding upon us until they have an exhausting effect. We can become so accustomed to the discordant sounds of repeated sin that we lose our ear for godliness. The forfeiture of a consistent prayer life can take from us a sense of something missing. That's why we need the tuning and adjusting which a daily quiet time with God can provide. Do you pray every day? The Bible says, "In quietness and confidence is your strength." Get alone with God today and get your heartstrings tuned up!

Read: Isaiah 30: 12 - 15

Heavenly Father, Satan wants so much to keep us apart. Keep me alert to his tactics and distractions. I ask for your constant reminder to find time and a place to alone with you.

The Lesson of a Broken Window

The Bible says that if a person commits one sin he breaks the whole law of God. But how can that be? How can one lie or one theft destroy the whole of God's law? Well…if someone threw a rock at a windowpane, the rock would actually strike the glass in only one specific spot, but, tell me, what would happen to the whole widow pane? Of course, the pane would be broken, even though the rock struck it in but one place. The point is that we cannot minimize our need of God's forgiveness by minimizing our sins. Nor can we reduce our guilt by comparing the severity of one sin to the severity of another. A Holy God cannot countenance any sin regardless how minor we may think it is. All of us have broken God's law and in doing so have broken God's heart. Nevertheless, He wants to forgive us and we need for Him to do it.

Read: Romans 3: 10 - 23

Holy and gracious God, I come to you with an honest attempt to see the sin in my life as you see it. I want my confession and repentance to heal the brokenness of your heart.

The Want-Ad

In one of the daily newspapers of a large city there can be seen this advertisement in the want-ad section: "Wanted: A man who has made a mess out of life." Our first response is to wonder what business could possibly be interested in seeking people who could qualify. That ad is placed in the paper by one of the downtown Gospel missions and is just another way of saying what Jesus said many years ago. He said, "I came not to call the righteous but sinners to repentance." (Mark 2:17) What He meant is obvious. People who are oversold on their goodness…. the "holier-than-thous", do not see any need for Christ to help them. So Jesus can help only those who see their need for Him. We don't have to search our own hearts very much to discover our need for Jesus. We need Him as Savior. We need Him as Lord. We need Him as Comforter. We need Him as the Friend He offers to be. An old hymn favorite says it well, "I need Thee, Oh I need Thee, every hour I need Thee, Oh bless me now my Savior, I come to Thee."

Read: John 6:35 - 40

I need you every day, Lord, but I come to you with today's sins, needing forgiveness. I come to you with today's anxieties, needing your peace. I come to you with today's blessings, needing to give you thanks.

Unescapable Responsibility

❧

Many years ago a very effective evangelist did something which captured the undivided attention of his audience. He began his sermon on that evening by leaning over the pulpit and in a confidential tone, saying, "I have a question to ask. I cannot answer it. You cannot answer it. Satan cannot answer it. Even an angel from heaven cannot answer it. Every eye was fixed on the preacher by then and he said, "The question is one written in the Bible. It asks, 'How shall we escape if we neglect so great a salvation'?" (Hebrews 2:3) Quite obviously there is no answer to that question because there is no way to escape the responsibility of ignoring God's offer of forgiveness through Christ. Neither can Christians avoid the responsibility of sharing Christ with those who don't know Him. In fact, that is the first application of this verse of Scripture. Indeed, if God's Word is always true and if every act of disobedience against God is a matter of record, what gives Believers the idea that our neglect to share Jesus with the world around us is not judged irresponsible behavior? To forfeit our opportunity to introduce friends and family to Jesus is not only to neglect their salvation; it is to neglect our own.

Read: Matthew 9: 35 - 38

Lord, you do not save us so we can keep it all to ourselves. To take stock of our lives, however, could give the impression that salvation is for private consumption. To be sure, salvation is personal but it is not private. So lead me to someone today with whom I can share Jesus, personally not privately.

❧

Hope is a refreshing word in a world like ours. With each day, however, it seems there is a new outbreak of war, or there is rioting in the streets, or there are new threats of missile firings, leaving us all too little foundation for much hope. "Disarm the race," shout some advisors. Yet the nearest fistfight reveals that man's problem is not a trigger but his trigger-finger. Peter, in the Spirit, admonishes: "… be ready always to give an answer to every man that asketh you a reason for the hope that is in you…" (I Peter 3:15) We do have hope for humanity and our planet, but it is a hope which exceeds the promises of treaties or truces, of political campaigns or elections. Our hope is for the birth of man into a new being. People can be changed from the inside out, and when they are, their world changes as the result. Oversimplified? I think not. Christ Himself is the reason for the hope that is in us. And since it is true, we must not reflect the despair of the hopeless as if we were one of them… nor hold our peace about who is our Hope. We know that we can live without food for longer than we imagine. Without water we can live only a few days. There are times in live, however, wherein we cannot live another moment without hope. Someone you know may be just that desperate and you are their link to Jesus Christ, their hope.

Read: Romans 5: 1 - 5

Father, I have been moved by pictures of starving people living in squalor. I have contributed to world hunger causes and I should do it again. Today, awaken me to those who hunger and thirst for hope. Lead me to someone with whom I can share the hope I have in Christ.

New Wine

❧

"Neither do men put new wine into old bottles; else the bottles break and the wine runs out and the bottles perish: but they put new wine into new bottles and both are preserved." (Matthew 9:17) Our Lord spoke these graphic words to His disciples; making plain the danger of putting His doctrine into the old, corrupt system of the Pharisees. In the ancient world, bottles were frequently made of sheep or goatskins. After long use, however, these containers would become brittle and easily ruptured. When new wine was put into an old wineskin, it would, by pressures of fermentation, often cause the skin to swell and burst. New wine was meant for new wineskins. We have lived our way into a new year and this is a time for thoughts about newness. However, to surround new intentions and new motivations with old patterns and old perspectives is to create a rupture through which all newness is lost. What we have left is just another old wineskin, which will eventually be so beyond repair, little hope of containing newness will remain. If some of us have hope about a fresh life in Christ, we will have to discard some of the old wineskins of self-satisfaction, inflexibility and sameness. If we intend to renew our faithfulness in matters such as church attendance, prayer habits and unselfish giving, we will have to rid ourselves of some old wineskins of divided loyalties and indulgences. New wine is for new wineskins. New commitments are for new years.

Read: Luke 5: 36 - 39

Your commandments are not new, Lord, but my commitments to you are frequently in need of being renewed. Forgive me for trying to keep your truth and your Spirit inside old attitudes and unrepented sins. Like David of old said, "Create in me a clean heart Oh God and renew a right spirit within me." (Psalm 51: 10)

Each winter most of us are looking for a change in the weather. It will be good to hear the birds sing and see the buds appear in a couple of months, signaling that change of seasons we call spring. That change in the weather usually prompts other changes; changes in perspective, appearances and motivations. Change can be good, good for you and good for those around you. But change can also spawn some less desirable results. All too often a change of address or a relocation of family will change that family's level of involvement in their church. There are parents who throughout their children's early years seldom missed a church service and they were among the most faithful believers. When the children left home for college, or work, or they married, the pattern of the parent's church attendance and the level of their church involvement declined. To be sure, there are some understandable changes in the patterns we take in our Christian lives. One's health picture can have a marked effect as can the health of one for whom we may be responsible. Work schedules and the limitations of age can have an accountable effect upon our Christian activity. It's the change in our zeal, our desires, our faithfulness, our sense of responsibility, our love for the Lord that we need to set our defenses against. Any change of the heart ought to be a good one and for all the right reasons.

Read: Hebrews 12: 1 – 3

Praise you, Oh God, for your eternal stability. Nothing can change you and I live in that assurance. But Lord, it is my changeability that concerns me. I pray that you can change me as I need it, but stabilize me in the face of a fickle and changeable world.

A Point of No Return

If you have traveled very much on interstate highways you are familiar with the dilemma of having missed a strategic turn and being unable to do anything about it until you come to the next exit. As you know, there are no "U" turns allowed on such highways and there are exits provided only every so many miles. It makes for a helpless, frustrated feeling to continue driving along an interstate, knowing you are traveling the wrong direction, but caught in consequences of your own error. The Bible says just such a condition prevails in someone who repeatedly refuses to invite Christ into his life or a Christian refuses the Lordship of Christ. That error of decision can be made so long that one becomes hardened to it. We are confronted with the truth of Hebrews 4:7, "He again fixes a certain day, 'Today,' saying through David after so long a time just has been said before. Today if you hear His voice, do not harden your hearts."

Read: Joel 2:12-17

Today, Lord, I am praying for friends and loved ones who have so long refused Jesus as Savior. I pray there is still time for them. I pray for the tenderizing of their hearts. And I pray that my habits and insensitivity will not stand in the way of what you still want to accomplish in me.

Not Birth but Rebirth

۶⸲

The oldest man in the world died at the reported age of 168. The mountaineer, named Shirali Mislimov, living in a Caucasus village all his life, never had a birth registration, but Russian scientists have estimated his age by various and sundry tests. In any event, the white-bearded gentleman from the Russian mountains was very, very old. Upon reading of the aged man, I was almost immediately struck with the thought: In all of his long, long life did he hear the exciting news of personal salvation through Christ Jesus? Long life and good health are blessings indeed, but of what significance is 168 years if they are coupled with an eternity apart from God? Then my thinking drew closer home than the Caucasus Mountains in the south of Russia. I began thinking of young people growing older and elderly people becoming more elderly who live within our reach and I wondered how many of them have actually heard the exciting news of personal salvation through Christ. How easy it is for us to presume that people who live in the presence of church steeples all their lives are "reached" by the process of familiarity. We can look about us on Sunday mornings and become impressed enough by the sight of a large congregation that we credit ourselves with "reaching" a city for Christ. The fact of the matter is that probably more than two-thirds of our community is not to be found in anyone's church on a given Sunday. That is to say nothing about the spiritual condition of those sitting in the pews. Not all those yet to be introduced to Christ live in places like the mountains in the south of Russia.

Read: Acts 1: 6 – 9

It is abundantly clear Father, that we have been given the opportunity and the authority to tell as much of the world about you as we can. Just keep me reminded of those parts of my world who work where I do and live in my neighborhood.

How Great is Great?

❧

We can live in the midst of greatness so long that we lose our perspective of greatness. Nuclear explosives are all tremendous to the scientific layman, but weapons researchers talk of "smaller" and "larger" megaton bombs. Professional footballers talk of "big" men but their "average" man is nigh a giant to most. Christians speak of the Great Commission but even its greatness has become all too commonplace. Jesus said for us to go to "all the world." Have we calculated the measure of "all the world"? That phrase has its geographic implications, yes, but also it possesses humanitarian implications. We are to go with the Gospel, to all nations and into every area of life. But familiarity has knocked the edge of magnitude off of still another aspect of the Great Commission. "Go," Jesus said, but to go into all areas where there is life and to all areas of life requires some considerable going! Every means must be utilized if we go that far and that deeply. The outreach of television is startling, provided one is interested in reaching the hearts of people with the heart of the Gospel. Communication in daily conversation, however, is probably the greatest, most available means for any Christian to flesh out the Great Commission. When someone is sharing the Gospel he is not engaged in "small" talk!

Read: I Corinthians 10: 16 - 23

You are great Oh Lord. Greatness begins and ends with you. Forgive me for being so impressed with earth side greatness that I forget how pale it is compared with the greatness of God. Help me realize that words of worship and words of the Gospel are the greatest words that leave my mouth.

Ready for the Unexpected

❧

I am writing these lines at 29,000 feet. It seems so much of what I do these days is done while flying from place to place. There's a lot to be learned about life in airplanes and airports. For instance, as we reached cruising altitude a while ago, the captain announced over the public address system, "Ladies and gentlemen, I have just turned off the 'Fasten Seat Belt' sign so you can move about the cabin. However, when you are in your seat, we ask that you do what we do here in the flight deck, keep your belt fastened in case we encounter some unexpected turbulence." There's a lot of that in life, isn't there? In fact, there's more of the unexpected variety than the kind you anticipate. That's reason enough to approach life like an airline passenger with a fastened seatbelt. What is it the Bible says? "Pray without ceasing." That hardly means we are to spend each waking and sleeping moment assembling words of prayer. If I understand the passage properly, it means that we are to always be in a spirit, a frame of mind, for prayer. I suppose you could say we are admonished to maintain an attitude, which could break out in prayer most any time. If we talk to the Lord often and keep a continuing spirit which is not a stranger to prayer, then we will be much more ready for that unexpected turbulence to which we are always subject. Hopefully, for you "rough air" will not be your lot in life any time soon, but if it's appropriate for an airline pilot to recommend that his passengers keep their belts fastened, I suppose it is even more appropriate for Christians to encourage other Christians to keep their prayer life up to date.

Read: Philippians 4: 6 – 13

Thank you, Heavenly Father, that there are no surprises to you. You know all things and you know them before they happen. I cannot get my mind around such a truth. This I know, if I want to be at peace in the face of the unknown, I need to constantly fasten my eyes on you.

For some reason, I was thinking back the other day to determine just which Sunday School teacher in my past had the greatest impact on my life. To my surprise, I found that the teacher whose influence seems to have been the strongest was probably the least equipped of all the ones I had. He was not a polished man. As I remember him, he was tall and thin with an oversized Adam's apple, which I could not avoid watching as it worked its way up and down his neck as he talked. He was usually more stern than suited my fifth and sixth grade fancy, but his discipline seemed always to be mixed with unshakable sincerity and love. Though I remember him as an excellent fisherman, he was always too anxious to deal with the Scripture lesson to spend much time spinning yarns about the "big one" he had caught during the week before. Perhaps the thing which remains most vivid in my mind about this Sunday School teacher, however, is the genuine personal interest he had for "his boys". I recall his "drop-by" visits at my home and his frequent phone calls. Even during college and seminary days, he maintained his interest in my life. Still another memory about my teacher lingers. There were times when he wondered if he was making any progress with us. Several times he told us that he felt like a dismal failure. I wish I had known then how important it was to reassure him and to appreciate him. Could it be that today someone would find us "famous" for encouragement?

Read: Ecclesiastes 4: 9 – 12

Thank you Father, for your reliable comfort and encouragement and thank you for the encouragers who have made the difference in my life. Start me on a search for more and more people who can say, I was "there" when they needed me.

Willingness is the Key

༜

"But we have this treasure in earthen vessels..." (II Corinthians 4:7) The more I consider it, the more astounding it becomes. As a Christian, I am a container in whom God has deposited a knowledge of his Truth. More importantly, as a Christian, I am an ordinary residence in whom the Holy Spirit of God actually dwells. And fellow Christian, you too are just such a residence. Think of it...all the life... the power...the peace...we so often say we seek is within us. We need not be looking, groping for these things "out yonder somewhere", they are residing within us waiting to burst through and fill our being as the shells of our will are broken and shattered. A confession is in order at this point, however. You and I must admit that we want the results of a Spirit-flooding but all too seldom do we want the process by which such an internal flood takes place. Borrowing Watchman's Nee's term of "being broken", perhaps our greatest need, man-for-man, is to pray for the willingness to be broken rather than praying only for "results-without-price". B.B. McKinney wrote it well into one of his hymn: "Holy Spirit, breathe on me, my stubborn will subdue...."

Read: I Peter 5: 6 - 11

Father, I guess I am like many other Believers; I want to be mature without the process of getting there. I want to know your will without surrendering my own will. I ask that you give me the hunger and thirst for your righteousness which leads to your fullness.

Clearing Out the Clutter

Often garages house the evidence that adult children have passed at least three major crossroads in their lives. They went away to college. They got married. They are now parents. To survey what has been collected in the old "garage" is to be like the "wizard of trash"! There are desk lamps, boxes of assorted clothes, artificial plants, coat hangers, cribs, broken chairs, curtain rods and an abundance of whatever else once figured into the dormitory domain or the newly wed world. Why do all these things have to be brought "home" to be dispensed with? Are there no systems for collecting these items in other places? At this point, parents of grown children are chuckling over what I am writing. They can readily identify with the problem. A few hard-nosed people though, want to ask me a revealing question or two…. "Why did you allow all this clutter to accumulate? The answer is obvious – I could have… should have…. And didn't. I guess I kept waiting for the "garage fairy" or for a son to appear at the door under heavy conviction that he should haul away his portion of the past. It's a study in procrastination. Such is the lesson, not only about garages, but about tithing and soul winning, daily Bible reading and prayer, apologies and restored friendships. Things change in our lives when we stop postponing the change and permit the Lord to clear out the spiritual clutter we've allowed to accumulate!

Read: Psalm 32

It is all too easy, Lord, to allow sin to clutter my life. I have chosen complacency over confession, thinking that guilt was a replacement for repentance. I want to make space for you today by confessing my sin, not to allow it back into my life.

Friend of God

❧

"Friend" is the word Jesus chose to describe those followers of His who do what He commands. A close look at what Jesus said on the subject reveals that He equated friendship with the spirit of sacrifice. Beyond servant hood and discipleship, friendship with Christ is to be sought. One of the highest of all compliments in the Bible is paid to Abraham who was called "a friend of God". In Proverbs we are told there is a friend who sticks closer than a brother. A "friend" is more than an acquaintance, a golf partner, a neighbor, or a classmate. A friend is one who has proved to be committed, faithful and generous. Would you call yourself a "friend of God"? We are almost offended at the suggestion that the answer is not obvious. A friend of God is a friend of His Word. A friend of God is a friend of His Church. A friend of God is a friend to the lost. A friend of God is a friend to the hurting. A friend of God is a friend of wholesome family life. A friend of God is a friend of the ministry. To be sure, a Christian is more than a friend of God; he is a child of God. Yet there is something very significant about a child becoming a friend. The longer I have lived and the older our sons have become, the more I realize how fulfilling and marvelous it is for parents and children to become friends. Especially significant is the joy of developing the best of friendships through the seasoning years of marriage. To be a friend of God is quite a role in life!

Read: John 15: 1 - 17

Heavenly Father, Eternal Friend, you are both to me. With Jesus as my Savior, I am your child, but I also want to be your friend. Keep me reminded of those things which I can do this very day which prove me to be a friend of God.

Our Schoolmaster

❧

God has established not only moral laws; He has put natural laws in place. And just as His moral laws apply to all and have consequences for all, His natural laws are no less persistent. When warm, moist air for the South collides with frigid air sweeping down for the North, things happen…ice happens, trees topple, power lines snap, schools close, cabin fever ensues and all our complaints change nothing. Maybe we need to remember that God's laws, natural and moral, are designed for our good, not our convenience. So we are to adjust to what God has ordained and in doing so, we become more resilient, patient, durable, flexible and appreciative. If jet streams and weather fronts answer to God's natural laws, surely those of us made to know right and wrong are answerable to God's moral laws. God's law, reflecting His perfection, is designed to bring us to the realization of our imperfection, hence, to bring us to Christ. God's moral law, then, confronts us with an accountability for which there is no solution except in Christ Jesus. It is only as Christ answers for our unrighteousness and gives us His righteousness that we can satisfy God's law. With Christ as Savior, we have His Spirit within us, thus the power to hunger and thirst for God's righteousness.

Read: Galatians 3: 10 – 27

Dear God, it is clear to me that your laws are unchanging in their purpose. They are not given for us to establish our righteousness but yours. Thank you that Jesus is our righteousness and your law teaches us how much we need Him.

❧

I owe a lot to sports. An athletic scholarship paid most of my college bills. Of course, with a tone of cynicism, one could say, "Yes and you're indebted to sports for two torn knee cartilages, a broken nose, two cracked teeth, a snapped Achilles tendon and a variety of sprains, strains, cuts and contusions." A single auto accident could produce the same results and worse, without any of the benefits. To be sure, some people are consumed with the subject of sports. There are super fans, who border on "athletic insanity".... There are sandlot sports-parents who drive their children beyond all reason in the pursuit of reliving their own past, or fantasizing about a past that never happened. There are even people who play on church athletic teams who have never learned to control their tempers, claiming some kind of exemption from moral responsibility because there is a "unique pressure" which belongs to competitive sports. There are Christian sports figures that are so lopsided in their mind-set that they exaggerate the comparison of good sportsmanship to good Christianity. Be all that as it may I am convinced there is much to be taught about life, its disciplines, motivations and relationships through competitive sports. Even more can be taught through a Christian approach to sportsmanship, physical conditioning and learning to live with triumph and defeat. The Bible challenges us to lead the Christian life with the zeal and commitment of a competitive athlete. Paul says we live like Believers should, not for trophies and ribbons, but so we do not disqualify our witness to the world around us.

Read: I Corinthians 9: 19 - 27

Lord, I don't want to be an undisciplined Believer, living my witness like a couch potato. Stir me within so that I may serve you with the zeal of a champion, not satisfied to forfeit my Christian potential.

Smoker's Cough

❧

<u>Reader's Digest</u> once related the amusing item of a California woman who became extremely irritated by the hacking cough of her pet bird, which was a macaw. When this distressing symptom continued, the woman took the bird to a veterinarian, who checked his patient, only to find it was in perfect health. Furthermore, the doctor discovered that instead of having some strange disease, the bird had merely learned to imitate his owner who had a raspy cough of her own, due to cigarette smoking. When the lady was informed of all this, she was shocked, but gained insight into her own problem and she immediately stopped smoking. Sometimes we are all too quick to be irritated by the weakness and faults of others, when if we took an honest look at ourselves, we would find we are guilty too. Jesus said, "Why look at the splinter in your brother's eye and overlook the plank in your own?' (Matthew 7:3)

Read: Luke 7: 39 - 45

I am embarrassed, Lord, when I have my critical spirit brought to my attention. You have told us to be discerning; to inspect the fruit in anyone's life to see if they are for real. But you have warned us about being judgmental and cynical. Purify my motives, Lord, and insist that I be as forgiving as I want you to forgive me.

Being Serious

❧

If I remember correctly, it was during the reign of Queen Elizabeth I that one of her secretaries of state became quite elderly and retired to a place in the country. When some of his friends went to visit him they told him he appeared very melancholy. He said, No, I am just serious, and it is proper that I should be. God is serious exercising His patience toward us. Christ is serious because He shed His blood for us. The Holy Spirit is serious. Satan is serious. All Heaven and Hell is serious. How can we afford to be trifling?" At first, the Englishman sounds like a killjoy. And certainly his example is no call for a sour approach to the Christian life. But the Bible does say we are to be sober-minded. That is we are to look at things as they really are. God is happily serious about loving you. How serious are you about your relationship with Him?

Read: Luke 9: 57 - 62

Forgive me, Oh Lord, for mistaking interest for dedication and habit for commitment. Help me find that walk with you that can be described as "happily serious".

Hanging on the wall of a television producer's office there is a penetrating sign. It says, "Everyone has 20 – 20 hindsight." Though hindsight is precise and accurate, it is always too late to be of much use. The Bible tells us about a man who spent his life with little thought for God and eternity. He died and went to hell. There is a place of eternal separation from God. He begged for a leave of absence so that he might return to earth and plead with his relatives not to make the same mistake he had made of leaving God out of his life. His hindsight, however, could not help him, nor could it help anyone else because even a brief return visit from eternity is impossible. While you have the opportunity of foresight, make your decision to invite Christ into your life. There will be no regrets later. And by the way, the idea of having no regrets because of foresight is an excellent approach for Christians to use when pointing out to an unsaved friend the need of a Savior.

Read: Luke 16: 19 - 31

As I pray today, Father, I am reminded to intercede for friends and loved ones who are without a Savior. I do not want to have hindsight about when I should have attempted to witness to them. Show me a way, and soon, that I can use foresight in sharing Jesus with someone close to me.

The Inside Counts Most

❦

Today's air travelers make interesting studies. I once saw a young woman on a plane whose attire was not particularly unusual among the traveling public of today. She wore grubby jeans, a denim jacket, comfortable shoes, oversized sunglasses and read a paperback novel. What was a bit unusual was her carryon luggage. It was a carpenter's tool chest. The tool chest being the open-sided variety, revealed her pocketbook, hair curlers, combs, scarf, another paperback novel and other items buried beyond recognition. Doubtless, by design, the tool carrier was dented, scratched and paint smudged.... Anything but new looking. To be sure, the whole get-up was assembled to create the relaxed casual... unpretentious look. The dark fingernail polish, however, somewhat betrayed the notion for a totally casual look. All of the externalities notwithstanding, just how natural and unpretentious the young lady is can only be determined by what she is, not by what she appears to be. The applications are legion. For instance, one church member's contribution envelope looks like every other member's contribution envelope. Even when sealed and the contributor's name filled in, offering envelopes look alike. It is what is on the inside that makes the distinction. Even more important, it is what is in the mind and heart of the giver that reveals the character and conviction of the gift. Is worship behind our giving? Do loyalty and sacrifice prevail? Is excitement and gratitude involved? "God looks not on the outward appearance. He looks upon the heart." (I Samuel 16:7)

Read: Matthew 23: 23 - 28

Father, whether it is in my giving, my praying, my worship or my business dealings, I want to be diligently responsible to you. If I answer to you first, what I am on the inside will be what I am on the outside.

Devoured By The Forest

❧

To compare the battle site of Ephraim's forest in King David's day to the environment surrounding our home life today makes for an interesting study. The witness of Scripture is that the forest devoured more than did the sword in the struggle between Absalom's rebels and his father's army. (II Samuel 18:3) It seems a fitting illustration of the environment that threatens to devour wholesome, enduring, family life in our time. In my view, that threatening, engulfing environment has developed by the influence of the following: The persistent secularization of our American culture; Humanism's takeover of the media; Materialism's makeover of our value system; The multiplying crusade to redefine the family; The surfacing of the spiritual underworld; The church's preoccupation with success divorced from the necessity of personal salvation. To study the "threatening environment", and to offer no comment about what we can do to combat that environment, would be only to cultivate a mind for discouragement. So, we consider six responsibilities and opportunities, which are ours in combating the "Ephraim" of our day, which is part of the battle for preserving our homes. First, we can seize the necessity of distinctively Christian individual behavior. Second, we must be perceptive about the influences which invade our homes. Third, we must model Christian home life and parenthood for children who will later follow those models. Fourth we should be informed and vocal about the politics of moral issues. Fifth we should reinforce the spiritual and moral impact of the church in the community. Sixth, we must allow prayer to be the weapon God intended with respect to the protection of our families.

Read: II Corinthians 6: 14 – 18

Help me, Lord, to be alert to the subtle enemies of a healthy family life. The culture around us claims to be family friendly when in fact, it promotes an agenda which is the opposite. I commit myself to pray for my own family and for a revival of the nation's home life.

Normal Christians

❧

Super Sunday is the day set aside for the Super Bowl. It is to be played by Super Power teams. But that is just the beginning nowadays of things being billed as "super". The celebrity world has its Super Stars. Professional athletes have theirs too. A TV network once aired its "Super Stars" competition in the winter and there is a gasoline called Super X. Even the world of glue has staked its claim to a product called Super Glue. With so many things now being called "super" we may be in a quandary as to what is ordinary. I am going to resist the temptation to pursue an explanation of the "super mind-set" which has become prevalent today. Needless to say, there are some very interesting theories to be considered. However, I must follow just one thought which has prompted me. We may have come to a time wherein we are so unfamiliar with the normal Christian life and so accustomed to sub-normal Christianity, that when we see a normal Christian we think of him as a "Super Saint"! The challenge of our times then, is not for super-sainthood but for an ordinary, garden-variety, normal commitment to Jesus Christ as Lord. It is at that level of surrender to Christ that we experience the normal happiness, normal assurance and normal strength, which normally belong to normal Christians. God does not call upon us to be super-saints, just normal ones.

Read: Matthew 18: 1 - 6

One thing I have learned, Lord, Satan is crafty in the distractions He darts before us. He wants me to believe that living a godly life is out of reach. Teach me, over and over the lesson of the indwelling Christ. I don't have to be an exceptional Christian, just allow Christ to be all that He is, and do it in my flesh.

❦

Forgiveness transpires not when it is offered but when accepted. Likewise... communication takes place when there is both projection and reception. Years ago, due to some telephone circuit changes, the "air-jack" from the church to the radio station was inadvertently cut. At broadcast time on Sunday morning, the station made their usual mechanical switch to our auditorium for the worship service only to find there was absolutely no reception. Literally thousands of people were unable to hear the broadcast. The telephones at the radio station rang repeatedly during that Sunday morning hour asking why the service was not being heard, giving graphic indication of the extent of the listening audience. It was a graphic illustration that we cannot communicate the Gospel without an audience. There we were; microphones in place, the choir ready to sing, the sermon prepared, but no radio audience to hear. To be sure, there were several hundreds of people gathered in the place of worship that heard and worshipped but not out there... where the larger potential lies... there was no communication. We can never subtract from the value of the gathered church in worship, for that is what we ever seek to enlarge, but to reach the yet-to-be reached we must get to where the people are. You are somebody's line of communication, fellow Christian. You are there where they are. Let them hear from you.

Read: Romans 10: 12 - 15

Father, at this moment I need for you to bring to mind some people in my life to whom I can be a line of communication. You have salvation to offer, forgiveness, comfort, encouragement and I need to tell them.

❧

Paradise was the name of a former weekly dramatic television program and Paradise was the name of the western frontier town which is the setting for the series. In one episode, the local mine shut down its operations and many of the townsfolk found it necessary to move away. With a sense of hopelessness about the future of Paradise, the central figure in the series, Ethan, came to the painful conclusion he and his four children would also have to move away. In an emotional scene, Ethan and the children were saying their good-byes to friends, including a mountain-man character that was very close to them. After embraces with the youngsters, Ethan and the log-haired sage are confronted with the unwanted parting of their ways. Haltingly, Ethan says, "I'm sorry". The friend's reply is full of implication. "No, it's not your fault. It's my fault. Years ago I decided to be a hermit. I should have stayed one." To be sure, to stay a hermit is to run no risk of having painful separations from friends but it also means to have no friends at all. And we need friends, next only to our Lord and our families. In fact, there are times when Christian friends are even more needed than certain family members. We need friends for affirmation and companionship. We need trustworthy friends to tell us the truth about ourselves. The Proverbs speak of a friend who is faithful enough to wound us. We need Christian friends for times of adversity and sorrow. Like Proverbs 17:17 says, "A friend loves at all times." We need to befriend others, allowing us to be encouragers and sowers of Gospel seed. By the way, Ethan and his children returned to Paradise after spending one night away from town. They said, "We need old friends more than a new town."

Read: Proverbs 18: 24 and Proverbs 27:6

Lord, Thank you for being a friend of sinners. Thank you for being my friend. Thank you for being the kind of friend who tells you the truth about yourself. And thank you for the privilege of being called your friend when I do what you ask me to do.

As a little boy and his parents walked from the church parking lot to Sunday School, he was given two dimes by his mother. One dime was for his offering at Sunday School and the other dime was for candy the next week. AS the little fellow walked along toward the church building he stumbled on the sidewalk and one of his dimes fell out of his hand and into a sewage drain. As he watched the coin disappear, the little boy said to himself, "Well, Lord, there goes your dime." Little boys are not the only ones who think they must look out for themselves even if it means to leave God out. But that approach to life only seems logical, it really leads to losing what is important. The Bible says, "But seek first His kingdom and His righteousness and all these things will be added to you." (Matthew 6: 33, NASV)

Read Luke 12: 13 – 24

Sometimes Lord, I really miss the obvious. I am the loser when I put other things before you. Today, I want to live like one who really believes he doesn't need everything he wants but you will see to it I have everything I need.

Who's In Control?

Many years ago, in the days of the horse and buggy, a man and his wife were traveling on a dangerous and narrow mountain road. The wife became very nervous and in her fright grabbed one of the reins out of her husband's hand. Very calmly, the husband offered his wife the other rein. She protested by saying, "Oh no, I don't want both reins. I couldn't ever manage that horse by myself." Her husband then gently said, "Well then, make your choice. It is either you or me at the reins. We cannot both drive the same horse!" At that, the wife gladly surrendered full control of the buggy to her husband. God says, in effect, "You and I cannot both control the same life." That's where we get into trouble. Saying we want to surrender to God's will while snatching selected worries and preferences out of God's hands. Satan wants us to think that he and the Lord are equal competitors, when in fact, Satan, is no competition when Jesus is put in charge!

Read: John 16: 7 – 11 and Ephesians 6: 11

Lord Jesus, you have resisted the Devil, you have conquered the Devil and you have bound him. Increase my wisdom in doing battle with him. Assure me that Satan cannot win over me when you are completely in charge.

Said A Different Way

Often the same spiritual principle can be expressed in two different ways. In many instances, one expression of a Christian truth has become almost commonplace, through familiarity. Then suddenly, the old axiom rises from a calloused heart simply because it is expressed in a different way. We have virtually grown up with familiar phrases like, "Let the Lord lead", and "I want God's Will to direct". Perhaps we need another approach to the same truth in order to regain our focus upon it. To be willing to follow His Will is but another way of permitting the Lord to lead. There is no virtue in a "readiness to be over-run" by the Will of God. To be sure, His ways are not always our ways but He doesn't want to defeat His own children. To be in the Will of God is not to be unwillingly imprisoned. Such confinement would indicate that the "prisoner" was out of God's Will, not in it. To be in God's Will is to be of the same mind, the same spirit, the same purpose as He. May God help us to become so absorbed in His Will that our mind and His are on the same page.

Read: Proverbs 3: 1 - 6

Heavenly Father, difficult it is for me to comprehend, your Word tells me you had a plan for my salvation before the world was made. That means you have had my best interest before I was even around. Press that truth upon me so I can see your will as actually in my best interest.

The Dream

❧

There is a passage in the Bible, found in the Old Testament, (Isaiah 29: 7 – 9), which describes a hungry man who dreams he is eating and awakes to find his hunger not satisfied and a thirsty man dreaming he is drinking and awakes faint with his thirst unquenched. That portrays the person who is deceiving himself to think he can find real satisfaction in life apart from God. We were made for fellowship and closeness to God, and apart from Him we are basically unfulfilled. We may pretend satisfaction. We may seek fulfillment in multi-various directions but we can never breathe the breath of fullness and contentment until we are in harmony with God. So how does somebody get in harmony with God? That is where Christ comes in… That is when you let Him in. When we allow Him, He can live out His life within us and through us!

Read: II Corinthians 4: 5 - 7

It is so emancipating, Father, to discover that living the Christian life is not a matter of trying to emulate Christ. I have tried that and met with failure. Today, I want to allow the indwelling Jesus to live out His life and do it in my flesh!

A Lesson On The Ice

I once did an unrehearsed "split" on some ice in a church parking lot. I opened my car door to drive home, only to find my right foot slipping farther and farther from by left one. All my efforts at coordination failed and I found myself in a gymnastic stance I had not tried in years! Comforted that I had avoided having an audience for this spastic display, I drove away pondering three split second lessons I had been taught: One on Caution; One on Confession; One on Compassion. This was not my first fall on ice. You would think a fellow would learn something from previous experience, at least the simple lesson of caution. I guess, however, we all have to admit we stumble and fall more times than necessary, simply because we are not as cautious as experience should have taught us. Not all our falls are simple ones on ice; sometimes we take serious falls on slippery territories of temptation. The fact is, we all have our spills, especially spiritual ones. Confession is not only more truthful than a cover-up, it frees us from pretense. Some of us all too easily forget when we were crushed, broken, and dependent upon the compassion of others. Such forgetfulness can make us harsh, sarcastic, and even judgmental. Far better is it to remember how you felt when you were down. It enables you to be "big" on compassion.

Read: I Corinthians 10: 12 – 13

Heavenly Father, when I think if how much you have forgiven me, I am embarrassed at how little I have forgiven others. I know its not that you want me to be soft on sin, but to be strong on compassion.

Having Authority

Some friends of David Hume, the agnostic, once reproached him for what they felt was an inconsistency with his unbelief in God. It seems that Hume went to church quite regularly to hear the powerful Scottish Bible preacher, John Brown. Hume replied to his friends, "Well, I don't believe all John Brown says, that is true, but I am sure He believes it. And at least once a week I like to hear a man who really believes what he says." That reminds us of what some critics of Jesus once said. They went out to hear the Lord teach one day with the view of finding fault. They returned saying, "We never heard a man speak as He does, for He taught them as one having authority." Jesus meant what He said. Do you and I mean what we say about Him? Talk is cheap, but not when it is a genuine Christian doing the talking.

Read Romans 12: 9 - 13

Lord, I want my life to be a genuine sermon which honors you. In other words, I want to walk the walk, not just talk the talk.

Deciding To Love

Dr. Gary Smalley is the one credited for the insight "Love is a Decision". The more his idea is considered, the more right it seems to be. Too often, we think love will function on its own, involuntarily, and in the purest of directions. To be certain, God given and God purified love is trustworthy and appropriately spontaneous. The problem, however, is that what we sometimes think is love, is a perversion, hence, not to be trusted at all. Other times, what we deem to be love may be infatuation or some other emotion enroute to disaster. We need to take our cue about love's character from what we know of God's love; for God is love. But love, even in the lives of God's twice-born people, must be directed by redeemed wisdom and discipline. That is where and how love becomes a matter of decision-making. We decide, by way of our commitment to Christ, what is right, wholesome and just, then let love serve "the decision". Love is a decision to accept a person as he or she is. Love is a decision to forgive before forgiveness is even sought. Love is a decision to seek to uplift the person loved, not to belittle that person. Love is a decision to make the well-being of the one you love reason enough to make sacrifices. An honest study of Romans 5: 1 – 8, with a particular focus on verse 8, will probably underscore in your mind the things it did in mine. Love is a decision…. A big decision…. a series of big decisions.

Read: Romans 5: 1 - 8

Lord, help me today to consciously love you and decisively so. And encourage me in the decision-making needed for me to love people around me. Your word tells me to even love my enemies. I really need some help with that one.

The Weight of Responsibility

৵৻

When the tribes of Gad and Reuben balked on the east side of Jordan, preferring the green pastures of Gilead as a residence to the unknown land of Canaan which God had given them, Moses persisted, ... "shall your brethren go to war and shall ye sit here? And wherefore discourage ye the heart of the children of Israel?" (Numbers 32: 6 – 7) Responsibility weighs heavy on God's scales. Responsibility for obedience to God is where we first step upon His scales. Responsibility for encouragement to fellow believers is a scale upon which we are weighed far more often than we know. In the parlance of today, Moses said to the irresponsible Gadites and Reubenites, "Why do you choose the careless privilege of discouraging the faithful people of God?" Compromising Christians discourage God's obedient children. Absence from worship is invariably labeled a loss to the absentee, but it is also a source of discouragement to those who faithfully sit in half-filed pews. Criticism which is destructive is more than destructive... it is a source of discouragement. Superficial Christianity is like foot dragging, discouraging whole-hearted Christianity. On the scales of responsibility we all could stand to weigh more. Being over weight is hardly our problem there.

Read: Deuteronomy 31: 7 - 8

Dear Lord, I am reminded today that there are many weary worried and aimless people around me. I need to see myself as responsible for making a difference. Call to my mind names of people who have encouraged me so I may remember to thank them, and call others to my mind that I may remember to help them.

The End of Anxiety

Sometimes well-chosen quotations say all that needs to be said on a given subject. For instance, here are a couple of quotes about... **Optimism:** "An optimist is a person who thinks he can find big strawberries in he bottom of the box." "An Optimist sees an opportunity in every calamity, a pessimist sees a calamity in every opportunity." And here's one about ...**Determination:** "Some people grin and bear it, others smile and change it." And another: "Life is like a grindstone and whether it grinds a man down or polishes him, depends on the stuff he's made of." Then, there is an excellent quote about.... **Challenge:** "There are two kinds of men who never amount to much – those who cannot do what they are told to do and those who can do nothing else." When a church faces certain opportunities and decisions, all the qualities, extolled in the foregoing quotations are needed. However, they will not be adequate without the most important ingredient of all.... **Faith.** George Muller, a Christian of great faith once said: "The beginning of anxiety is the end of faith and the beginning of faith is the end of anxiety." As we pray about our tomorrows, let's use our heads.... and our faith. "For whatever is born of God overcomes the world and this is the victory that overcomes the world, even our Faith." (I John 5:4)

Read: 1 John 5: 13 - 15

Heavenly Father, keep getting into my head that, as a Christian, I have the Mind of Christ. I actually can choose victory over defeat.

The Big Difference

The longer I live, the more impressed I am with God's integrity. He is so truthful and honest it is almost shuddering. For instance, He never has misled us to think that being a Christian is the way to be exempt from life's difficulties. To the contrary, He has said in the Bible, "In this world you will have tribulation." At this point, someone is bound to ask, "Well then, what advantage is there to being a Christian?" If you mean by "advantage" to be excused from life's problems.... very little, but if you mean by "advantage" to have endless resources to see you through life, being a Christian does make the difference. So all people have problems...Christians have them too. But tell me my friend, to whom do you turn when you have nothing left? That is where Christ can make the difference. "Casting all your care upon Him for He cares for you". (I Peter 5:7)

Read 1 Peter 5: 6 – 11

Father, to know that you always have my best interest is more that comforting, it makes the difference in a cold, hard world.

The Diagnosis

There is an old, old spoof that is frayed with use, but it illustrates a point. A man sped up to a drug store and rushed to the druggist, asking if he had something for hiccups. Without a word, the druggist socked the man right between the eyes. As the man slowly got to his feet, the druggist said, "You don't have any more hiccups, do you?" The man said, "No sir, I never did, but my wife out in the car does." All too often we are like the mythical druggist, jumping to conclusions and trying to solve our problems with the wrong diagnosis. Man's greatest problem is with his sinful nature. A change of environment may help. Financial aid may assist, but man needs a remedy for his sin-problem. That remedy is God's forgiveness and re-creation through Christ. If your sin-problem has been dealt with by God's forgiveness, live today like the re-creation you are! "All we like sheep have gone astray; we have turned every one to his own way; and the Lord has laid on Him the iniquities of us all." (Isaiah 53; 6)

Read: Ephesians 2: 8 - 10

Lord, sometimes we have as much trouble with living like forgiven sinners as we do with seeking Your forgiveness. We ask that You convict us of our forgiveness as well as of our sins.

Personalized Love

With precious upturned eyes, a little girl approached me to show me the things she had made during the Sunday School hour. One such item she and the other children had made was a familiar heart shaped valentine decorated with bright red yarn. She turned the valentine around so I could see what she had printed on the reverse side. There I saw meticulously printed letters, spelling out "I love". I commented, "I see you wrote 'I love' on your valentine, but you did not say who you love." In a guileless six-year old tone of voice my "vestibule valentine" answered, "I didn't have time to say who I loved". A child once again leads us. She provides the insight needed. Of what significance is it for us to say, "I love", lest we take the time to personalize it? That we are loving is desirable. That we individualize and declare our love to persons, by name, is even more desirable. The calendar says it is the season of love, Valentine's Day. The Scriptures say it is always the season for love. Every day is a day to "Take aim" at a life and love that person in an individual way. "And so I am giving a new commandment to you now…love each other just as much as I love you. Your strong love for each other will prove to the world that you are my disciples." (John 13: 34- 35, The Living Bible) Start at home, fellow Christian, someone there needs to hear you say, "I love… you".

Read: Romans 5: 1 - 8

Loving Father, teach me how to love like you love. You love us but don't indulge us. Your forgiveness does not come from a reluctant love. You love us, and tell us so in your Word. Increase my capacity and desire to love the way you do it.

On The Inside

A little boy stepped upon the scales to be weighed. He was anxious to outweigh his schoolmates, so he puffed up his cheeks with his breath. His teacher chuckled a bit and said, "That won't do you any good, Ben, you can only weigh what you are". That is a good reminder for all of us. Regardless of what we may do to alter what we are by making <u>external</u> changes, we are still what we until the changes are made on the <u>inside</u>. You see, reputation is not what people think you are, it is what God <u>knows</u> you are. The Bible says, "As a man thinketh in his heart so is he". (Proverbs 23:7) Little wonder the Greek word for "character" literally means, "*to engrave*", or "<u>to cut an impression</u>". That is what our character does. It makes lasting impressions upon people.

Read: I Thessalonians 1: 6 - 8

Lord, you know me altogether. My life, even my thoughts, are an open book before you. The people around me do not know me as well as you, but they probably know me better than I think. Help me to seek and to live out the character of Christ likeness.

Every generation has its set of false philosophers, who insist God and His ways are out-of-date. Let's consider a verse of Scripture. It says, "Jesus Christ is the same... yesterday... and today... and forever. (Hebrews 13:8) The world may change... but God never does. Societies' ways may come and go... but God's Word stands forever. Nations rise and fall... but the Kingdom of God marches on. Popular opinions vacillate... but Jesus... Jesus is the same as when he walked this earth bodily. Jesus ever lives! The Bible tells us He is now seated at the right hand of His Father God, and that His Spirit dwells in every twice-born child of God. Search the pages of your Bible. Claim all that He is for yourself. He is the same... forever! "Before the mountains were brought forth, or even you formed the earth and the world, even from everlasting to everlasting, you are God." (Psalm 90:2)

Read: Deuteronomy 4: 39 - 40

Dear God, forgive me for being so easily deceived by the world's temporary attractions. Give me a heart and a hunger for what Jesus said would be fulfilling to me, and lasting.

Divine Approachability

Insights often come at unexpected moments. It was during a Life of Christ Pageant that I was provided such an insight. It came during the scene wherein the Beatitudes were given. Just before the cast of disciples and the listening crowd were seated to hear the words of Jesus, several children ran onto the stage excitedly shouting "Jesus! Jesus!" One of the men portraying a disciple intercepted the children before they reached Jesus. Then, dramatizing the Scripture passage: "Let the little children come unto me." Jesus stepped over to the children, reached down and drew them to himself. Then came the simple, tender, spontaneous move, which contained a wealth of insight. As Jesus picked up one of the children and held her in his arms... she spontaneously hugged him. A little child lovingly hugged Jesus. I seriously doubt that many people envisioned that side of the Lord's magnetism and availability. Oh yes, we have imagined Him holding children in His lap, but... children hugging Him? For me it was a scene, which beautifully illustrated the truth of: **Divine approachability**.

Read: Matthew 11:28
John 6: 17
Revelation 22:17

Thank you, Oh Father, for your great grace and abundant love which makes it possible for us to draw close to you. In the name of Jesus I come to you now with my worship, my repentance, my needs and my thanksgiving.

Bearing His Likeness

Years ago, following the death of Gustavus the Great, the statesmen of Sweden met to decide who would succeed his throne. Some suggested the throne be offered to the king of Poland. Others suggested a republic. The Chancellor said, "Few people know it, but the king has a daughter, who is now 6 years old." The statesman questioned if this was only a trick of the Chancellor, but he quickly removed their suspicions when he left the room and returned with the child. She was placed on the throne and carefully inspected. One statesman said, "This has to be the king's heir for she bears all the features of the great Gustavus!" And that is the way people will really know if you and I are Christians, the Bible says, we will be "conformed to the likeness of God's Son." (Romans 8:28)

Read: II Corinthians 4: 5 - 7

Lord, I'm not being honest when I say I don't care what people think of me. I really want to be known by my best qualities. Remind me throughout the day that it matters when people see in me those qualities, which reflect the very likeness of Jesus himself.

A Sermon in the Snow

Once while watching the heavy snowfall, I was reminded again of a familiar analogy. As I watched the Saturday night skies filled with falling flakes and saw the ground being heavily covered with that blanket of white, I first thought of the singular beauty of fresh fallen snow. Of course, I entertained a few thoughts about the effect the snow would have upon church Sunday's attendance. Then came to mind the analogy; like the unmarred snowfall covers everything with an equal appearance of whitened cleanliness, so God's forgiveness covers all sin for those who are in Christ. Covered in the righteousness of Christ, God sees us not as sinful but as if we had not sinned. As both ugliness and attractiveness are equally covered in the snowfall, making all things share an equal beauty, our sinfulness and comparative goodness are equally covered by the all-surpassing purity of God's forgiveness. Try as we will, there is no improvement to be made upon the natural appearance of a snowfall. Most anything we do to it falls into the realm of trifling. Any attempt on man's part to "add" to, or tamper with, God's forgiveness is little more than trifling. Isaiah said it well. "…Though your sins be as scarlet they shall be as white as snow…." (Isaiah 1:18)

Read: Psalm 51: 1 - 7

Dear God, your handiwork is such a thing of beauty and your forgiveness is no less a thing of beauty. Like the Psalmist, I want a clean heart buried under the snowdrift of your forgiveness.

Bird Sketches

Dr. Donald Grey Barnhouse, a well-known Bible teacher of the past, used to tell about the time when the Emperor of Japan commissioned an artist to paint a portrait of an exotic bird. After many months of waiting, the emperor went to see how the artist was progressing. Upon his arrival, he found the final touches were being put on the finished canvas. When the emperor asked the artist why the painting had taken so long, the artist went from cabinet to cabinet producing armloads of separate sketches. There were sketches of feathers, wings, claws and beaks. The emperor then expressed how much he appreciated the painting knowing better all that went into the finished product. Christians are not molded into Christ-likeness overnight. In fact, that is what a Christian's life is all about…day-by-day, permitting God to change us unto the likeness of His Son.

Read: I Peter 2: 1 - 5

Today Lord, I want to act more like a child of God than I ever have. It's not that I want to be a spectacular Christian, but a normal, growing Believer.

The Taste of Salt

Jesus' descriptive statement to those who follow Him, "Ye are the salt of the earth", is replete with varying applications. Perhaps we are most conscious, even if glibly so, of the interpretation which depicts the Christian as a personal soul-winner offering the "seasoning" of Christ to otherwise spiritually "savorless" lives. There are still other dimensions to this saltiness principle, however. In an earthy society, what if anything, makes Christians distinguishable? I suppose the matter reduces itself to the basic question, "What accent in our living wins the comment, 'They are different'!" Of what significance is our professed religion if we contribute to the blandness of living? If our attitude is one perpetually sour, negative, critical and argumentative, how are we different from one who is yet unseasoned by salvation? Perhaps our problem is that we assert our human rights to have any attitude we please, somehow forgetting that we have a more sublime "right" to salt the earth with a different kind of life. Someone has said, "Life to many is a battle and they are not happy lest they are fighting with someone." For others, life is a treadmill of insignificance, while still others live only by the exhilaration of emotional thrusts. How are we, as Believers, different from these? The early Church shook the world, but how? While the world was flavored by spite and hatred, of the Christian it was said, "See how they love one another". While an evil culture entertained itself by the massacre of human flesh, the Christians sang enroute to the arena. They were different.... are we?

Read: Matthew 5: 13 - 14

Dear Father, help me get beyond the fear of being ridiculed for my faith. Increase my courage to risk being distinctly Christian.

The Red Bible

John Wanamaker, a famous wealthy businessman of the 1800's, was 11 years old when he bought his first Bible. It was years and years later, after he had made his fortune that he said, "I have made purchases involving millions of dollars, but it was as a boy that I made my greatest transaction. It was then that I bought a red leather Bible for $2.25, which I paid for by installments. As I look back, I see it was the wisest, most important and far reaching investment I ever made." Probably you already have a Bible in your home, perhaps two or three of them so you do not need to buy a Bible. But, tell me, do you "buy" what the Bible says? The Bible says God loves you and gives you a new future when you invite Christ into your life. "Buy" that and it will be your best "Buy" ever!

Read: Isaiah 40: 6 - 8

Lord, Mr. Wanamaker bought a red Bible. I want to buy into a well-read Bible. As I read my Bible today I ask that the Holy Spirit will make clear every sentence I read.

Translating Prayer Language

Anyone who takes prayer seriously will come to those moments in life when the question of "how" to pray is a hard one to answer. When the content of prayer is both general and habitual, there is very little power as well. It is when we take to heart the Scripture's admonition to be specific in our requests and persistent in our petitions that we encounter the unique "exhaustion" of prayer... the exhaustion of vocabulary.... the exhaustion of expectancy... the exhaustion of motivation. How do we continue to pray for change in people who make it clear they see no need to change? How do you pray for restoration and healing among those who have self inflicted wounds they insist were unavoidable? How do we cease not to pray for a moral awakening in the face of rising popularity for dumping old moral standards? Is God unaware of our weariness? Is He somehow indifferent to the frustrations, which can accompany the attempts to "Pray without ceasing?" At this point the discovery of Romans 8:24 – 27 is like staking claim to a gold mine: "Who hopes for what he already has? But if we hope for what we do not yet have, we wait for it patiently." In the same way, the Spirit helps us in our weakness. We do not know what we ought to pray, but the Spirit himself intercedes for us with groans that words cannot express. And he who searches our hearts knows the mind of the Spirit, because the Spirit intercedes for the saints in accordance with God's will." (Romans 8:24 b – 27) Think of it! There are times when we cannot put into words what we want to express in prayer, but we need not despair of prayer. The Holy Spirit translates the speechless into prayer language.

Read Hebrews 12: 1 - 3

Heavenly Father, it is so encouraging to know that you not only hear my weary prayers, you translate them into words which have real meaning. I want that truth to help me resist self pity and discouragement.

Sharing and Bearing

ЖС

"Would you like a peanut butter sandwich?" To which our five-year-old gave this answer to his mother, "No it sticks to my braces". Now, mind you, our five-year-old had no braces on his teeth, but one of his older brothers did. It is amazing how little children so readily identify and actually empathize with others. Vicarious sharing is something to which they seem naturally to respond. Our Lord so often illustrated a spirit, which he extolled by pointing out the ways of a child. Through the quill of Paul, the Holy Spirit instructs us: "Rejoice with them that do rejoice, and weep with them that weep." (Romans 12:15) "Bear ye one another's burdens and so fulfill the law of Christ." (Galatians 6:2) Through the Spirit of Christ, who dwells in us, we have the capacity to genuinely rejoice and weep with others. However, such capacity goes untapped if we do not know one another well enough to be aware of the experiences through which we are passing. Simply knowing people is necessary for a spirit of Christian empathy. Furthermore, we cannot expect others to share the needs and blessings we may have, unless we trust one another enough to reveal ourselves. The Scriptures say, "Bear one another's burdens"... and thereby imply this admonition, "Share your burdens".

Read: Matthew 9: 35 - 38

Help me, Dear God, to be loving enough to care about what other people are experiencing. And give me an increased incentive to try to do something about it.

Lesson At An Airport

༺

It was a stormy day and flight connections were delayed on every hand. As we waited for various flight connections some passengers began to grumble about the way the weather was interfering with their plans for connecting flights and "ruining their day". I overheard one passenger talking to another, saying, "That's the trouble with this part of the country. The weather is forever posing problems. Now when you get out to my part of the country you don't have all this to contend with. In fact, it's sunny and 75 degrees today our where I live!" It was tough to listen to someone downgrade my section of the country, especially while extolling his as being so much better. It's true his area enjoys a lot of sunshine and basks in sunny days with cloudless skies, but I've been to his part of the country and have experienced days that were far from sunlit and cloudless. In fact, I remember being caught in one of the worst ice storms I've ever experienced in his hometown! On that particular day the flights were not just delayed, they were cancelled. Unquestionably, I am biased about my part of the country with its flower-laden springs and its colorful mountainous autumns and I become defensive when someone demeans it. But I think the overheard airport conversation revealed a truth for me. Before we become too smug about our own strengths and so critical of others' shortcomings, we need to be honest with ourselves. And maybe there is still another lesson: Before we so quickly complain about temporary circumstances we need to take stock of the usual set of blessings we more often enjoy.

Read: Psalm 27: 13 – 14

Today, Lord, I want to thank you for the blessings and comforts I have gotten so used to. I expect them. And when the unwanted or unexpected comes remind me to wait on you, for you are the God of the unexpected as much as the usual.

The Pans (pronounced P-ah-ns)

❧

I once saw a television documentary and was not particularly surprised at the beautiful music I heard on the program until I learned the source. It sounded like a keyboard instrument but in reality was a band of drums, called pans (pahns), played with mallets. In the West Indies, after World War II, British soldiers left behind, as refuse, empty oil drums. The oil drums were ugly and corroded. But some natives of the island saw in those drums, what they <u>could</u> become. The drumheads were cut, cleaned, honed for pitch and polished until they were recreated into things of beauty. Then it struck me: That's exactly what Jesus does with a life He recreates…. even one scarred and blackened with sin. There is a popular Christian song, which says it all well: "All I had to offer Him was brokenness and strife, but Jesus made something beautiful of my life."

Read: Zechariah 3: 1 - 5

What a thrill it is, Lord, to discover the power of your re-creation. You created everything at the beginning and nature itself is your autograph. But then you stepped in and offered re-creation through Christ to a fallen humanity. I want to be your autograph on re-creation.

Truth Is The Truth

A child of the great Depression, I have a perspective those later-born do not. I have lived long enough to watch the nations' moral "playing field" undergo radical changes. Not only has the field changed, the rules have been revised so any times there is little comparison between how the "game" was played then and now. Some delight in what they view as a tolerant progress. What concerns me so much is that many Christians labor under the impression that there remains in America a respect for the virtues and values, which were broadly recognized in days gone by. They sit back, remaining silent, oblivious to the fact that ideals taken for granted years ago are struggling for survival in a land enamored by tolerance and indulgence. Influenced by the so-called virtues of pluralism, some Christians fear being called a bigot. We can no longer assume that right and wrong have clear meanings or that there is universal truth. In his classic novel, The Brothers Karamazov, the 19th century Russian novelist Dostoyevsky essentially asked, "Can man be good without God?" In every age, the answer is a resounding "no".

Read Ephesians 5: 6 – 13

Father, convict me when I am judgmental, but also convict me when I am intimidated by the unbelieving world around me. I pray for the courage to stand by your Truth and live by the Truth.

Missing the Mark

❧

Regardless how good a shot I might be on a basketball court, I would miss every now and then. Even All-Americans and NBA players don't make all their shots. In other words, we are not perfect. We all miss the mark. But we miss the mark other than on a basketball court… we miss the mark of perfection in life. The Bible says, "All have sinned and fallen short of the glory of God"… or to put it another way, "we have missed the mark of God's perfection." If that's the case, how can we ever hope to get to heaven? That's where Jesus Christ comes in, He is perfect. But, He also loves imperfect people and forgives them. That's why He died on the cross. When you receive Jesus into your life He takes care of the imperfection problem. Though forgiven of our sin, however, we Christians still commit sins. Yet with the Spirit of Christ within us, we actually can resist sin. So bottom line, Jesus is the answer to our need of sin's forgiveness and His Spirit is the answer to our need to resist sin's temptations.

Read: Romans 7: 14 - 25

Lord, don't allow me to settle for the rationale, "Nobody's perfect". I know I am a sinner but I also know Jesus forgives those who ask Him. What I need most is the reminder that I don't have to cave in to temptation. As a forgiven sinner, I can actually resist temptation and put Satan on his heels!

The Misprint

A small town newspaper once carried an article, which admitted a misprint. It said: "Our paper carried the notice last week that Mr. John Johns is a defective on the police force. This was a typographical error. Actually, Mr. Johns is a detective on the police farce." Such is often the plight of attempts to correct things we have said about people. Too frequently one careless statement leads to still another one. Once the feathers are out of a pillow they can never be totally retrieved. Neither can all the choice morsels of gossip be recaptured once they are scattered about. Far better would it be if we tried always to speak carefully and accurately the first time we said something about another person. The Bible says, "Behold, we put bits in horses' mouths, that they may obey us: And we turn about their whole body... even so the tongue is a little member, and boasts great things." Put life and lips under Christ's control and our tongue can be a blessing.

Read: Proverbs 6: 16 - 19

Forgive me, Oh God, for allowing my tongue to be used to serve my temper, my jealousy, my pride, my dishonesty. Increase my desire to hear words from my mouth which praise you, encourage the discouraged and serve the truth.

More To Come

❧

Many believers are convinced there is more to the Christian life than what they have experienced. They know there is bound to be more to salvation than their conversion but just where to find what is yet coming to them remains a hidden frustration. It is not that God has made the deeper Christian life hard-to-find or hard-to-get. To the contrary, the truth of the thorough Christian life is clearly taught in the Scriptures. The fullness of the indwelling Christ is not only available to all Christians; it is the result of the obedience God expects from all Believers. How then do we explain the gap between what so many of today's Christians have experienced and what they have yet to experience? A partial explanation is to be found in an unofficial, even subconscious idea, which stresses Salvation by grace and implies Sanctification by works. Another explanation can be attributed to the aversion to an identity with groups which equate the deeper Christian life with "a second blessing". Perhaps the greater portion of the explanation lies in the fact we have been led to think that average Christianity is normal Christianity, when by Biblical standards, the deeper Christian walk is the normal life for the Twice-Born.

Read: Galatians 2: 20 and Colossians 1: 25 - 27

Lord, it saddens me to think how long and how often I thought living the Christian life was up to me and how hard I worked at it. Today, I rejoice in the wonderful awareness that the Spirit of Christ lives in me in order to live out the life of Christ through me.

Winter Weary

"Winter weariness" can be a mid-winter malady. Snow, ice, sleet, freezing rain, traveler's advisories, school closings, potholes in the streets, take their toll during the year's coldest months. Little wonder the early sights and signs of spring are so welcome. To simply see the grass after its being covered with snow for weeks is a delight. To hear that certain bird-song we have not heard since fall is refreshing. To lay aside the heavy coats, gloves, boots and hats is a relief. To bask in rising temperatures and squint at the sun in a cloudless sky is exhilarating indeed. Spring is a season with a message – a message of new life… renewed hopes… corrected perspectives… bolstered spirits… lifted confinements… inhaling the fresh air which prevails on the other side of perseverance. Spring is God's parable in nature telling Easter's story. That Thursday night… Friday and Saturday in the long ago were like an endless winter to our Christian forebears. They waited through the hard chill of death, dejection, defeat and despair. It must have seemed like an eternity as they waited for their spiritual winter to pass. Then the Eternal Spring burst onto the scene on Resurrection Morning. Since that Day of Days… we can, if we will, live in the power of the Resurrection… we can live above and beyond the chill of death, the bitterness of sorrow, the overcast of sin, the winter of pain. Thank God for Spring… His Spring… His Eternal Spring!

Read: I Peter 1: 3 - 9

Praise you, dear God, for hope! Forgive me for being so preoccupied with problems that I cannot celebrate your hope. At this very moment, I hand over to you whatever I see as burdens and I take a deep, full breath of your encouragement!

Polishing the Heart

⁂

I am indebted to a friend for sending me the thought which prompted these sentences: "Only foolish men polish brass rails on sinking ships." The more I ponder that sentence, the more significant it appears to me. This statement presses upon us the issue of stark realism. Are our churches, often engaged in the pointless task of polishing the externals while more serious matters go unattended? Even we, as individual Christians can busy ourselves with appearances while ignoring the things that really count. In the final analysis, the subject of "brass rails" versus "sinking ships" is a study in our sense of values. For instance, of what avail is a bright smile "aboard" the sinking ship of hidden anger? Of what advantage is the hue of a well decorated sanctuary "aboard" a sinking ship of shallow worship? And what meaning has self-righteousness aboard a sinking ship of unconfessed sin? Like relentless waves pounding the surf, this matter of pretense versus truth breaks upon our hearts demanding honest attention. Neither our individual Christian lives nor the ministry of a church can spiritually succeed "aboard" sinking ships with only "polished rails".

Read: Matthew 23:25 – 26 and I Samuel 16:7

Dear Lord, put your mirror before me so that I can see myself as I am, not as I present myself to be. I'm too good at pretense. Lord, you have the honesty I need.

A Christian English teacher was teaching his Sunday School class and said, "All of you know how the verb 'to be' is used, 'I am, you are, he is." The teacher went on to say, "Verbs are conjugated that way not only in English but also in German, French, and Italian, but that is not the best way to arrange a verb. The Hebrew people arranged their verbs the other way around: 'he is, you are, I am'…" Then the teacher added, "That is the way Jesus taught us to look at life: Fix your attention first on God…. then focus on others…. and last, consider yourself." That is precisely what Jesus was talking about when He said, "Thou shalt love the Lord thy God with all thy heart…and love thy neighbor as thyself." (Matthew 22: 37, 39) KJV

Read: I John 4: 20 – 5: 2

Dear Lord, you love me without reservation. I want to love you that way, but I need to learn that it is my obedience to you which expands my love for you. I guess one of the best ways I can say I love you is to be able to say I'm serious about obeying you.

It is a foregone conclusion; we live in a troubled world. Of course, the world has been in trouble since Adam. Read history, re-read the Bible and page after page records the growing consequences of garden variety sin. Add to the mix, the full-blown results of greed, hatred and indulgence and the outcome is a dangerous world. Behind it all the Ruler of this world stirs the pot. Hopeless? Intimidating? It should not be for the people of God. We have not only been saved from this world, we have been saved for it. Salvation is not for our private consumption. Rather we are meant to be God's merchants of hope in an otherwise hopeless world. Fellow Believer, what a door is opened to us by such despair! It is our moment to shout, "Christ is the Answer!" Parade magazine published a story captioned "The World's Ten Worst Dictators". As I read the article I suddenly realized we have Christian friends and fellow servants of the Lord living under some of those very dictators. With God-given courage those Christians work to penetrate their surroundings with the Gospel of Jesus. It is our privilege to pray for and support them. But isn't it dangerous to do all that? That is the point. If Christ is the answer it is inherently risky to say so. There are sensitive Christians today who want to run some risks for Jesus' sake. That is why they are looking for churches with bigger things in mind than customizing the status quo. What an opportunity for those who know Jesus to dare to say to the surroundings of a troubled economy and a troubled world, "We have the Answer!"

Read: I Peter 3: 13 – 15

Thank you, Father, for my fellow Believers who know first hand the price to pay for a courageous faith. I pray for their protection today and pray for an increase in the risk factor of my own faith.

God Needs No Translation

❧

Have you ever felt utterly alone…I mean have you been in a place where you felt really stranded? I think the most stranded feeling I ever had was years ago when in Kyoto, Japan. Unlike Tokyo, I discovered in Kyoto very few people who spoke English. There I was, wanting to make a purchase in a large Japanese department store, but no salesclerk, no supervisor could I find who spoke my language. I left the store frustrated. We would feel stranded in life if we had a God who could not understand us and speak our language. But God took a human body, and His name was Jesus. It was in human flesh that God tasted of life, as we know it. So God does understand you and your problems, my friend. Turn to Him. He understands and speaks your language.

Read: Hebrews 4: 13 - 16

Dear Lord, it is both comforting and exciting to realize you hear my prayers. It is equally encouraging to know you not only hear my words but you understand my fears, my hurts, my confusion which I can't put into words.

Ultimately In Charge

❧

One morning after breakfast, following family prayer time and a few minutes with the morning newspaper, I said, "I just don't know how to pray about a lot of world news developments." A revolutionary and his rogues had just taken over their country. The Prime Minister had resigned and had been taken into custody. Some were celebrating the victory of the poor and common man over the wealthy and privileged few who had ruled the country. Yet there was amidst it all, the tragedy of hundreds dead and wounded, the waste of leveled buildings and the anxiety over future relations with countries like our own. The situation simply made me again aware of how often we must turn to the sovereign will of God and trust Him with matters beyond our ability to decipher, much less to articulate. It also made me conscious of how much world missions lives at the heart of the world situation. The greatest contribution we can make as Christians is to introduce the world to our Lord. To be sure, that is a task which boggles the mind as much as trying to live peaceably with a politically restless world. Be that as it may, we have before us the hard privilege of world evangelism and prayerful citizenship. Thank God we also have the peaceful confidence of trusting a Sovereign God.

Read: Psalm 31: 19 - 24

Eternal God, history and hope are on your hands. I have to admit that I get troubled over things beyond my control. Lord, I need a strong reminder that you are eternally changeless and ultimately in charge.

Two Epitaphs

᭰

I understand there is a cemetery in England where there are two gravestones with these intriguing inscriptions. On one are the words: "She died for the want of things." And on the next stone, which is along side the first, are the words: "He died trying to give them to her." Aside from being worth a laugh or two, those two epitaphs portray the folly of spending one's life only for this world's goods and riches. It all goes along with that cracker barrel slogan you and I were taught, "The more you have the more you want." The Bible says, "Put your affection on things above and not upon things on the earth." (Colossians 3:1, KJV) That does not mean we are to be lazy and fail to provide for our loved ones and ourselves. But it does tell us we need to keep our priorities in order.

Read: I John 2: 15 - 17

Lord, increase in me my sales resistance about all that Satan advertises as harmless or exciting. Your Word tells me he is a liar and I need the courage to quote you to his very face.

Opportunities to Celebrate

Our Christian forebears had the right idea. They felt there should be a Christian answer to what otherwise would be an occasion completely dominated by a godless mentality. Both Christmas and Easter are Christian celebrations, which originally were such replies to pagan festivities. When I hear some well-intended person insisting that Christians should not celebrate Christmas and Easter because it is a quasi-endorsement of two godless occasions, I want to tell them I think their approach would lead us to forfeiting an opportunity and failing a legacy. If we Christians bury our Christmas and Easter celebrations under ribbons and clothes, an omnipresent rabbit, an overweight myth, boxes and baskets, candy and eggs, we have little chance of seizing an opportunity and protecting a legacy. It is for us then to see what a tremendous opportunity these celebrations provide for us to keep faith with our spiritual predecessors, calling attention to our reasons for the festive spirit: Christ was born. Christ has risen. God cares. God saves. The world has hope. History makes sense. We can share deeper truths as we seize opportunities to protect legacies, that is, if we are verbal about the difference Jesus makes.

Read: Colossians 3: 12 - 17

Heavenly Father, thank you for the realization that every day can be Christmas or Easter, if it is Jesus we are celebrating. At this very moment, I claim the day as an occasion to celebrate my salvation and my Savior.

In the Old Testament book of Proverbs, there are some extremely helpful sentences aimed at the Monday through Friday world where we spend most of our time. Listen to some timeless hints for that workaday world offered to us by God's counselor:

"Mortals make elaborate plans but God has the last word. Humans are satisfied with what looks good; God probes for what is good." (Proverbs 16: 1 – 2, MSG)

"The first speech in a court case is always convincing – until the cross examination starts." (Proverbs 18: 17, MSG)

"People ruin their lives by their own stupidity so why does God always get blamed." (Proverbs 19:3, MSG)

"A thick bankroll is no help when life falls apart, but a principled life can stand up to the worst." (Proverbs 11:4, MSG)

"There's a way of life that looks harmless enough; Look again – it leads straight to hell." (Proverbs 14:12, MSG)

One only has to read a few sentences from the Bible like these and to realize the Bible is as up-to-date as the experiences we are encountering. Let God's Word advise you my reading some more of it today. Here are a few suggestions:

Read: Proverbs 12:22, Proverbs 15:10, Proverbs 28:9

Thank you Lord, for giving us a Bible which never grows old. I have to confess that I often get distracted from Bible reading by doing what appears to be important. Remind me, Lord, that few things are important enough to deprive me of a fresh lesson from your Word.

Twenty-one Words

❧

There are no less than 600,000 words in the English language. The range of one's vocabulary then is a definite indication of his culture, education, general intelligence and personal discipline. The average American has a "use" vocabulary of about 10,000 words and a "recognition" vocabulary of some 35,000 words. When a youngster enters the first grade, he might have a personal vocabulary of some 3,000 to 4,000 words, which will expand to 40,000 words by his graduation from college. Such a growth of word use is dependent upon the extent to which one reads, listens and has a pride in expression. These things being true it seems strange to suggest that anyone can be articulate with a 21-word vocabulary. Nevertheless, there are ten sentences, consisting of three words each, utilizing twenty-one words, which provide some of the most appropriate, adequate and articulate language anyone can speak: "I love you. I thank you. May I help? I was wrong. Please forgive me. I understand you. I will pray. You look nice. You did well. Take your time." Learn to speak that language… conquer that vocabulary… and you will be able to communicate like you never believed possible! There is another language, brief, to the point, and it requires few words. It is the language of caring, helping, tangible compassion. To help a hurting or needy person requires little translation, but it speaks volumes about what a Christian is and how he got that way. In fact, to help someone in real need, and to do it for Jesus' sake, is a giant one-volume commentary on the Biblical claim, "It is more blessed to give than to receive." (Acts 20: 35)

Read: James 1: 22 – 25

Father, I have the vocabulary but I need the wisdom and compassion to choose my words and use them well. Increase my awareness of the Spirit of Christ within me and the opportunity I have for Him to be heard through me.

Pillows

🌿

Just before surgery, a Christian woman told her friends she had found three Bible verses which she called "pillows" she was going to rest on while she underwent this period of anxiety in her life. Following the operation, as she was coming out of the anesthesia, she reached or a pillow. The nurse said, "No, no, you cannot put a pillow under your head just now. You must lie perfectly still and flat on your back." The patient was alert enough to say with a smile, "All right I may not be able to have my bed pillow but I have three others I am resting on!" "Nothing separates us from Lord's love. (Romans 8:39) "I have trusted His mercy." (Psalm 13:5) "I am saved by grace." (Ephesians 2:8) Such pillows promise a lot of peaceful, restorative sleep. As you fluff your pillow tonight and settle in for a night's sleep, remember still another verse of Scripture. It too, can combat anxiety and restlessness: "He who keeps you will not slumber." (Psalm 121:3b)

Read: Psalm 121

Lord, you created us with the capacity and need for inward peace. It is a peace that passes all understanding and it can't be manufactured. As I understand it, unconfessed sin disturbs that peace. So I claim your peace today, first by confessing my sins.

Captive to the Bible

God has promised to bless the rightly divided preaching of His written Word. "It pleased God by the foolishness of preaching to save them that believe." (I Corinthians 1:21) I cannot find where He has pledged growth or health to a Christian by any other means. Of course, the objector cannot resist his reaction to my rather simple stance on the matter. "You Bible loyalists are all alike! You are narrow-minded, authority figures who overprice the Bible antiques you convince naïve people into buying." Now that I have devoted a couple of sentences to the voice of "rebellion", let me devote one or two to the voice of this preacher: A firm commitment by anyone to the centrality of the Bible will not cramp or stifle his mental and social sensitivity, rather it will enhance and purify it. I am as much opposed to making an idol of the Bible as anyone, but to the rightful authority of the Scriptures I am captive!

Read 1 Corinthians 1: 18 - 19

Lord, it is exciting to know that every time I read my Bible I am hearing from you. I firmly believe that your Word is like your voice in black and white. What I am asking is the will to do your word, not just hear it.

Missing Words

Years ago, I watched news coverage given to Yitzhak Rabin's funeral service in Jerusalem. The Prime Minister of Israel had rightfully won his recognition as a key figure in the Middle East peace process. He took risks and paid the price for his peace overtures toward some of Israel's enemies. It was not an enemy without, however, who gunned down Rabin. It was a twenty-eight year old Israeli law student who assassinated the Prime Minister upon what he called "God's command". Needless to say, God gave no such orders, for He would not contradict His sixth commandment of centuries ago, "Thou shall not kill" (Exodus 20: 13). As I listened to the eulogies offered by selected world leaders and Mr. Rabin's family members, I found a number of things which impacted me. I was struck by the personal touch woven into the remarks made by a few of the international figures who spoke. Perhaps I was most touched by the remarks of the Prime Minister's granddaughter. The tears on her cheeks were real and her loss was greater than that of an international figure. She had lost a grandfather. I was struck with the brevity and simplicity of Mr. Rabin's funeral, when compared to other state funerals. With more than the funeral's brevity and simplicity, I was struck with the absence of comfort's language, the glories of the eternal after-life and the hope beyond the grave. It made me remember what God's Word says: "I would not have you to be ignorant, brethren, concerning those who are asleep that you sorrow not as those who have no hope. For if we believe that Jesus died and rose again, those who sleep in Jesus will God bring with Him." (II Thessalonians 4:13 – 14)

Read: I Corinthians 15: 20 – 26

Thank you, Oh God for the comfort and power of the resurrection. Remove any smugness I have because I have a living Savior. Rather give me a burden for those who do not have that Savior and who sorrow without hope.

Authentic Tooth

The famous military figure of World War I, General Pershing, once had a tooth pulled sometime after he became and international figure. It is rumored that the dentist who extracted the general's tooth decided to sell it as a souvenir. When the General heard about it he was angry and instructed some of his officers to assume the task of getting his tooth back. Reportedly, those officers collected 317 so-called "authentic" Pershing teeth, which of course, meant at least 316 of them were fake and palmed off as genuine. Isn't it amazing how far some people will go to make a dollar? No less amazing is how far some people will go trying to palm off their commitments to God as genuine when, in fact, they are only counterfeit. God knows a real Christian though and He is not impressed with deception regardless how good the counterfeit may be. In fact, as you may remember, the Lord turned a deaf ear to the spiritual braggart in order to hear the honest prayer of admitted failure, "Lord, be merciful to me a sinner." (Luke 18:13).

Read: Matthew 23: 23 - 26

Praise you, dear Lord, for your integrity. You are the Truth, both now and for eternity. I am so thankful that I can put my whole weight on any promise you make. I want to be molded into someone you can trust. So I pray today as David of old, "Create in me a clean heart, Oh God."

If there are enemies of the home, and there are, the so-called "sexual liberation", the resurgence of secularism, and the clamor for upward mobility, the neutralizing of values in the classroom and the downsizing of morality in the entertainment industry are such enemies. There are friends of the home as well. **Priority** is a friend of family life. As old fashioned as it may sound in our day, Christian absolutes of moral purity are the best foundations on which to begin a marriage. The home which honors God's purposes for human worth the sacredness of life, the beauty of marital lovemaking, clean speech and wholesome laughter, is a home from which come future husbands and wives who know something about building such homes in their tomorrows. **Time** is a friend of the home, or I should say, time spent at home is a friend of the home. Even as I write that sentence, I feet some pangs of guilt in my own heart. Those who say it's not the quantity of time families spend together but the quality of that time are probably playing a little too much with words. **Self Control** is friend of the home, too. Though much attention these days is understandably given the problem of domestic physical abuse, verbal abuse is equally damaging. If parents could only hear replays of the verbal explosions, the nagging, the relentless criticism the threats they heap on their children, they would probably be embarrassed if they have much of a conscience. And what about **Love**? Isn't it the greatest friend of the home? Indeed it is, but if love is all it says it is, it is pure, patient and capable of waiting.

Read I Corinthians 13: 4 – 7

Lord, I want to be a friend of God and to do so, I need to be a friend of the family. I pray for the spiritual well being of my own family. And Father, for those young children in our family, I ask you to protect them from the wicked One.

At Any Moment

❧

It has been reported that an assistant to the Postmaster General once found himself in a very perplexing situation. It seems that a man telephoned him and insisted that a stamp be issued honoring the second coming of Christ. The postal official was at first bewildered about how to handle the situation without appearing to be atheistic or sacrilegious. Then he gathered his wits and said to his caller, "If you will tell me the exact time and place, I will prepare a stamp for the occasion." The postal official was chagrined several days later though, because he had received 12 letters from different people who predicted the exact time and place of Christ's return to earth! Jesus said, "Of that day and hour knows no man, no not the angels of heaven, but my Father only. Watch therefore, for you know not what hour your Lord is coming." (Matthew 24:42)

Read: I Peter 4:7 - 11

At any moment, Lord, we are told you could return to this earth. That is exciting to know. I want to be ready. I want to be equally excited about your presence right now, in me.

The Well Within

Oil is a subject of enormous importance these days. As go oil resources, so goes life to the modern and mechanical world. Events in the Middle East punctuate the role of oil in the minds of those who seek to determine and control the destiny of their nation and other nations as well. There has been, in the past, an experiment used in Canadian oil production. By means of electrodes placed deep into the earth, the crude oil is heated at its source, thus becomes more fluid and flows more rapidly up through the lines which have been drilled. What this process has done in extracting more oil, more readily, I don't know, but it certainly makes for a great illustration of how we Christians can become more spiritually productive. It stands to reason; a warm Christian heart will produce a quicker, compassionate and more direct witness, while a cold heart is slow to seek out the lost. A warm Christian heart seeks to worship and enjoys it, but a cold heart has all too little desire for praise. And what spiritual "electrodes" reach deep into our hearts to warm them? The discipline of daily Bible reading and Bible study sets higher the thermostat of the heart. No Christian's heart stays warm apart from honest, frequent prayer. And surely a regular fellowship with God's people is essential to priming the flow of praise.

Read: II Peter 1:1 – 11

What a discovery Lord, to find I have in Christ everything that pertains to life and godliness! Help me this very day to use all you have given to me to prime that abundant resource.

Doctor's Orders

All of us need to experience love and acceptance. But we seem to forget that sometimes, don't we? We talk about how gifted someone's talent is, or how magnetic someone's personality is. We say things like "He can really preach or she is a super manager!" But all too seldom do we hear anybody say of another, "Great Day! He loves people!" A doctor once gave some orders to a nurse regarding the care of an infant patient of his. Among his orders was this one: "Love the baby every 3 hours." There is an official diagnosis sometimes given to infants and children who lack expected mental and physical development. That diagnosis goes by the initials, FTT, "Failure to Thrive", and it can relate to the neglect of loving attention of a baby. A baby needs to be loved and made to feel secure. For that matter, so do older people and teenagers and widows and hardnosed businessmen. Little wonder Jesus said, "A new commandment I give to you, that you love one another as I have loved you." (John 13:34)

Read: I John 4: 7 - 14

Loving Father, I want not only to realize your love for me, I want to pass on your love to others. Teach me how to love without enabling sinfulness and how to nurture without indulging failure. In other words, Lord, teach me to love like you do.

Though I love my chosen home in the foothills of the Blue Ridge, the ocean has a charm for me. Maybe that's built into me since my boyhood was spent on Florida's southeast coast. It matters little what the weather is – the sounds of the surf, the sea breeze and salt air are like an invigorating tonic to me. I find myself in reflective moods while walking the beach. Once while watching dusk become darkness across God's great ocean, four distinct emotions overtook me. First, I felt **awe**. Remembering the Biblical account of creation, I was struck with the thought that God "moved upon the face of the waters" (Genesis 1:2), and He said, "Let there be a firmament in the midst of the waters" (Genesis 1:4). And the earth was spoken into existence. Then, watching the night stars appear, I said with the psalmist, "What is man that you are mindful of him"? (Psalm 8:4) What an awesome God we serve! Then I sensed **gratitude**. The lyrics, "from sea to shining sea", came to mind and I thanked God for the privilege of living in a country whose shores remain intact, bordering the greatest place in all the earth to live. **Concern** interrupted my gratitude though, as I prayed for the salvation and for the moral awakening of America. Next came thoughts about what lies beyond those ocean waters and I felt **accountability**. Jesus not only died to save America but He died for the other billions of people who live beyond our shores. It is expedient that we keep our nation and that world at the forefront of our mind.

Read Psalm 95: 1 - 7

Lord, you have lessons for me everywhere I turn. Open my eyes and my heart today to see the work of your hands and to learn things which will make a difference in my life.

Little Things

Following a fatal airplane crash, the investigators traced the cause of the accident to the absence of one small rivet in the framework of the plane. The absence of an inexpensive fastener, in their opinion, had led to the eventual collapse of part of the plane and then led to the loss of scores of lives. Needless to say, little things are important. And little things can be very damaging. It is like the Bible says of the tongue: "It is a little member which can set on fire the course of nature." (James 3:6) Watch out for small irritations that cause you to say little cutting things, which in turn, hurt and wound deeply. Look out for little suspicions and jealousies, which lead to thoughts and words that damage lives, homes and reputations. Be careful about the sarcasm you use. You may find it coy and amusing but it may have inflicted a wound hard to heal. Recognize exaggerations and half-truths for what they are, lies by any other name. Use the little things instead to encourage and lift someone nearby today.

Read: James 3:13 - 18

Lord, the more I think about it the more I realize my tongue gets me in more trouble than any other part of my body. Yet it is with my tongue that I worship you, I pray and I spread the truth. My tongue can be a blessing but I need you to take charge of it.

Never Out of Sight

Sometime ago, I was driving into our city by way of a main street and I was quickly passed by a car traveling much faster than the posted speed limit. I noticed the car, after passing me, darted in and out between cars, weaving its way toward downtown. Suddenly I saw the speeding car slow down and the driver began observing all the rules of good driving. And what brought about this sudden change of behavior? You guessed it. The driver spotted a city police car a few feet ahead of him. Amazing, isn't it, how well behaved people are when they know the authorities are watching them. But you know, we are always being watched by the Authority of Authorities. God knows our every action and thought. Like the Bible says, "God is not mocked. Whatever a person sows, he will also reap." (Galatians 6:7) Live like God is always looking, because…. He is! Live like you want to please God, because you can.

Read: Psalm 139

It is too much for me to take in, Lord. You are always and everywhere present. That is beyond my comprehension, yet your word says it is true. So, I will find peace today in your presence. I will also be reminded of my accountability to you. I thank you that you never let me out of your sight.

❧

Once I heard a man pray on Easter Sunday. He began like this: "Lord, we thank you so much for Easter. We need Easter so much this year." His second sentence so captured my attention. I listened even more intently as the man continued this conversation with the Lord. "There has been so much heartache, disappointment and sorrow in recent months. We need the hope and assurance that Easter means." Not just because of our difficulties and adversities do we need Easter's message; we need it because it is the celebration of the crossroads of human history. Easter means there is hope for winning the war against every evil obstacle and godless force we have. We need Easter to be reminded of how thoroughly our Lord defeated Satan. We need Easter to underscore for us the lengths to which Jesus went to deal with our sin and guilt problem. We need Easter to realize that there are no ultimate reversals for us. We need Easter to be able to spend time in hospital rooms with certainties which surpass diagnoses. We need Easter to strengthen our grasp on those we embrace in funeral homes and those who need us in the hard months of adjustment thereafter. We need Easter to remind us of how important it is that we invest in reaching a world God went so far to redeem. We need Easter to keep life in such balance that we do not allow an encroaching attitude of pessimism to overshadow our testimony. We need Easter to help friends bewildered by life's injustices, to understand this is not all there is. We need Easter to reinforce that constant perspective. There is more to come

Read: I Corinthians 15: 50 – 57

Lord Jesus, we not only need Easter, we have Easter. Praise you for your glorious resurrection and thank you for the power of the resurrection. I ask you to help me today to live like someone who has been given the power of the resurrection.

A Resurrection Confirmation

Most of the major motel chains in the country now have a system of communications by which they can make advance reservations for their guests. When reservations have been made for you, you are usually supplied with a confirmation which you present upon your arrival. There is real security in having that printed reservation in your pocket, especially as you are driving along late in the afternoon, assured that a comfortable room awaits you. God has supplied us with a written confirmation regarding a Christian's reservation in heaven. You will probably recognize the wording of this Biblical confirmation as it appears in John 14. This is the way *The Living Bible* expresses it: "There are many homes up there where my Father lives and I am going to prepare them for your coming. When everything is ready, then I will come and get you so that you can always be with me where I am." (John 14:2) With Christ as your Savior you have a reservation in heaven!

Read: John 14: 1 - 14

Praise you, Father, for your trustworthiness. When you say something, you mean it. When you promise something, you intend for us to bank on it. Today, I claim my place in heaven because you have paid for it and reserved it.

࣪ৎ

13 feet… 7 inches is the bold-letter wording on two large signs located in front of an underpass through which I drove the other day. Those signs, of course, are to forewarn truckers in particular, so they will not try to drive their oversized loads through an undersized passage. The signs, however, said still something else to me. They graphically underscored an illustration of our Lord's Incarnation. To experience man's world… to taste man's temptations… to encounter man's earth… God had to travel through the narrow passage of self-retraction. Is that not what is meant by the Scripture passage: "…being in the form of God, He thought it not robbery to be equal with God; But made Himself of no reputation and took upon Him the form of a servant and was made in the likeness of men; And being found in fashion as a man, He humbled Himself and became obedient unto death, even the death of the cross." (Philippians 2: 6 – 8) "He humbled Himself,"… Paul wrote of Jesus. Better translated, "He emptied Himself", was Paul's way of describing the Incarnation of Christ. Let us be mindful of our Lord's entry into this world as well as His departure from it. He came to do and to be what he did and was… to taste of our world and show us the Father in the process. He traveled the narrow passage of human birth and dwelt among us. He traveled the narrow passage of temptation and conquered it for us. He traveled the narrow passage of death and triumphed over it. And because he lovingly humbled Himself to do it all, we have confidence in his power to defeat whatever enemy may attack us.

Read: Hebrews 2: 14 - 16

Oh God, what a lesson you teach me about the power of humility! The world around me insists I must try to be greater, smarter, and bigger in order to succeed. I see the importance of setting goals to achieve, but I see the greater importance of submitting my ambitions to what you have in mind.

The Stable

A missionary in London once make a visit to a professional jockey in order to talk with him about his relationship to Christ. He found the jockey in a stable and when he began talking about religious matters, the jockey stopped him. The jockey said, "A stable is no place to talk of religion, so that is the end of that!" The missionary calmly and warmly said, "Oh no, that is not the end of it. A Stable is really the beginning of it. The whole wonderful story of Jesus Christ began in a stable. So, my friend, if Jesus was born in a stable, you can be born again in one." The missionary's approach was effective. The young jockey listened and eventually committed his life to Christ. Most anywhere you are can be a fitting place to talk about Jesus if it is done prayerfully, carefully and genuinely. So today, if the opportunity presents itself, you can be God's messenger of encouragement, His witness to salvation, His interpreter of the Truth. It doesn't matter about the surroundings as much as the opportunity.

Read: Colossians 8: 12 - 17

I confess, Lord, I am not nearly as alert as I ought to be about situations which are tailor made for my witness. Increase my attentiveness and my readiness to share Jesus with people around me.

A Place To Pray

꙰

"Neath the old olive trees, 'neath the old olive trees, went the Savior alone on His knees...." With the songs of Gethsemane we are familiar. The picture of our Lord, framed in olive branches, engaged in prayer's agony, is well imprinted in our minds. There is however, even more to be said about Gethsemane than it was a place of prayer for Jesus, a place of slumber for His disciples and the place of betrayal for Judas. Too often, our eyes by-pass the helpful little things in Scripture. Do you remember seeing the following brief passage about Gethsemane? "And Judas also, which betrayed Him, knew the place; for Jesus oftimes resorted thither with his disciples." (John 18:2) John tells us that Gethsemane was a familiar place of retreat to the Lord and the Twelve. Before and after busy moments in their ministry, Jesus and the disciples slipped aside for times of spiritual refreshment, evaluation and His instruction. This garden of olive trees was just one of their places of retreat. Indispensable to their ministry seemed places like Gethsemane. In like fashion, places like our own favorite prayer spot are indispensable to our daily walk with Jesus. Establish some familiar places to which you are drawn to pray and which become landmarks in your Christian Biography.

Read: Mark 6: 30 - 45

Dear Lord, you have told us that a closet is an effective place in which to pray. You led your disciples to find places of retreat and seclusion to pray. I suppose where we pray is a good place if it helps us keep our minds on you. Help me find times and places where I am not distracted and where I can build memories of conversations with you.

There is a day called Good Friday on the Christian calendar. But knowing what is remembered on Good Friday people understandably ask, "Why do you call the anniversary of Jesus' cruel death on the cross <u>Good</u> Friday?" It would seem more fitting to call it <u>Bad </u>Friday or <u>Dark</u> Friday. No, <u>Good</u> Friday is a well-chosen name for this day, not because we revel in the suffering through which Jesus went on the cross, but because His death made possible the celebration of <u>our</u> forgiveness. Christ offered His life as the One to bear our guilt and then He arose from the grave to tell us that forgiveness is available to all who will accept it from Him. The day all that transpired was a good day for us. It is not a good day to be taken for granted. It represents the seriousness of sin, the magnitude of God's grace and the centerpiece of His forgiveness. Bottom line: Good Friday is good because God is good.

Read: Psalm 118: 1 - 9

Oh God, you are great and you are also good. When I consider all you are and all your give I am overwhelmed. When I take a long look at the cross of Jesus and why He died there, I am at a loss for words. Simplicity says it best, Lord, you are good.

It was our first March in Virginia after living in Texas for three years and we were taking note of the first evidence of spring. To say the least, my wife and I were pleased the weather was turning warm enough for our then two-year-old to play outdoors. We were also excited about the jonquils, which were starting to sprout, and the forsythia putting out their bright yellow blossoms. Embarrassed as I am to admit it, we both had the idea this was just the beginning of what our yard and neighborhood would look like for months to come. You can imagine our disappointment when we saw the forsythia losing their flowers to the green leaves which replaced them. And the jonquils only lasted a month. The dogwoods were beautiful for three or four weeks and then they too, became flowerless trees. Our Florida background had not prepared us for the other side of spring's beauty in the mid-Atlantic. It only lasts but so long. There is a lesson about Easter in the fleeting passage of spring. What makes Easter such an exciting celebration for God's people is not that it is observed one spring Sunday each year. But Resurrection truth is not applicable to just one day; it is the truth by which redeemed people live every day of every week! Easter is a special day indeed. Thank God, however, when Easter is over, the glory of the Resurrection is not over like some seasoned shrub or an annual spring flower. The Resurrection has a year round glory!

Read: I Peter 1: 3 - 10

Praise God, you are the same, yesterday, today and forever. Your Word does not fade. Your promises do not wilt and the power of the resurrection does not weaken. So I claim your strength for what faces me today.

The Door

❧

Years ago, while watching the antics of our youngest son, I had a lasting impression made upon me. Our son was then 16 months old and persistent. He had demonstrated his disgust at a closed door, which he wanted open. The interesting thing was that, just a few feet away, there was another door to the room and it was very much open. Like little children, many people insist upon forcing open the doors to happiness and fullness when God has already provided doors, which are open to such a life. Jesus said, "I am the door, by me if any man enter in he shall be saved and shall go in and out and find pasture." (John 10:9) Jesus also said, "I am come that they might have life and that they might have it more abundantly." (John 10:10) Satan is an expert in designing attractive doors which lead to failure, sin and guilt. As enticing as those doors appear to be, we need to leave them shut. When God opens doors to us we can trust what lies beyond. So the lesson for today is to consider what lies beyond before choosing a door.

Read: John 10: 1 - 10

You are the door, Lord, which leads to eternal life. I need to be reminded you are also the door that leads to good choices, wise decisions, a clean conscience and no regrets.

Alive Unto God

Our Lord is alive! There is more to that announcement than fact alone. The fact that Jesus was raised from the dead two thousand years ago is not a kind of sanctified display along God's "midway of miracles". Too often, it is thought and by too many, that the purpose of the Resurrection of Jesus is to dazzle us with God's ability to overpower the laws of nature. The empty tomb is not simply "exhibit A" in the case of God versus Satan. The fact that Jesus arose and is alive has something to do with us and it has something to do with us now! Jesus said, "Because I live, you shall live also." (John 14:19) There is an inseparable connection between the resurrection of the Lord and our resurrection to newness of life. There is assurance of our final resurrection because he is the "first fruit" from among the dead. But equally important…. is the relationship between the resurrection of Jesus and our vitality of life here and now. To the degree that Jesus is alive in us, we are vital in Him. To the extent we appropriate the truth that Jesus not only arose from a tomb in Jerusalem but He actually is living in the Redeemed, our living is done in the "power of the resurrection". "Now if we be dead with Christ, we believe that we shall also live with Him… likewise reckon ye also yourselves to be dead indeed unto sin, but alive unto God through Jesus Christ our Lord." (Romans 6: 8 and 11)

Read: Job 19: 23 - 26

You are a Risen Savior, Lord. I believe that with my whole heart, but I want to be a reason others can believe it with their whole hart. Remind me, and often, that to the extent I allow you can live out your life in me for all the world to see a Risen Savior.

A Moment In Time

❧

Daylight Savings Time and Standard Time takes command of our clocks on Sunday mornings at some unheard of hour of the night. But why must these time changes take place on Sundays? Why couldn't Daylight Time or Standard Time be introduced on a Saturday or a Monday? Why Sunday? In a way, it seems like an irreverent intrusion into church life. Is it though? Is it an intrusion, or is it actually an illustration? Think about it a moment. Christians worship on Sundays because it is a weekly celebration of the Resurrection of Jesus. Nothing so changed history and eternity, as did the Resurrection. So for time to change on Sunday morning figuratively underscores the impact of the Resurrection. When the crucified Jesus stepped from His tomb, all time and eternity changed. When he arose, the opportunity for change in our lives and in our testimonies was made possible. And for someone to reject the Lord of the Resurrection is to refuse the greatest of all time changes there is! Not only does the clock change in the predawn hours of a couple of Sundays each year, all time and eternity changed in the predawn hours of the first Resurrection Sunday. So when your alarm sounds on a Sunday morning, reminding you of what hour it is, lay hold on some thoughts about time: It is time to thank God for the change in your life because of that moment in time when Jesus walked away from His grave. It is time for you to again make your way to the house of God, reminding your neighborhood that you are a regular worshipper, a Believer in the risen, living Christ. It is time to awake from our spiritual sleep, as the Bible puts it, realizing how many around us have never allowed the Lord of the Empty Tomb to change life and eternity for them.

Read II Corinthians 5: 17 – 6: 2

Oh God, than you for knowing all about time though you are timeless and eternal. History is all about your timing as is eternity. Keep me aware that just as there was a moment in time for my salvation, I need to part of a moment in time for someone else's salvation.

My Assignment

❧

Advising the Thessalonian Christians, Paul wrote, "…study to be quiet, and to do your own business and to work with your own hands…that ye walk honestly toward them that are without and that ye may have lack of nothing." (I Thessalonians 4: 11-12) Notice the accent upon the little possessive pronoun, "own"? Here is a distinct assumption that a Christian is going to engage in honest work. The Christian is endowed with abilities unique to him and it is simply assumed that he will utilize those abilities. In the course of daily life then, the Christian is able to have inward peace in that he commits to God's control those things with which he is unable to deal and he works honestly at that which God has equipped him to do. As a result of this principle in living, the Christian has his testimony among those outside of Christ and he has, at the same time, the needs of his own sustenance met. This is a strong Scriptural appeal for honest Christian work and, at the same time, a stern disapproval of laziness, indolence and dependency. This principle applies also in the life and influence of a church. Each of us within a church family is to "do his own business" and "to work with his own hands". In the highest sense of the word, we can only testify to those who are "without" (without Christ) and we can only lack for nothing "within" (in Christ) as each does his own work and works with his own hands.

Read: Colossians 3:17. 23 – 25

Sometimes Lord, I am so caught up in doing what I like to do I forget the importance of doing what I need to do. You have gifted me and assigned me according to your purpose. I am now reporting for today's assignment.

A few years ago, I read that the hidden secret to a healthy life is eating onions, but believe me, it cannot be a kept secret for long. Whether eating onions can contribute to our health may be questionable, but one thing is for certain, eating onions cannot be hidden! The things that produce good spiritual health are not so questionable. Daily Bible reading, frequent prayer, regular worship, and Christian friendships are like a balanced diet and supplemental vitamins for a healthy Christian life. And when we are spiritually healthy, that cannot be hidden either. The Bible says a healthy Christian is one who can look into the mirror, as it were, and see himself more and more changing to reflect the image of Christ-likeness. Soon enough it will be obvious to all. "But we all with unveiled face, beholding as in a mirror the glory of the Lord, are being transformed into the same image from glory to glory, just as from the Lord, the Spirit." (II Corinthians 3:18, NASV)

Read: II Corinthians 4: 7 - 12

Lord, I don't want to be a hidden Christian. I don't want to appear almost like a Christian. I want to be more and more like you. Help me know it is possible to be Christ-like, allowing you to be yourself in me.

❧

Like a splendorous ray of sunlight piercing the foreboding clouds, Easter in the Christian sense, stands glorious in our otherwise darksome day. If the resurrection of Christ means anything, it means that God's own have a certainty. We can predict, yes, we can anticipate an experience while living in an unpredictable era. Foreknowledge is an attribute of God and it is God's to share if He chooses. We ourselves cannot forecast the tomorrows. It is obviously good that we cannot, for had it been best for us, doubtless God would have given us that capacity. Although we cannot forecast our future, we can accurately predict the ultimate victory of God. If we are His and He is ours, then we can predict a victory for ourselves, since He has said that His triumph is ours to share with Him. This is no small comfort in a day like ours, for we are, at this very moment, subject to "attack" by our adversaries: death, sorrow, distress, disease, and earthly enemies as well. For such a time, we who are God's own by faith in Christ, have a reassuring forecast: God wins! Paul has such a good word for us...".. Nay, in all these things we are more than conquerors through Him that loved us." (Romans 8:37) He says there is something more valuable than being a conqueror. He says we can be more than conquerors, we can be victors. That is strange jargon for this age, isn't it? Though we have equated victors and conquerors, they are not always synonymous. Death seemed a conqueror on Friday, but Jesus was victor on Sunday! Because He is victor we are more than any conqueror of ours. The eloquence any Easter is that His victory is our victory too!

Read: I John 5: 1 - 4

Father, forgive me for living one minute like a victim. I know there are many adversities and adversaries I have to face, but none of them are more than conquerors. Your Word tells me that you have made me the one who is more than a conqueror.

Insurance Policy

Once a mythical cowboy applied for an insurance policy and when the agent asked him if he had ever had an accident, he replied, "No, but a bucking house kicked in two of my ribs last summer. And a couple of years ago a snake bit me on my ankle." The agent said, "Wouldn't you call those accidents? The cowboy answered, "No…they did it on purpose!" Seriously now…. A Christian knows that life is not just made up of bad luck, good luck and accidents. We know that God never promises any of us exemption from life's problems, but He does promise to bring something for our good out of every experience we have. That is what the Bible means when it says, "We know all things work together for good to them that Love the Lord and who are the called according to His purpose." (Romans 8:28)   Notice the verse does not say all things are food. That's just not true. To lose your job is not good. To lose your home to a fire or a flood is tragic: to be given a diagnosis of cancer is frightening. The verse says, "All things work together for good". Out of loss, God can lead us to gain. Out of fear, God can lead us to peace. Out of guilt, God can bring us to forgiveness. When all is said and done a sovereign God makes sense out of the senseless and that is good.

Read: James 1: 2 - 12

Father, thank you for being patient with me when I fret and worry. I know you are ultimately in charge of life and eternity, but I often forget. Help me get a glimpse of you beyond whatever discouragement crosses my path today.

The Power of Choice

❧

One is hard pressed to single out the greatest of blessings from God. To be sure, at the top of the list would appear such suggestions as: Christ Jesus Himself, love, forgiveness, heaven, companionship, family... and health. It appears to me, though, one of the most important of all God-given blessings is one, seldom ever mentioned. Perhaps it is just one of those blessings so attached to life, we take it for granted as much as the air we breathe. The blessing of which I speak is the **power of choice**... the very privilege of **Will**. Even our relationship to God rests squarely upon our **power of choice**. Many a marriage has been saved because someone **chose** to forgive. Many a heart has been healed because a son **chose** to come home. Many a friendship as been salvaged because someone **chose** to understand. Many a missionary has staked a claim for God because some Christians **chose** to tithe. Many an evil has been dealt a blow because a Christian **chose** to speak out. Thank God, even the very form of American government is predicated upon our God given right to choose. So when you and I approach a national holiday we are not only blessed with political privilege, we are charged to appropriate a God-given blessing... our **power of choice**.

Read: Deuteronomy 30: 15 - 20

Heavenly Father, the Bible tells me that you have chosen me. That boggles my mind. I can't begin to understand what love drives you to choose me for yourself. This I do know, I choose to accept your love and today, I choose to prove my love for you by doing what you ask.

We are not asked to believe in the Resurrection of our Lord without there being a purpose in such belief. The Empty Tomb of Jesus is not a "Haunted Cave" or a dazzling sideshow along God's "carnival" of doctrines! I readily agree with the oft-repeated quotation, "One would do as well to place his faith in the Tomb of the Unknown Soldier as to vest his hope in an unresurrected Christ". By the same token, I would think one might as well embrace a "Believe It Or Not" of Ripley as to believe in a Resurrection which has no purpose for those who accept it. The Resurrection is part of all that Jesus told us of Himself. If we reject the Resurrection, we cast suspicion upon the trustworthiness of His other claims. He said He would rise the third day. He also said He loved all men. Shall we believe one thing He said and not another. The Resurrection is our victory as much as it was His. Christ won the victory over sin and death and He did so garbed in the flesh of humanity! We are not asked now to assume the role of partisan fans in a hometown stadium, cheering Him for His triumph. His triumph says to us, "Make Christ your Lord and permit Him to conquer the same sin and death which now surround your humanity!" Resurrection's purpose is the message of Paul's testimony to the Galatians: "I am crucified with Christ, nevertheless I live, yet not I, but Christ liveth in me." (Galatians 2:20)

Read: I Peter 1: 3 - 9

Lord, you had me in mind when you were on the cross. You had me in mind when you stepped out of the tomb. You have me on your heart when I pray. Thank you for caring so much. It makes today worth living.

Three Short Sentences

৯৫

God knows.... God cares... God wins... By the simplest terms, these three statements serve as a commentary on Easter's meaning and message. **God knows....** That God took a body, was miraculously conceived in the womb of a virgin and that He experienced life as we know it means that He understands us from the inside out. "We have not a high priest who is unable to sympathize with our weaknesses, but one who in every respect has been tempted as we are, yet without sin." (Hebrews 4:15) So when you hurt, He understands. When you shed tears, He understands, having wept Himself. When you feel abandoned, be reminded of His experience with crowds who turned away and with disciples who forsook Him and ran. **God cares...** That God planned for our restoration before the worlds were made; That Jesus was nailed to a cross which was ours and buried in a tomb which was more ours than His, means that His care for us exceeds mere sympathy and sacrifice. His care for us caused Him to become a substitute for us. "For scarcely for a righteous man will one die; yet peradventure for a good man some would even dare to die. But God commendeth His love toward us, in that while we were yet sinners, Christ died for us." (Romans 5: 7 – 8) **God wins...** That Jesus left behind an empty tomb means not only that He won the victory over sin and death; it means we can as well. The Resurrection was a victory for all who will make Jesus Lord and Savior, claiming His triumph over their trials, temptations, sorrow, and death. "I am the resurrection and the life; he that believeth in me though he were dead, yet shall he live: And whosoever liveth and believeth in me shall never die." (John 11: 25 – 26)

Read: Romans 6: 8 – 19

Dear God, whether it be three short sentences or a thousand long ones, Easter's meaning cannot be put into words. I can be one of the best commentaries on Easter by living out the victories of Jesus' Resurrection. Help me do it.

If...God could empty Jesus' tomb and make Him live again...He can make love to live again in a marriage, which seems to have lost its hope of survival. He can make hope live again in the hearts of parents who yearn for a son or daughter to come back to the Lord. He can make joy return to a Christian's life after guilt or compromise has all but buried it. He can lift the spirits of a church beset by division and distracted from its vital lifelines of reaching the lost and discipling the saved. He can revive the zeal for Christian service in the heart of one weary with well-doing or bitter with disillusionment. He can make friendships come to life again by the power of a humbled spirit and by an exchange of apologies between people who seek to forgive because they have been forgiven of God. He can bury a cynical tongue and resurrect one that speaks the language of encouragement. He can bury a skeptic and raise him up an optimist. He can return Sunday's excitements to one who lists them in the subtle shifting of weekend priorities. Heaven's doors are open to the twice-born because of our Lord's empty tomb...and so are some other doors. Because we serve the God of resurrection power, we have a living Savior...a lively hope...and we can have a resurrection-quality to the life we now live in the flesh.

Read: Hosea 6: 1 - 3

Forgive me, Lord, for burying anger, resentment, cynicism and allowing them to fertilize roots of bitterness. Raise up in me the spirit of forgiveness and trust and empower me to claim a newness of life.

Faithful In Least

❧

A bank employee was due a very good promotion and he had received word the promotion would be announced the following week. Needless to say, he was really pleased. However, at lunch one day, the president of the bank saw the employee indulge in petty deceit as he passed through the cafeteria line. He slipped two patties of butter under his slice of bread so they would be hidden from the eyes of the cashier. That little incident changed the president's mind about the employee and the promotion was not given to him. Think of it! A man let a few cents rob him of a gratifying promotion. But the bank president was probably correct in his judgment. Like the Bible says, "He who is faithful in that which is least is faithful also in much." (Luke 16: 10) Our best insight into the meaning of faithfulness is that quality as God exhibits it. Can you imagine the impact upon our prayer life or assurance or our expectation if every now and then God failed to keep His word? What if He didn't keep faith with us in just a few little things? Our whole ability to trust God would be destroyed. Isaiah stated the case well: "Behold, God is my salvation; I will trust and not be afraid..."

Read: Isaiah 12: 1 - 6

What a thrill it is, Oh God, to realize you can be trusted all the time under all circumstances. Turn Satan away from my ears today as he lies to me about your reliability.

Years ago, I read Reuel Howe's book, <u>Man's Need and God's Action</u>. Howe penetrates well into some of our inmost needs. It is a kind of helpful shock to see in print the description of things you have felt in secret. In my opinion, the most vital thoughts in this volume rotate around the idea: "God created persons to be loved and things to be used… we are tempted to love things and use people." Will you not agree that inward hurts are far more painful than outward hurts? A wounded spirit aches differently but more lastingly than wounded flesh. Why so? Because to be hurt by another person is to sustain the fear of being cut off from him. This is basic in the anxiety that surrounds death; the fear of ceasing to be. We are dependent upon one another and to be alienated from each other is to hurt with the pain of "not-mattering". Of course, we often have built-in defenses and insulations against these hurtful rejections. Sometimes we become super-sensitive and ache before we have really been hurt. Occasionally, we will withdraw from people so as to remove the threat of what we have convinced ourselves will happen. Sometimes we will become extremely critical of those we want to notice us most so that it will appear their attitude toward us does not matter. In any event, these attitudes represent the fear to love because of the fear of being rejected. Perhaps these observations will give us another insight into what our Lord meant when He said, "Perfect love casteth out fear." (I John 4:18) Simply stated, we need each other.

Read: I John 4: 16 - 21

Father, admittedly I take your love too much for granted. I know your Word tells me that you love me even in the face of my sin. But I need a fresh realization that your risk to love me is my opportunity to rejoice in that love and to love you in return.

Excitement Fits the Occasion

How do you describe…a child at an Easter egg hunt? With the very little ones, there is first timidity, bewilderment and hesitation. Then slowly follows the discovery of what the "hunt" is all about. Soon enough there are dancing eyes, excited screams, carried about on hurrying little feet which are hard to hold still while cameras attempt to preserve the whole occasion on film. Of course, there are some who question whether Christians even ought to plan such events for their children. After all, to focus children's attention on bunny rabbits and jellybeans is easy to do but misses the meaning of Easter by a country mile! I would readily agree we need to start early with our children and stay consistent with an emphasis upon the life and love of Jesus in holiday seasons like Christmas and Easter. The fact is, the more we emphasize the reality of Christ on a year round basis, the more easily Children will be able to understand His rightful place on special days and occasions. Whereas I question how much profile we ought to give to an Easter egg hunt, it seems the element of excitement and the delight of Easter's meaning is illustrated by the sight of children on an egg-hunt, running from discovery to discovery on a warm sunlit spring day with new life everywhere, putting in an appearance! Yes indeed, our Lord is alive and when we live in the joy and strength of His life there are discoveries everywhere to be found!

Read: I Peter 1: 3 - 8

Dear Lord, excitement too often describes my reaction to things which don't deserve it. Stir in me a holy excitement about your resurrection and about the life you want to live our in me.

Standard Equipment

꒰꒱

Some things come and go: like birthdays... and clothing styles... and hairstyles... renegade governments... and food fads... music trends... and sports heroes. Some things come and stay: "forever" things... like God's Book... "The grass withereth, the flower fadeth, but the Word of our God shall stand forever." (Isaiah 40:8) Whatever the moment in time, the Scriptures are designed for us as "standard equipment". Whether printed on parchment or captured on microfilm, whether read by candlelight or by a florescent fixture, the Word of our God is a step ahead of history. Choose the year, past or future and you will find God's Written Voice is "standard equipment" for the human race. Not long ago I read of an interesting fact, which belongs to the days of the western frontier in America. The pony express route was a 1900 mile trek from Missouri to California which required ten days of horseback travel by 40 men, each riding hard 50 miles a day. To conserve the weight the pony express riders wore the lightest clothing, rode on small thin saddles and carried no weapons. The mail pouches the riders carried were very light and letters to be delivered by pony express were to be written on thin paper, posted at $5 an ounce. Yet each rider carried the large full-sized Bible, which was presented him when he joined the elite band of horsemen who comprised the Pony Express. Why? The Scriptures were considered "standard equipment". It is forever stabilizing to a Christian who lives in a changing world to have God's Book as "standard equipment".

Read: Isaiah 55: 6 - 11

You are holy, Oh God, and so is your Book. You Word is also timely and timeless. Indeed, it is standard equipment for Believers, but it is never ordinary or commonplace. Keep me aware, Lord, that as I stay in touch with your Word, I stay in touch with you.

Get Into The Game

❧

Bjorn Borg was once the undisputed number one tennis player in the world. Upon his convincing defeat of Jimmy Conners, the young Swede virtually eliminated all doubts about his superiority on the tennis court. Following their Wimbledon Championship Match, Jimmy Conners had little to say other than to compliment Borg and to assure tennis fans everywhere he was not going to let his defeat end his aspirations to return to the number one ranking he once enjoyed. There was one comment Conners made, however, which was an important admission and observation. Regarding his play against Borg, he said, "I never really got into the match mentally." Needless to say, you cannot play good professional tennis without unyielding concentration. In fact you can't play good amateur tennis without it... or for that matter, good leisurely tennis. By the same token, we cannot fully experience the joys and the impact of the Christian life unless we concentrate upon it. This is not to suggest that the way to live an abundant Christian life is through tension and pressure. It is to say that life must be focused upon the priority of Christ likeness. When priorities are established and the energies of life are Christ-centered, there follows a capacity for the flesh to do what the will desires. That is precisely what Paul was talking about when he said: "I press toward the mark for the prize of the high calling of God in Christ Jesus." (Philippians 3:14)

Read: Philippians 1: 20 - 21
Colossians 3: 1 - 2

Today, dear Lord, I want to keep my head in the game. Of course Christ likeness is no game to be played, it's a life to be lived. Drive Satan's distractions away and help me keep my mind on the prize you have put before me.

Quick To Encourage

❧

Encouragement is absolutely essential to the life and health of a Christian. Life can deal some heavy and low blows to God's people. The Enemy is an opportunist. When he sees a Christian down, he doubles his efforts to keep him down. When he sees a Christian in despair, he exaggerates the problem to multiply the despair. When he spots a Christian weary of the battle with a given temptation, he beautifies the temptation to make resistance all the more difficult. When he finds a Christian asking, "Is it worth it all?" he is swift with his reply. "Certainly not"! You would think Christians would be more alert to the situation than we are. So often we miss our opportunity and responsibility to encourage one another by way of a positive spirit, an encouraging remark, a timely compliment or an understanding ear. And where does "constructive criticism" fit into all this? Too often it fits, but not very well. Some of us have so long lived in a critical mood that we do not realize how discouraging we can be to other Christians. Too often we see what is wrong, not what is right. We take the good for granted, ignore thanksgiving and dwell on failures. Is this to say we are to be indulgent with each other? No. Are we to be satisfied with sloppy performance just because we are Christians? Of course not. Are we to condone carelessness and shabbiness in the Name of Jesus? Never. Just what is the answer? Be as constructive as we are critical. And be critical of ourselves when we are not constructive. "A friend loves at all times and a brother is born for adversity." (Proverbs 17:17)

Read: Ecclesiastes 4: 9 - 12

Lord, I have been encouraged by thoughtful people so many times. It is too easy to take and not to give in that situation. Remind me throughout the day that you mean for me to be an encourager for someone too weak or too defeated to handle it on his own.

The Difference

"It is amazing the difference a day makes." Such was my comment as I looked out a kitchen window to see the dogwood blossoms making their annual appearance. Just the day before we had taken note of the dogwood buds but they did not appear ready to blossom. The warm temperature, sunlight and overnight rain of a single day, however, combined to make blossoms from buds – open beauty from what had been a growing promise. Easter is just such a day... a day symbolizing another day, which made the eternal difference! Friday had been a long and frightening day. Saturday had been a lonely and sad day. Then came Resurrection Day. What a difference a day makes! The power of God, the love of God and the Will of God combined to make life from death... open victory from what had been a Divine promise. To be sure, Christians celebrate the Resurrection of Christ every Sunday, but there is a special place for the celebration we call Easter. It should be approached as the Day of Days, the day which wrought the difference... in our own destiny, in our outlook on death, in our approach to life, in our sense of hope, in our slant on history, in our view of the Bible, in our expectancy of Christ's return. It is amazing the difference a day makes! It's the difference in broken hearts, lonely lives, guilty minds, discouraged spirits and weakened hopes.

Read: 1 Peter 1:17 - 21

Lord, we celebrate your resurrection every Sunday and every year on Easter Sunday, but I rejoice in the resurrection every day. Every day, because you live, I live also! And because you live in me, I live with hope. At this very moment I lay claim to the power of the Resurrection!

The Table

❧

"Jesus took bread… and said… this is my body. And He took the cup… saying… this is my blood… During the Lord's Supper, we share the symbols of our Lord's sacrifice, the bread and the cup. There is, however, another symbol we share during the observance of the Lord's Supper. That symbol is the Table itself. The setting of the first Lord's Supper was the Passover. The Passover was a family experience as the Jewish nation observed it. The Lord and His Disciples were like unto a family, in fact, spiritually closer to one another than to some of their own family members. The Lord's Table is to be shared by the spiritual family of Christ in the spirit of the Upper Room occasion. Thus the Table about which we gather symbolizes our **relationship to Christ**. We are the sons of God, having experienced mutual birth into the Redeemed Family. The Table symbolizes our **relationship to each other**, as well. As children of God we are indeed relatives, brothers and sisters. The Table symbolizes our **responsibility to one another**. As a family, we are to make mutual the concerns of our joys, our sorrows, our anxieties, and our victories. Consequently, the Lord's Table symbolizes both our remembrances of Him and remembrance of one another. We first remember who He is to us, subsequently to remember what we are to each other.

Read: I Corinthians 11: 23 - 34

Dear Savior, forgive me for the times I have partaken of the Lord's Supper with a preoccupied mind. Admittedly, I have participated in communion services with little thought of me responsibility for fellow Believers around me. Thank you for my place at your table and thank you for that reminder of my responsibility.

Short But Not Cheap

❧

The Bible says, "Your life…is even a vapor, that appears for a little time and then vanishes away." (James 4:14) Is this to say that life is no more significant than a quickly evaporating puff of steam? Is it to say that we are here today and gone tomorrow, thus life cannot be but so important? Of course not! The Bible's emphasis at the point of describing life as a vapor is upon its uncertainty, not upon its insignificance. The very fact that God chose to create the human race indicates the worth of mortal life. God sought to spend His love and share His life with those He brought into being. And those He brought into being He created in His own image. That spiritual image in which we have been created involves those unique capacities for fellowship with God, which belongs only to humankind. Hence, the true worth of life is not found in its earthly length but in its heavenly capacity. There is an eternal dimension, which enters into life's worth that far exceeds the dimension of its earthly length. Beyond the life of the human body there is the life of the human spirit, which will never die. Before even the conception of life in the womb, there is the foreknowledge of God and the provision of our salvation. If there is any conclusion to be drawn, it is that life is too sacred to be discarded because it is unwanted. To be sure, there are some situations wherein hard decisions have to be made about life-termination, but I am convinced it is never right to eliminate the life of an unborn child in order to be rid of an undesired pregnancy. Nor is it right to mistreat children or the elderly because they get in the way. Nor is it right to destroy someone's worth by way of an uncontrolled tongue or temper. To put it simply, Life may be short but it is not cheap.

Read: Jeremiah 1: 4 – 8

Heavenly Father, I know I am unworthy of your blessings but I thank you that you find worth in me. Forgive me for putting myself down for all the wrong reasons and help me treat people around me with the worth you gave them.

Starting Over

When two of our sons were eleven and eight, they were having Saturday lunch together at the kitchen table. Their mother was washing dishes but watched them bow their heads, each offering silent thanks. Momentarily, the older boy raised his head but he noticed his younger brother was still praying. So he waited for the finish to his brother's prayer. To the eleven-year-old, it seemed a long wait so when the eight-year-old finally looked up, he asked, "You been praying all this time?" The younger brother said, "Yea, I was almost finished but I muffed it up and had to start all over again." As you look at your life today, do you see a need to start all over? If we will come to Christ, admit that we "muffed it"; he will give us the chance to start all over. The Bible calls it being "born again". Not only does God give us the chance to begin again when we are born again, He places before us a life of new beginnings as we confess and repent of our sin and receive His forgiveness day after day.

Read: Ephesians 4: 17 - 24

Thank you Lord, that with Jesus as my personal Savior I am a new person, but Lord, I don't often live like the new person I am. Help me see myself as a new person with a new wardrobe, inspired to live in what the Bible calls newness of life.

Get With It

❦

"Go to now"... is the way James says it in his New Testament epistle. These days, we would say something like "Face facts".... or "Get with it". In any event, the phrase is to awaken the reader to the truth, which follows: ".... you know not what shall be tomorrow. For what is your life? It is even a vapor, which appears for a little time then vanishes away... Therefore, to him who knows to do good and does it not, to him it is sin." (James 4:14, 17) Life is all too brief and unpredictable for us to be careless about its use. I had the fleeting nature of life and time graphically brought to my attention one weekday morning a few years ago. Among the items in the mail that day was a media guide sent to me by the football office of a major university. As I leafed through the colorful magazine with the action shots, crowd pictures and information typical to a sports guide, I came to the section of player photographs and the thumbnail sketches printed beside their pictures. I spotted the picture of one player and saw an unmistakable resemblance. The young man was a 250 lb. nose guard with an impressive list of accomplishments in his athletic background, but no doubt about it, he was his mother's son! The features were there in that young but sizable face. And why would all this be of such keen interest to me? The football player's mother was the first child I baptized as a twelve year old in my first pastorate. Where has the time gone? It's gone where all time goes...it's gone by.... and in a hurry. We all have some things we need to do for the Lord.... and some things to be for Him. We had better "get with it" while there's time to repent, time to love, time to befriend, time to pray...time to grow into the likeness of Jesus.

Read: Ecclesiastes 3: 1 - 11

Lord, time just flies by. I so need to learn how to use it not waste it; enjoy it not lose it. Today I seek your wisdom about where to invest my spare time and how to be fulfilled in my workday.

The time-worn phrase, "Be sure your sins will find you out", is no mere speech figure. It is a quotation from the Bible. A tragedy occurred many years ago when a circus performer was attacked by one of his own trained animals. After the animal trainer had shown his mastery over several lions, tigers, and leopards, he concluded his act by introducing an enormous 30 ft. boa constrictor. He had owned the reptile for nearly 25 years. But as the snake coiled itself around its trainer and as the people began applauding the trainer's courage, suddenly a horrible sight took place before the spectators. Without warning, the snake, which had appeared almost harmless for 25 years, resorted to its serpent nature and squeezed its trainer to death. Sin often looks harmless, but be sure it will find you out! It is no coincidence that the Bible describes Satan as a serpent. His fate is predicted as being crushed by the heel of our Lord, but, in the process, the serpent will deliver his bite! Satan is a defeated foe but we need to take seriously this ability to leave behind sin's unmistakable wounds.

Read: Genesis 3: 1 - 15

Help me, Oh God, to see sin as it really is. Sometimes it seems so harmless, but it is never harmless. Remind me that sin's first result is that it hurts you and in the process, it leaves ugly scars on my conscience and on my character.

A news story of several years ago told of a nineteen-year-old young man, who had become a drug addict and gave some of his narcotics to his fourteen-year-old brother. The boy's father, who was the mayor of the town where they lived, and who had attempted to help his older son with his drug problems, finally went to the authorities and painfully filed charges against his older son for distributing narcotics to a minor. When asked why he took such steps, the father said, "Sometimes you have to confront someone with the consequences of his guilt before you can really help him." God has said in His book, "All have sinned and come short of the glory of God." (Romans 3:23) "The wages of sin is death." (Romans 6:23) When we realize that we are imperfect, sinful and undeserving of any favors from God, we are in position to accept God's love and forgiveness.... through Christ. And when we realize the lengths to which God went to give us that forgiveness we despise sin and cherish forgiveness all the more.

Read: Jeremiah 17: 9 - 11

Heavenly Father, at this very moment, I confess my sins and repent. I realize you dealt with the consequence of my sin on the cross and in the resurrection, but I seek your renewed grace day to day. Thank you not only for daily bread but for daily forgiveness.

On God's Mind

❧

The speck of planet we live on is part of a solar system of approximately 100 billion stars that are like a planet pinwheel around the sun. But our galaxy of 100 billion stars is only one of a billion other galaxies and the closest one of those is 200,000 light years away. When we think of the enormity of the universes around us, we understand why King David once said to God: "When I consider your heavens, the work of your fingers, the moon and stars, which you have ordained, what is man that you are mindful of him?" (Psalm 8:3 – 4) But He is mindful of us. The Bible tells us that we are more valuable to God than anything He created. He even sent His Son to tell us so. Remind yourself often of how important you are in the mind of God. And the next time you have the opportunity to encourage someone who is suffering at the hands of low self esteem, tell him how important he is in God's scheme of things.

Read: Psalm 8

Dear God, it boggles my mind to consider all you have created and how you have ordered its survival and future. It's all beyond my comprehension. But to realize that I am on your mind and that you love me is even more incomprehensible. Thank you that I don't have to understand it, just take your word for it.

When driving down a highway, well within the speed limit, surely you have been passed by cars zooming along at excessive speeds. You probably have wondered to yourself, as I have, "Just where are the police at a moment like this?" You have reasoned, "Now if I was to exceed the speed limit by even a few miles an hour there would be troopers on every hand to arrest me!" Quite often we fret ourselves over how much other people seem to get by with, while we wonder if the honest life is really worth it all. Then we read something God led King David to write years and years ago: "Fret not yourselves because of evil doers, neither be envious against the workers of iniquity. For they shall soon be cut down like the grass and wither as the green herb." (Psalm 37: 1 – 2) Satan would have us to believe that the road to success is paved with whatever we can get by with but he hides the fact that any such road eventually leads to destruction.

Read: Psalm 37: 1 - 9

Admittedly, Lord, I want my share of success. I'd rather succeed any day than fail. But, Lord, I know I cannot really succeed while disobeying and dishonoring you. So keep me alert to temptations which are just not worth it all.

❧

"Bible-bunglers"… is one of the tags we have tied to misusers of God's book. "Bibliolaters" is a name given to those who, usually without awareness, make the Bible an object of worship… almost a personified object of that worship. "Bibliognostics" are Bible know-it-alls, who do not attract lesser students of the Scriptures to greater study as much as they intimidate them. "Biblioscientists"are Scriptural researchers who know all about the seventh heaven, the last Adam, the first earth and the bottomless pit, but who will not leave their studious hot-houses to rub shoulders with human need. "Bibliocynics" describes those who presuppose the Bible's need for their intellectual grooming before being introduced in acceptable company. Such embellishments and naturalistic explanations supposedly are to help a "Bible-in-overalls" say what it really intended to say. "Bibliotherapists" are those so preoccupied with applications of Bible truth they leave unattended Scriptural specifics. In warped Bibliotherapy, the target is relevance without obedience. If a title can be attributed to a wholesome and healthy use of the Scriptures, it would be "Bibliodynamics"… the internalizing of God's Word so that it becomes the food-source of our energy and stamina… our nutrition and health. "… for he is strong that executeth His Word…" (Joel 2:11)

Read: Psalm 119: 73 - 80

Lord, between the covers and binding of my Bible is your voice put to print. Within me the Holy Spirit dwells to illumine and interpret your Word. The dynamics are all there for me to understand and obey your Book. I pray for the discipline and reverence to rightly handle your written Voice.

Being Yourself

If you remember the old and popular television program called "Candid Camera", you recall the sound of the program's host, Allen Funt, as he introduced the show with words like these: "Smile, you are on Candid Camera. Candid Camera simply catches people in the act of being themselves." Many a time have I laughed till it hurt watching those antics of people, which were caught on the Candid Camera film. But there is a sense wherein we are all, and always, on a kind of candid camera. People are forever seeing us in the act of being ourselves. Christians, then, need to especially see that their actions match their beliefs. It is like the Bible says of Christians. "You are a letter...known and read of all men.... written not with ink, but written with the Spirit of the Living God". (II Corinthians 3: 3)

Read: Ephesians 5: 1 - 4

Father, I don't want to pretend my Christianity. I really want to be me. I pray there is not a contradiction found in who I am and the Christian I should be. Truth be known, however, I am more often like me than I am like Jesus. Remind me throughout this day, the Spirit of Christ is in me in order to live out the likeness of Jesus in my flesh.

As Real As the Wind

❦

The next time you feel the wind blowing against your face and tousling your hair, ask yourself this question, "Where does the wind come form?" It is a probing question. We know the wind exists because we feel it and see the effects it causes. But as to where it starts and where it finally ends, nobody knows. The Bible talks about the wind a lot. In fact, it says that what happens to a person when Christ comes into his life is a lot like the wind. You can tell Christ is there because you sense and see changes in a person's life, but you cannot easily explain it. One has to experience Christ in his life to know what it is like to have Him there. Have you ever thought about letting Christ do for you all that He promised to do for anyone who invites Him to take over his life? All the potential for godliness is ours in Jesus. We don't need to attend a required number of conferences or read a specific number of books in order to qualify for Christ likeness. We need, rather, to realize that holy potential is in us from the moment we receive Jesus as Savior. As we yield our will to His will, He lives out His godliness through who, what and where we are.

Read: II Peter 1: 2 - 8

It is an eye opener, Lord, to learn from your Word that you have given to me everything that I need for godly living. I have tried to live like Jesus and failed so much. Then I put myself down for my failures. Keep reminding me that the open secret is to let Jesus be Himself and do it in me.

In more polished circles, the word is "recalcitrant". In household terms, the word is "bullheaded". Regardless the choice of words, the condition is the same. We are to "be strong in the Lord and in the power of His might". On the other hand, the same Bible teaches us to be teachable, humble and obedient. It seems there are several words, which can help us in seeking the teachable spirit that sacrifices no firmness of conviction over our own Christianity. **Concession**…It is important that we concede to ourselves and others that we are not yet totally versed in all matters of the Scriptures and the Spirit. To be sure, there are no additions or subtractions to be made to the Bible. It is a finished revelation. Yet there remains before us a lifetime of study and application of the timeless revelation of God. **Consistency**… God does not contradict Himself. Because He is timeless, He does not say one thing in the first century and mean something else in the twenty first. We must always be sure what we are taught can be scripturally verified, not with isolated passages, but by the whole of Scripture. **Consideration**…As Paul wrote the Corinthians "knowledge puffs up", but "love builds up". If any idea, by its nature, poses an obstacle to another Christian's growth in Christ, it must respect our consideration for each other. **Concentration**…. We cannot be careless or casual in our Christianity and expect to have a teachable spirit. It is a hunger and thirst for righteousness which God delights in filling.

Read: Ephesians 4:11 - 16

Lord, my opinions are so often stronger than my beliefs. My opinions can make me opinionated and unloving. I ask you to strengthen my belief in your Word and to expand my love for those with whom I share it.

The Evidence Becomes The Proof

A nine-year-old boy, who felt he had more chores to do about the house than he should, wrote out a price list for his mother, leaving it on the kitchen table. It read: "drying dishes, a dollar a week; mowing the yard, five dollars; emptying trash, a dollar; Total, seven dollars a week." Seeing the price list, his mother wrote one for her son leaving it on his pillow to find. It read: "cooking meals, no charge; washing clothes, no charge; making beds, no charge; nursing wounds, no charge: Total: I love you." We can never claim that we deserve God's attention, His care or His forgiveness, but He gives us those things because he loves us. It is difficult to understand how God could love us sometimes, but He sent Christ to earth to show us He does. What an insight there is for us! We can claim we love God but to say it does not prove it. When we demonstrate our love for Him, the evidence becomes the proof.

Read: I John 4: 9 - 21

Heavenly Father, sometimes when I tell you I love you I have to admit I don't love you enough. I need to be about loving you in concrete ways. Keep that thought before me throughout this day so that I can feel authentic when I say I love you, Lord.

With Him In Mind

I am told that when the famous artist Rembrandt painted his canvas called "The Crucifixion" he painted his own face upon one of the people standing about the cross the day Jesus died. Such was Rembrandt's way of conveying the truth that he had a part in the reason for our Lord's death. Indeed, Rembrandt could have painted my face…and yours….onto one of those people standing about the cross. Because it was for all of us…each of us…. that Jesus died. He died as our substitute, for we were the ones upon whom guilt belonged not He. He was sinless. There is a spiritual, the lyrics of which ask a rhetorical question: "Were you there when they crucified my Lord? Sometimes it causes me to tremble…" Yes, you and I were there…in the Mind of Christ who loved us and died for us. He died for us with us on His mind. We should live with Jesus on our minds.

Read: Colossians 3: 1 - 17

Dear God, daily spiritual warfare is a battle for the mind. I know that, but I can get so distracted by the Enemy. I find myself dwelling on earthly things and losing the battle. Help me make more and more space in my mind for you and allow you to win the battle.

Always In Style

❦

Like wide ties or narrow ones and pleated trousers, many things come and go in style. Of course the world of retail business would not stay long in existence if styles did not change. It is by changing styles that the motive to buy is perpetuated. It is interesting, though, how certain items go out of style, but if kept long enough, they are eventually replaced by items, which look very much like them, only new. Thankfully, some things never are out of style. Thoughtfulness, gratitude, courtesy, integrity and love are never a part of the style-market because they cannot be revised, replaced or duplicated. God, the Father, never changes, nor the Son, nor the Spirit. The Scriptures describe our Lord as "the same yesterday, today and forever". (Hebrews 13:8) So our God is predictable; yet His ways, His blessings, His wonders are never predictable. His ways are past finding out. No one can ever complain of a dull, uneventful life if he is in fresh touch with a God whose character is unalterable but whose ways are forever new. The Gospel never changes. The written Revelation of God was given centuries ago to some forty different writers, over a span of some 1500 years and there is no need to revise that revelation. The heart of the Gospel – its truths, the way of salvation, the commandments of God, the promises verified in Heaven – will never change. Certainly the ways to communicate change, as we seize every advantage to make Jesus known to every corner of the earth. The message however remains changeless, while ever fresh.

Read: Psalm 19: 7 - 14

Praise You Lord, for your reliability and changeless character. I come to you right now depending upon promises you will surely keep. But I also thank you for your fresh and unexpected ways of doing things. I will keep my mind fixed on you but I will keep my eyes open for divine surprises.

When someone comes back from a trip to Israel, the land of the Bible, he is usually asked about what impressions were made upon him. When I am asked about my most vivid impression upon visiting the ancient land of the Bible, I find myself saying the same thing again and again. When you are in places like Jerusalem, along the shores of Galilee or near towns like Bethlehem and Jericho, you feel a kinship to Bible days and it just does not seem it was all that long ago that Jesus was here on earth. Actually, one can sense the nearness and presence of Christ anywhere in the world and right now. The Bible describes Him as being the same yesterday, today and forever. The same Christ who lived on earth years ago wants to live here today and tomorrow... and He wants to do it in your life. Think of it, people who live around you can get an idea of what Jesus is like by watching how you live in your world.

Read: John 12: 20 -26

Lord, to visit the land of the Bible is a privilege, but it is even more exciting to realize we are where Jesus lives right now. Help me to be a guide for others to see where Jesus is at this moment, not just where He used to be.

❧

I spent a year in the hospital during a week some years ago. Before then, I knew as much about being hospital sick as a Wall Street executive knows about scalding pigs. I found there is only one place to know how to be hospital-sick. Advisers to the sick, who have not been there would be wise to advise less. I learned other things: Hospital beds are not designed for two-hundred pound, middle aged grandfather types who are accustomed to the roaming rights of a king-sized bed at home. CT scans are best tolerated by marathon runners who have twenty-six miles of endurance in them. Walking an IV tree is not nearly so enjoyable as walking a dog. And there's nothing normal about a normal temperature, it's downright exciting. Double sanitation packages of hospital silverware are really devices to test the determination levels of a patient's appetite. Something else, it takes longer to spend a night in the hospital than most places. I have still other, deeper, impressions. Christian doctors who pray as thoughtfully as they study x-rays and progress charts are very special healers. And Christians are very special people when they don't think their cards and notes are too small to matter. As for nurses and hospital personnel, they have every vote, which is mine to cast, and I'll cast any others for them I can find. I thank my Omnipresent God that there are no prayer chambers, no preaching platforms, no Christian concert halls, no televangelism specials, no sanctified spots in Israel, no cathedrals.... stone, brick, or glass.... where He's any more real and powerful than He is in a hospital room.

Read: II Corinthians 1: 3 - 7

Father, though I would rather experience only good health, good days and good fortune, I know that is unrealistic. Remind me, then, that when I encounter the unwanted, unpleasant and painful moments in life, it is my chance to live in your strength and to qualify for ministering to others with understanding.

The Right Equipment

❧

Once, two of my sons were playing football in the back yard. One of them kicked the football and it landed high in the limbs of a tall tree. The boys came to me for help and we tried a number of methods to retrieve the ball. We threw rocks and sticks at the football and finally, resorted to throwing an old tennis ball at the limbs and branches, hoping to break their grasp on the pigskin. But none of our attempts met with success. A neighbor noticed our plight, brought out his extension ladder and a long tree pole. In a matter of minutes, using our neighbor's equipment, we retrieved the ball. Afterward I said, "It is amazing what you can do with the right equipment!" God has the right equipment for life: the Bible, prayer, the leadership of His Spirit, the fellowship of His people, confession, repentance, forgiveness. It will amaze you what God can do with your life, using His equipment!

Read: Ephesians 5: 15 - 21

Thank you, Lord, for never expecting us to do what you have not equipped us to do. I need forgiveness for all the times I've tried to serve you in my own strength. I acknowledge that I need your wisdom and power for what is ahead of me today.

With Commencement programs and Graduation events there is always an abundance of advice, references to the future and challenges to make the best of one's opportunities. That, I suppose, is as it should be and I imagine it is somewhat natural for the average graduate to listen to all those things with preoccupied ears and a wandering mind. Hence, I will not add to the "endurance load" by making the sounds of a commencement speaker. Rather I would like to make sounds like a friend... a friend who really cares about what happens now and in the years to come. It is not so much advice I offer then, as it is a set of observations: Beginnings have more to do with results than any other part of that which you undertake. Life goals are absolutely essential to prevent aimlessness and the lack of motivation. A choice of friends can make or break your attitude toward life or values. Leaving God behind with your childhood or teen years is neither freedom nor progress, it is disastrous. Being truthful with yourself about yourself is the brand of honesty, which pays the highest kind of dividends. For whatever they are worth, thanks for letting me share these observations... friend to friend.

Read: Proverbs 2: 1 - 22

Lord, thank you for the capacity to learn, but I pray for teachability more than for knowledge. Guard my path from wrong turns and warn me when I am given ungodly advice. I give you my mind and will today and thank you for your holy leadership.

The life cycle of a common Caterpillar provides us one of the best insights into a basic truth of the Bible (John 3:3). The Bible tells us that we must be born again in order to become a member of God's family. Naturally, we wonder how this new birth can take place (John 3:9). Then we remember how the caterpillar spins a cocoon, enters it, then sometime later emerges from the cocoon, but it has changed appearance altogether. It is now a butterfly. It is the same creature, but it is also a different one. The name we have given to that process is a "metamorphosis" and that is interesting because the root meaning of that word is simply "born again". Jesus says if we will invite Him into our lives, He will give us a whole new nature…a new outlook…. a new future. Indeed it is like being born all over. To experience the New Birth is too exciting to keep to yourself; others need to learn about it from you. Think of it, someone can have a whole new life and eternity just because of you.

Read: John 3: 7 - 16

Dear Lord, sometimes I don't feel like a new person. In fact life gets somewhat old at times. Thank you for the reminder from your Word that I am a new person in Christ, not because I accomplished it, or always feel like it, but because of your miracle of rebirth.

MAY 7 *Circumstances Reveal The Difference*

✿

Driving home amid the wet and windy aftermath of a hurricane, I had some lessons on the Christian life underscored. No less rain fell on my car than on the hundreds of others sharing the Interstate with me. The wind, which whipped across the highways, shook my car, too. And the fog, heavy downpours, and limited visibility, awaited me as well as anyone else who found it necessary to travel that day. There was a difference, though, for me and doubtless for a few others like me, on the inside of the car. I chose the occasion to play some of my CD's. While heavy clouds dominated the skies and the rain pelted my windshield, I listened to the soothing sounds of the rhythmic pounding of the ocean on the beach. Then I played a CD of instrumental Christian music called "Quiet Streams". So, while my eyes were confronted with a dismal day, my ears were treated to messages of peace, assurance, hope and confidence. So it is for Christians in this present world. Our relationship to God does not exempt us from life's outer circumstances. Like the Scriptures acknowledge, "The rain falls upon the just and the unjust." (Matthew 5:45) It's not that circumstances are different for Christians; it is that the circumstances reveal the difference in Christians. Cars are driven from the inside, not the outside. Life changes, some days are easy on Christians; other days are tough. There are unexpected hardships and sometimes, dreaded adversities. But the drive to endure comes for within, where Christ indwells us.

Read: John 6: 29 - 33

Heavenly Father, whether today turns out to be one of the good ones or not, I am going to take my assurance from your promise to keep those in perfect peace whose mind is fixed on you.

What Is Important

❧

The three sons in our family were once like those in your home, in that they kept up with the names and records related to college and professional athletes in various sports. Back then, however, those sons might not have been able to remember such details when it came to world history or English literature. Does that sound familiar? I guess it is only added proof to something we all know is true. We make it a point to remember the things, which appeal and are important to us. Perhaps this is one of the most revealing ways to measure our thoughts about life. What occupies your mind and interest most? Could it be that the place we insist Christ has in life is not reflected in the focus of our concentration? I have a suggestion for myself and for you. Let's give some time, detail and special effort today to reveal how important Jesus is to us and our families. In other words, let's let our enthusiasm for the Lord be reflected in how well we know Him and how comfortable we are when He is the subject of our conversation.

Read: Matthew 16: 13 - 18

Thank you Lord, that you know everything there is to know about me. It is so comforting to realize that you not only know me but you understand me. Such knowledge is too high for me to achieve but I want to know you and all that I can know about you. It is important to me.

Side by side.... two advertisements appeared in the morning's newspaper. One ad bore the caption: "Lose Pounds and Inches Fast". The other displayed the headline: "Lose Weight and Feel Great"! The claim of one advertisement was a weight loss of 15, 20 even 25 pounds by way of an appetite suppressant. The other promised a loss of 17 to 25 pounds in six weeks provided one is "really serious about losing weight". Having glanced at those two uniquely American advertisements, I turned one page of the paper... then two.... and there I saw four glaring photographs of five people who were "really serious about losing weight". I studied the faces of those five people caught in the act of hunger by an Associated Press photographer. It was not the first time I have looked at photographs of hungry Africans but thank God, I am still capable of shock when I see frail little arms and legs, swollen tummies and hollow eyes. I have had similar feelings when exposed to the starving faces of Bangladesh. Even more vivid are the memories of the poverty I saw, first hand, in remote barrios of the Philippines and southern Sudan. Is it enough, however just to be shocked or hurt...or disturbed? Is there something I can do about the starving millions in the world? Can I help in any way to change the despair on the face of a little boy who clutches his collapsing baby sister in his arms? Pray? Yes. Reprimand my selfishness? Yes. Arouse others who have half-a-heart? Yes. And I can take to heart the Biblical admonition, "To whom much is given, much is required". (Luke 11:48)

Read: James 2: 14 - 16

Forgive me Lord, for living with so much plenty, feeling entitled to it. What I should feel is privileged and responsible to find ways to change the tide for those who have little or nothing. And don't let me forget the Bread of Life is my greatest privilege to share with a hungry world.

At our house we used to have a little dog named "Hercules" and a kitten named "Goliath". I suppose the names we gave those very small pets were supposed to compensate for their size, which hardly matched their names. But that is not so unusual. People are forever compensating for small realities by over describing them. For instance, we over-sell the appeal and results of sin in order to justify our sinfulness. The truth of the matter is that a sinful life-style is not nearly all it is pretended to be. A person who lives apart from God's way has bought an over-advertised "Mess of pottage" at the price of a home in heaven, perhaps a home on earth, and a peace which neither time nor circumstance can destroy. That hardly seems a bargain, does it? We defend retaliation and spite by exaggerating the ill-treatment some has given to us. Then we feel guilty from the over action. We tell lies and describe them as "little" and "white" but often pay the price of a liar reputation. All the while Satan tries to convince us that we are safe in our bad choices. Don't be a pushover today for the false advertisements of the Deceiver.

Read: I John 2: 15 - 17

Heavenly Father, I don't want to be a pushover for Satan. I need discernment and sales resistance when temptation comes my way. Today, I ask that you help me to be mindful of sin's consequences every time temptation puts on its best face.

Several thousand people, from different parts of the world, spent a weekend some years ago promoting what they called "harmonic convergence". These people met in numbers of what they called "sacred places" and hummed in vibrations with what is supposed to be a cosmic change in the direction the world is going with respect to peace and human relations. If I understand these people properly, they have shaped their ideas around some of the thinking ancient South American Indians had about world history being determined by "sun periods". These latter-day harmony cultists think we are entering the era of the "sixth sun" which promises peace and harmony among earth's mortals. I am sure the people who follow such superstitions do not appreciate my oversimplified explanations of their beliefs, but I hardly think a sophisticated presentation of their ideas would make them any more believable. What amazes me is that such ideas can marshal the followings they do. I guess novelties or resurrections from the distant past will always hold an intrigue for some. Christians, however, need no fascinations or deviations to chart a course for changing the world. We need not wait for the appearance of the sun-eras or the synchronizing of cosmic vibrations in order to effect change in people's lives. We need only to share Christ with them and when they invite Him into their lives, a new Son-era begins for them and a peace which passes all comprehension settles upon them. I suppose the lesson is simple. While people search and lunge for ways to change their world, for whatever reasons they want to change it, we must keep kindled our zeal for sharing Christ, the One who indeed can change anybody's world.

Read: John 3: 31 – 36

Dear Lord, the truth is so much better than anything less. I remember the Bible says your Word is truth. Increase my hunger for your Word and deafen my ear to the lure of superstition, gossip and error.

In Step With Spring

❧

I once saw a billboard advertising a local shoe store. The sign read, "Get in step with Spring!" That seems like a good word not only for potential customers for a shoe store but for people in general. Spring represents fresh, new life, following the dreariness of winter. The Spring of the year also illustrates the kind of life God wants us to have, a life which is full and fresh and which does away with the dreary existence of leaving God out of life. Is your life in step with what God planned for it? Get in step with the newness of life God has already worked out for you and breathe the fresh air of a new season! And realize that when people around you sense a freshness in your life, they will be impacted by it. Those who do not know Christ will wonder what makes you different, increasing your opportunity to tell them about your Savior. Fellow Christians will be encouraged in some of their darkest days to take heart. Young Believers will learn there is more to salvation than just the early excitement of conversion. Enjoy the extended season of Spring with your Lord and encourage them to share it with you.

Read: I Chronicles 16: 23 - 36

Help me dear Lord, to get in step with you. So often I march to the cadence of this world, jumping with passing excitement, dragging through every trial. You are the refreshment and newness in every season of life. Keep me focused on you and not on life's changes in the weather.

Affection and Expression

❦

Affection without expression leads to depression, while expression without affection leads to dissatisfaction. These are basic premises related to emotional abnormality. They are also rudiments related to Christian stewardship. Affection for the Lord must be expressed else the soul sags with depression. God's plan for His people to be stewards is not only His method of maintaining His Kingdom within the Christian, it is His provision of spiritual therapy. The natural and immediate desire of a redeemed life is to express affection for Him who did the redeeming. The Christian who loses awareness of Christ's life in him will be someone who neglects the expression of his affection in the Lord. In time, such a believer becomes like the careless husband who bristles when his love for his wife is questioned, "What do you mean, do I love her? She ought to know that without me repeating myself. I told her that years ago." Equally tragic, of course, is to see the person an unsaved person trying to go through the motions of church "loyalties"…contributing, attending, when there is no real affection for Jesus to be expressed in the first place. If we love the Lord, my friends, we will worship, we will give tithe, and we will sacrifice. To do otherwise is to cramp the strings of our hearts, becoming spiritually depressed, and unbalanced of soul. "But whoso keepeth His word in him verily is the love of God perfected; hereby know we that we are in Him." (I John 2:5)

Read: I Corinthians 4: 1 – 5

Dear Jesus, may my life today be an evidence of my love for you. If I know my heart I want there to be a match between what I say about you, how I feel toward you and how I live for you.

Road Signs

❧

Once, when driving along on a main thoroughfare, I was confronted by a sequence of road signs. The first one said, "One lane ahead". A few feet further, there stood another sign. It said, "Merge to single lane". Then came the third sign saying, "Single Lane Only". As I obediently did what the road signs instructed, I thought to myself, "What would happen if I was a hard-headed driver who refused to follow the advice of the road signs". I took stock of the situation and saw that I would either plow into a high bank on the right side of the road or into oncoming traffic on the left. The Bible says the way to heaven and eternal life is like a single lane, a narrow way and a precise gate. The way to God is through Jesus Christ. We can refuse to take God's Way, but the consequences are just not worth it! We need to remember this truth when accused of being bigoted and narrow minded by those who insist the Jesus way is not the only way to God. Maybe a good reply to such an accusation is to say, "If it is narrow minded to believe what the Bible says, I am guilty."

Read: Matthew 7: 13 - 20

Thank you God, that you never lead me astray. I confess that too often I follow the lines of least resistance or I choose to be headstrong about my opinions. By your Word and the Indwelling Holy Spirit I have the directions and road signs to keep me on course.

Within the space... of four sentences in the sixth chapter of Paul's letter to the churches of Galatia, there appears to be a glaring contradiction: "Bear ye one another's burdens, and so fulfill the law of Christ." (Galatians 6:2), "For every man shall bear his own burden." (Galatians 6:5) Without pursuing the matter further, one might conclude Paul could not remember what he had written in verse two when he penned verse five. There was no problem, however, in Paul's capacity for memory, but there is a need to understand, in our language, what he wrote in his. The "burden" to which Paul refers in verse two derives from a word describing an unusually heavy load, but the word translated "burden" in verse five refers to the ordinary load most anyone would be expected to bear. Hence, the apostle presents not a contradiction, but a healthy guideline for Christians who are genuine about ministering to their friends and fellow Believers. Consider the following paraphrase of the two verses in question: "Help bear the unusually heavy and unexpected burdens which your fellow Christians have to sometimes carry and thereby, fulfill the law of love Christ gave us." (verse 2) "Every Christian should be expected to carry his equal and ordinary burden in life so as not to be burdensome and problematic for other people." (verse 5) Paul's exhortation to those spiritual forbears of ours is no less good instruction for us today. We ought to be able to provide abundant support and help to our fellow Believers in times of unusual need. And the other facet of Paul's sensible guideline is worthy of equal attention. We should never be a burden to others simply because we don't carry our own weight.

Read: John 14: 31 – 35

Loving Father, you have made our burdens your burdens. You took the burden of our guilt to the cross and dealt with it. You said you would not leave us as orphans, but you would come to us. If ever I had an example of shouldering burdens, I have it in you.

❧

Thoughts about my own mother were prompted when a friend told me of a comment his adult daughter made after completing her college and graduate studies. She said, "I noticed one day that you and Mother had some new clothes. Then it struck me you had done without such things for a long while so that my brother and I could have the opportunity for our education." My friend went on to say how fulfilling it was to have made those sacrifices because he and his wife felt it was in investment in the best of goals, not in passing desires along the way. It was good to be in the presence of such a gratified father. Later I began thinking again about my own life and the sacrifices which were made by a widowed mother, an aunt and uncle, who all gave me opportunities I now know how to value. My mother lived in two rented rooms on the second floor of a house owned by a family in the church where she worked. My aunt and uncle, whose home was mine for a number of years, could have done otherwise, but they made my future some thing in which they had a major investment. To be sure, as a student at Fork Union Military Academy, I had necessary work scholarships, waiting on tables and working in a storage room. Perhaps I thought I was virtually paying my own way, but as an adult, I came to realize I was the object of willing sacrifice on the part of people who loved me enough to do without things they chose not to have. I have also come to realize the greatest joy of having grown children is to discover your sacrifices have not really been sacrifices, they have been rewarding investments.

Read: I Samuel 1: 26 – 28, 2: 18 - 21

How do I thank you, Lord Jesus, for those sacrifices of your which made my salvation possible? And thank you for loved ones in my life who invested in my future just because they love me. What a privilege to have done the same for my sons. Help me to be an investor in still other lives while you reap the dividends.

Few people nowadays need an explanation of the word "addicted". We are all too familiar with the problems of drug addition, alcohol addiction and other habit-controlled life-styles. However, there is a **good** form of addiction. There are indeed, **good** habits by which one styles his life. "I beseech you, brethren, (ye know the house of Stephanus, that is the first fruits of Achaia and that they have addicted themselves to the ministry of the saints.)" (II Corinthians 16:15) The portion of that verse which catches your attention, is in these words; "they **addicted** themselves to the ministry of the saints." It was no small compliment then, that Paul paid to the "house of Stephanus" when he said they were "addicted to the ministry of the saints". Would to God it could be said of our families and our Christian friendships, that we are addicted to the "ministry of the saints". May I suggest several "addictions" which would be good for us? A ministry of **awareness**.... Being conscious of each other's needs. A ministry of **intercession**... Praying for one another in personal matters. A ministry of **encouragement**.... Offering comments which uplift one another. A ministry of **adventure**.... Pledging our support to missions on the cutting edge. A ministry of **giving**... keeping faith with our stewardship as God has prospered us. A ministry of **help**... offering our time and availability to man the church's leadership needs. A ministry of **strength**... "being there" to fortify and reassure one another.

Read: Ephesians 5: 15 - 21

Lord, though I may not be addicted to alcohol or drugs, I have to confess television occupies a lot of my time as can my favorite hobby. I know I need diversion just to stay healthy, but keep me honest about how committed I am to giving myself away in your name.

Imagineered

❧

Once, while in Niagara Falls, Canada, I saw an intriguing exhibit in one of the shopping malls. It was the model of a future city, one century hence. As we all know, there is no way to conceive what our cities will look like even a few years from now, but as the Canadian exhibit marker indicates, some things are "imagineered". That word caught my attention, "imagineered". Even at its best, however, imagineering the future cannot accurately depict what the real facts will be. There is a passage in the bible, found in I Corinthians 2:9, which addresses itself to this matter of what God has in store for those who love the lord. Here is the verse: "That is what is meant by the Scriptures which say that no mere man has ever seen, heard or even imagined what wonderful things God has ready for those who love the Lord." All too often that passage is quoted with reference to heaven and the promises which await us there. That is a misapplication, however, because this particular promise is for the here and now. There will be experiences in heaven which defy our farthest imagination, but even now the Lord intends for us to claim a foretaste this side of glory.

Read: II Peter 1: 2 - 11

Keep me aware, Lord, of how exaggerated Satan is when he tempts me with his deceptions. Thank you that it is impossible to exaggerate your promises. They are for real and they are beyond imagination.

No Private Matter

❧

"Religion is a private matter," say some of those who are uncomfortable when talking openly about their Faith. There is more likelihood that they have all too little to talk about instead of being convinced that their relationship to God should be confined to privacy. There may be a few, though, who have bought the lie, and they think to be open about their Faith is characteristic of an insensitive extreme. But where does this line of thinking originate? It certainly cannot be found in the pages of Scripture. To the contrary, the Bible declares, "The redeemed of the Lord should say so". The Great Commission, which Jesus gave, is predicated upon the assumption Christians would seek to make disciples "as we go". It is actually intolerance in the name of tolerance, which calls upon Christians to keep their Faith to themselves in American culture. By no means should Christians be overbearing, judgmental, and harsh in sharing our Faith with friends and neighbors. However, we are not "wearing our religion on our sleeves" when we seek to tell a friend about the most exciting relationship we have in life, our relationship to Jesus Christ. Every single year, there may be as many as 1 ½ million more people in the United States added to the number who are not professing Christians. Can we, in the name of tolerance, or awkwardness, or acquiescence, keep our Faith to ourselves while our nation becomes less Christian by the day?

Read: II Timothy 1: 7 - 14

How good it is, Lord, to be reminded I not only have a testimony to give, I have been given the courage to do it. Greater is the Spirit in me than he who is in the world. That very Spirit gives me the boldness and the good judgment to not only have a testimony but to give it when I should and how I should.

Jesus once said, "Inasmuch as you have done something for the least of people you have done it to me." (Matthew 25:40) That is a good reminder because often we get discouraged over how little noticed are the kind and good things we attempt to do for people. Oh yes, we are quick to say something very appropriate like, "What I do, I don't do for sake of recognition." Yes, but every one of us, if we are honest, like to feel that our efforts at love and consideration are appreciated. Because God is so lovingly entwined with people, He shares the joys and the heartaches people have. In that sense, He is blessed when we are thoughtful, sympathetic and helpful toward someone who needs us. This is part of what the Apostle Paul was talking about when he wrote these lines to the Christians in Corinth: Blessed (Happy) be the God and Father of our Lord Jesus Christ, the Father of mercies and God of all comfort, who comforts us in all our affliction so that we will be able to comfort those who are in any affliction with the comfort with which we ourselves are comforted by God." (II Corinthians 1: 3 – 4) Isn't it rewarding to realize that thoughtful, encouraging thing you do for someone today will cause a smile to break across the face of God?

Read: Matthew 5: 13 - 16

It is alarming, Father, to realize I am constantly asking you to bless me, my family, my undertakings, with no thought of how I can bless you. I really would like to be a source of joy to you so I will set my heart on obeying you and serving the needs of others in your behalf.

In our country, we live by two different standards of time, Standard Time and Daylight Savings Time. Thinking about this arbitrary changing of our clocks twice each year, prompts certain thoughts. There may be merit in gaining an hour's time during the months of the year with longer days and shorter nights, but we cannot create more time than there really is. We can fit our schedules into the cycle of time, but when all is said and done, we have no more hours or days to live than those, which are given to us. The Bible talks about time a lot. Obviously, it is important for God's people to view time as the gift it is. Because time stops for none of us, it is "taken" or it is forfeited. Hence, we must take the time to do what is important. We have to take the time to pray and read God's Word. We can offer thanks at the breakfast table, over lunch and supper and call it our prayer life. Better still, we can take the time to do more than repeat our usual table blessing and actually pray awhile. We can profit from having a Bible in hand on Sundays to follow the sermon, but that is hardly a Bible reading program. We have to take the time to open the Scriptures to be read at home, at the office, over lunch, or at break time. Some of the best time can be taken when recordings of Scripture are played in a car, driving to the next appointment. Soul winning time is seldom easy to find. That is why there is no such thing as "accidental evangelism". Friends, neighbors and working associates of ours will hear of Jesus because we take the time to start such conversations. Changing clocks only changes the time of day. Seizing time for the Lord can change eternities.

Read: Colossians 4: 2 - 6

Lord Jesus, Thank you for the gift of time though I have taken so much of it for granted. Obviously, you have given us time for work, rest, leisure and worship, but to waste time is not an option you intend for us to use. At this very moment, I want to devote the remainder of my day to the purpose of seizing time as the gift you meant it to be.

A farmer and his son once went into a field to work together. The boy was told to throw all the large stones he could find into a nearby ditch so they would not interfere with his dad's plowing. The little guy called out to his father, "Dad, here's a rock I can't lift. I've tried to do it with all my might, but I can't do it." The father responded saying, "No son, you haven't tried with all the strength you have. I am here to work with you. You and I together are strong enough to move that rock!" God is ready and willing to be our strength when we are not strong enough. Like God said in the Bible, "Call unto me and I will answer and will show you great and mighty things which you know not!" It is important to realize that while there are some things wherein we need God's help, there are other things only He can entirely do. Then there are still other things He intends for us to do ourselves. He will not show up on time at work for us. He will not study and take an algebra test for us. He will not read the Bible to us. The key to the matter is knowing the difference between the time we need God's help or need His intervention or when we need to shoulder our own responsibilities. It's not an issue of "God" helping those who help themselves, it is a matter of knowing where our strength ends and His begins.

Read: Psalm 46: 1 – 7

Thank you, Father, for never giving us an assignment without the resources to carry it out. To be sure, we know you are always present to help us but too often we are wanting you to do it for us. The help we need so often is the discernment by which we do not undertake only what you can do.

Praying in a hard hat was a new experience for me, but such was my assignment at the groundbreaking ceremonies for a new downtown office building. What struck me about the whole experience, however, was not the unusual attire for prayer. Actually, prayer has not designated clothing style, or specific posture; it is more appropriate than time, place and appearance could ever make it. The thing which did impress me was that each of us who occupied the so-called "dignitaries platform" was dressed in coats and ties… and hard hats. Of course, such an unlikely clothing combination has recently become traditional for such groundbreaking ceremonies, where speeches and picture taking are more in order than construction work. Following the ceremonies, each of us who had a part on the program returned our hard hats to the contractor who issued them. As the crowd dispersed and we all went our separate ways, the construction crew, who wear hard hats for real, stepped onto the site to start erecting the building. Like speech making "dignitaries", all too many of us offer our comments and opinions about church… its program… its preachers… its money matters… its failures, then go our separate ways, leaving the work for someone else to undertake. Hard hats are really to be worn by those who do the work. So pick up your hard hat of sacrifice… of responsibility… of prayer… and leave the speech making for a time when your work is well on its way, if not completed.

Read: James 2: 14 - 20

Lord, talk can be cheap, but I do not want my prayer talk to be cheap. Increase my conviction, Lord, to be a doer of the Word, not a talker only.

Building Temples

❧

Legend has it that a Persian king once commissioned three architects to each design and erect a temple to honor the sun. He offered an enormous prize to the one who, in his opinion, had produced the most beautiful shrine. After their work was completed, the king inspected the temples. The first was made of stone and symbolized the durability of the sun, which ceased never to shine. The second temple was constructed of burnished metal and reflected the sun's radiance. But the third temple met the king's approval. It was made of glass allowing the sun itself to be seen in every direction. The Bible says a Christian is the temple of God's Holy Spirit who dwells within. Like the architect's glass temple, our lives are to be transparent and clean, so as to make it possible for the Spirit of Christ to be seen whenever we are looked upon. Can Christ be seen in you?

Read: John 3: 27 - 36

Whether I feel like it or not, Lord, your Word tells me that I am the dwelling place of the Holy Spirit. As a Christian, I distract people's attention from the lord Jesus or, if I get my sin and selfishness out of the way, He can be seen in me. That is what I want, Lord. Make me clean and transparent so that Jesus can be seen when people look in my direction.

✢

A college student was once asked what God was like to him. The young man studied the question and answered, "God to me is an oblong haze." Perhaps you are shocked at that answer. Maybe you feel the young man was just being sacrilegious. But wait…. before we ride off in a thousand directions reacting to the disappointing description of God, let me ask, "What is God like to you?" To be sure, God is not easily described for He is a Spirit and our best adjectives are only human. But the Bible gives us the help we need at this point. It says, "In Christ dwells the fullness of the Godhead bodily." Do you want to know what God is like? Take a long look at Jesus, for He is God in a body and written into words. Then invite that same Christ to take charge of your life today, allowing yourself to be a living commentary on the likeness of Jesus.

Read: John 14: 1 - 12

Praise you, Heavenly Father, for wanting me to know you and to know you personally. You have spared nothing to reveal to us who and what you are. We see you supremely in Jesus and you allow people around us to catch a glimpse of you in our behavior. Than you for such an existing privilege! Increase my desire for Christ likeness.

First Line of Defense

❧

We can accuse Satan of many things but being stupid is not one of them. He knows how to erode foundations. He knows how to camouflage consequences. He knows how to attack the point of weakness. He knows how to go for the jugular. And he knows a prime target when he sees one. The family is just one such target. It is always threatened because Satan knows the family must be weak and in disrepair if the nation is to fail. Without doubt, no country's future is ay brighter than the condition of its family life! Christians concerned about the home, the nation and the future must, of necessity, be alert to some of the crafty, subtle enemies, which Satan has enlisted to accomplish his goals. What was once being called the "Me Society" is little more than selfishness with a new name. The indulgence, lack of discipline and disregard being espoused in the name of self-fulfillment nowadays could very well threaten the family, but its effectiveness can also be obliterated by a strong, wholesome home life. The preoccupation with sex may tickle the fancy of many but we will never be able to have a great family life with this kind of emphasis on our bookshelves and television logs. Although, thankfully, there has been some apparent improvement in the situation, we still must contend with the modern disdain for authority. The home is the indispensable training ground for learning the basic lessons on authority. This is the day for Christians to commit themselves more than ever to a wholesome, durable home life. It is our first line off national defense!

Read: Deuteronomy 6: 1 - 9

Heavenly Father, the family is your idea. You created us with marriage and parenting in mind. You have established the principle of "as goes the family so goes the nation". I pray today for the protection and spiritual well being of my own family and I pray for an awakening in the nation to the importance of the Bible's model of the home.

An occluded front is what the weatherman often reports to be the cause of a heavy, drenching rain. As I understand it, an occluded weather front is one, which has cold air aloft and warm air beneath, thus presenting a situation that is very difficult to predict. Occluded fronts do not help churches…. in more ways than in the weather they prompt. There is both a weakening and a potentially devastating result in the unpredictability of "occluded religion". Cold air aloft and warm air beneath describes not only an occluded weather front; it characterizes "occluded religion" as well. John recorded a penetrating commentary of Christ in this matter: "I know thy works, that thou art neither cold not hot: I would thou wet cold or hot. So then because thou art lukewarm and neither cold not hot, I will spew thee out of my mouth." (Revelation 3: 15 – 16) A church, which is neither cold not hot, is more than tepid in spirit and repulsive to our Lord's taste, it is a threat to its own stability. To be unpredictable in our relationships with people is to keep enough threatening clouds astir so as to make moments of sunshine untrustworthy. How can we trust overtures of apparent friendship, which may suddenly thunder, with the threat of fickle-rain? To be occluded in our spiritual loyalties is to encourage fellow Christians on one day and disappoint them on the next. It is to strengthen fellow Christians in Bible study discussion and to disillusion them with a display of anger loud with profanity. Weather fronts will remain unpredictable. We Christians should not be.

Read: Matthew 22: 34 – 40; II Corinthians 5: 17 - 21

Lord, you did not put your Spirit in us to misrepresent you, but to reflect the truth of all you are. Help me to keep that in mind when my attitude and behavior are about to send the wrong messages.

Flies In The Ointment

꩜

A conversation prompted my reading of Ecclesiastes one night recently. This is not the verse I was looking for but it was one of those helpful rediscoveries in passing: "Dead flies cause the ointment of the apothecary to send forth a stinking savor; so doth a little folly ruin the reputation for wisdom and honor." (Ecclesiastes 10:1) Just as a few of those poisonous insects typical to the hot countries of the Near East would spoil a whole jar of perfume, a bit of error can spoil a whole witness of good. The applications of this axiom are obviously unlimited, but for our use we will focus its meaning upon Christian living of our day. Flies in our ointment are of several breeds: There are those theological flies with no spine. And there is another variety of theological fly with plenty of spine... also possessing a bite like an adder. There are hypocritical flies, which are happy in any pile of garbage. And there are treacherous flies who feed on other treacherous flies... and some not treacherous at all, just annoying. Regardless the breed, these are the flies which spoil the sweetness and the strength of Christian friendship and fellowship. Flies can be screened out, sprayed, swatted.... But I suppose there is only one effective way to stop them... eliminate the breed before they start. For Christ's sake... let's protect the ointment.

Read: I John 3: 4 - 22

What a privilege, Lord, to bear your name. I must confess, though, I have often failed to represent you well. Forgive me for that. By the convicting work of the Holy Spirit, keep me focused on what you would say or do as my model. I really don't want to be a fly in your ointment.

The Resurrection Connection

Our Lord is alive! There is more to that announcement than fact alone. Jesus was raised from the dead some two thousand years ago not as a sanctified display along God's "midway of miracles". Too often it is thought, and by too many, that the purpose of the Resurrection of Jesus is to dazzle us with God's ability to overpower the laws of nature. The empty tomb is not simply "Exhibit A" in the case of God versus Satan. The fact that Jesus arose and is alive has something to do with us and it has something to do with us now! Jesus said, "Because I live, you shall live also". (John 14:19) There is an inseparable connection between the resurrection of the Lord and our resurrection to newness of life. There is assurance of our final resurrection because He is the "first fruit" from among the dead. But equally important.... is the relationship between the resurrection of Jesus and our vitality of life here and now. To the degree that Jesus is alive in us, we are vital in Him. To the extent we appropriate the truth that Jesus not only arose from a tomb in Jerusalem but He actually is living where our living is done we demonstrate the power of the resurrection. "Now if we be dead with Christ, we believe that we shall also live with him.... likewise reckon ye also yourselves to be dead indeed unto sin, but alive unto God through Jesus Christ our Lord." (Romans 6: 8 and 11)

Read: II Corinthians 13: 1 - 4

Dear Lord, I empty myself of sin by confession and repentance. I open wide my inner person so as to allow you to fill me full of yourself. I want to power of your resurrection to be at work in me so there can be no question about the connection of my life to yours.

❧

A reasonable life-style once became the basis for a divorce settlement in Florida. A twenty-one year marriage was dissolved between a 71 year old corporate owner and his 51-year-old wife, after his attorneys agreed to accept the terms and demands outlined by her counsel. According to the wife's attorney, the standard of living to which she had become accustomed in this marriage was "anything she wanted." Since her estranged husband was worth close to $100 million, it seemed reasonable to the judge to award her a continued monthly support for those things, which had typified her marriage. These "things" included flying to New York in a private plane to have her hair styled, $2,600 allowance for eating out and gas and oil for her $100,000 Mercedes. An itemization of the monthly financial settlement in this divorce reveals both a life-style and an insight into priorities. As you read over this following set of requests, be sure you take note of the final one. It provides its own commentary: Vacations - $10,446; Clothing - $6,452; Dining Out - $2,600; Groceries - $1,592; Beauty Parlor - $1,440; Miscellaneous - $1,407; Pet Care - $171; Church (Charities) - $20. There is no comfort to be found in making ridicule of how other people live, even if there is "plenty of money to go around". What can be learned by all of us is that our priorities tell more about our character, values, and perspectives than we know. How do we spend our money? How do we spend our time? How do we spend our Sundays? How do we determine what we give to the Lord…and from which end of the money available – the first of the check or what is left? Establishing priorities is not just a need for the rich it is a need for us all.

Read: Matthew 6: 25 – 34

Dear God, it is so easy to get caught up in what the world thinks is important. Sometimes I fall easy prey to the idea that I must have certain things or I will miss out on what I think I deserve. Remind me that you deserve my first consideration or all else will never satisfy.

The Bluebonnet Perspective

While touring a university botanical laboratory, an old farmer was invited to look into a microscope. He gazed through the powerful lenses for an extended time, obviously engrossed in the details of the object being highly magnified. He inquired, "What is this I am seeing?" "A section of a blue bonnet petal," was the professor's reply. The farmer, with eyes still peering into the microscope, broke a period of self-made silence with the comment, "Why it's absolutely beautiful and to think that I have walked upon thousands of them!" This incident effectively captures the illustration of how we al have learned to glibly accept the commonplace while living in "forgrantedness". By analogy, the blue bonnet petal could be a multitude of objects. It could be our salvation when appreciatively examined through the "microscope" of realization. It could be our church, when examined through the "microscope" of fellowship and purpose. It could be prayer, when examined through the "microscope of trial or tribulation. It could be food and shelter, when examined through the "microscope" of what most of the world possesses. And then the illustrations of the magnified blue bonnet petal applies to the people who surround us. How very easy it is for us, to by-pass the multitudes, taking their unfit spiritual conditions for granted. The millions who share this earth, as a dwelling place can become so obscured in digits that their ignorance of our Christ is an undisturbing normality. Even a neighbor or a loved one can become so commonplace we do not see the potential beauty of redemption within him.

Read: Philippians 4: 4 - 13

Forgive me, Dear Lord, for missing my surroundings. I am surrounded by your love. I am surrounded by more friendship and prayer than I imagine. I am surrounded by lost people who need to hear form me. I am surrounded by blessings I take for granted. Open my eyes, Lord, before I miss it all.

Staking Tomatoes

Garden season reminds me of some tomato plants we tenderly nurtured in our back yard many years ago. A long look at tomato plants can teach us a great deal about healthy and fruitful Christian living. The Scriptures liken the Christian to the fruit-bearing branch and compare the Lord Jesus Christ to the life-giving vine. Jesus said so plainly, "As the branch cannot bear fruit of itself...no more can you except you abide in me." (John 15:4) I have seen highly potential branches bend and break until they no longer received any life-supply from the vine. They soon wilted and thus became barren, incapable of carrying out the innate desire for fruitfulness. We already know and which we have heard repeated. Let me call to your attention a lesser-emphasized parallel to another spiritual truth. Tomato plants must be staked and tied, lest they easily break and lose their very life ties to the vine. It's quite obvious that no person, regardless how "green" his thumb, can transmit the life-giving juices of the vine to the branches. Such a process is beyond the realm of human power to perform. However, the gardener, regardless how ungifted he may be in the so-called knack of growing things, can stake and tie tomato plants. He can provide support while resources beyond his own provide fruitfulness. The analogy is plain. Christians cannot make other Christians spiritually productive. That is the work of God's life-giving Spirit. However, it is our capability to stand beside one another, binding the brokenness and weakness of some to the strength of others. Indeed.... fruitfulness among Christians requires not only the life of the Vine; it requires the support of God's people bound to God's people with ties of caring.

Read: I Corinthians 2: 1 - 9

Dear Lord, I need the reminder that I require the support of other Christians. You did not intend for us to live in Christ likeness without Christ or without other Believers. I need constant connection with you and with fellow Christians. I need you within and them without.

A Willing Offering

Can you envision a Sunday morning worship service in a typical church, with the pastor making the following announcements: "We respectfully request that you bring no more offerings to the church. We have much more than enough. Please restrain yourself from giving any more." Many would say, "Why, that's unheard of". No, actually it is not unheard of, because that is precisely what happened when the Israelites got excited and involved in building the ancient tabernacle of worship. Moses challenged the people to bring their offerings of a "willing heart", itemizing a long list of suggestions about what they might give or provide. The result is recorded in Exodus 35. "And they came, everyone whose heart stirred him up, and everyone whom his spirit made willing and they brought the Lord's offering to the work of the tabernacle of the congregation and for all his service, and for the holy garments." (Exodus 35:21) The account, which unfolds in Scripture, is thrilling to say the least. It is a story of what God's people can do when their hearts are really into something that has captured their imagination. "The children of Israel brought a willing offering unto the Lord, every man and woman, whose heart made them willing to bring for all manner of work, which the Lord had commanded to be made by the hand of Moses." (Exodus 35:29) The amount of what those spiritual forebears brought as gifts to build a place of worship is not nearly as important as the spirit which prompted and accompanied those offerings. When togetherness and willingness prevail, the people of God are of an obedient mind. The results of such an atmosphere are astonishing.

Read: Exodus 35: 20 - 29

Sometimes Lord, I feel so dense. Satan wants me to begrudge everything I give to you so he can deprive me of the joy that you have awaiting willing obedience. I choose to obey you here and now and to enjoy you in the process.

Discipline Matters

༉༄

"Discipline means that somebody cares"... That is what several high school students told me a few years ago as I was leading a college preparation seminar. Only seniors attended the seminar, and our discussions centered on three general topics: Freedom and Restraint; Faith and Intelligence; Integrity and Conformity. In one session, the group was reacting to a thought, which I had introduced to the discussion, something I called for lack of a better label, "The Monster Standard". Frequently, the adult world in general, and parents in particular, say or imply to teenagers, "When you are older, you may do certain things that I do. Until then, you are too young to do them." The natural desire of any developing teenager is to appear older than he is. Hence, this "do as I say, not as I do" approach to moral standards becomes an invitation to older-looking things. The "when you are Older" standard then becomes the monster which turns on its creator! The high school seniors in the group admitted to their predictable complaints when they are refused their numerous wants, but they acknowledged their desire and need for discipline from those who claim to love them. They rightfully asked, however, "Why is something morally wrong for a person because he is too young to do it"? If it is morally wrong, or if it is bad for you, why is it not wrong for any age," they asked? The parent who sets the example is the parent who obviously cares even if his approach seems unappreciated. The parent who disciplines a child but cannot seem to discipline himself.... or herself.... encourages that child to become an understandable skeptic. So, parents, grandparents, teachers, role models of all sorts, prove that you care by being an example of what you extol.

Read: Hebrews 12: 9 – 11

I thank you God, for the discipline you give me. You love me too much to allow me to go long without restraint, consequence and instruction. Thank you for the encouragement I get from learning by my mistakes.

The Juggler

꙳

I once found a quotation in a magazine, which really caught my attention: "You have to be quite a juggler if you have one reputation to keep up and one to live down." Being yourself, being true to yourself, being honest with yourself are all necessary antidotes to pretense and phoniness. Every time we pretend to be something we are not we are saying, "I do not like myself the way I really am." How does someone come to himself and be real? We start by seeing ourselves as God sees us. Then we must want ourselves as God wants us. His measurements are actually the only ones we can trust, for he lovingly tells it like it is. Do you want to be free of pretending with yourself? Allow Christ to have your life. He will free you from the confusion, the fear and the exhaustion which come with deceit. Perfection is not a regimen for inner peace, but integrity is. The scripture offers a simply stated assurance, "Thou wilt keep him in perfect peace whose mind is stayed on thee." (Isaiah 26:3)

Read: Psalm 24: 1 - 14

I really don't like the thought of it, Lord, but I have been a hypocrite more often than I like to admit. Satan appeals to my weaknesses and I forget that I am going to regret what I am about to do. I ask you to give me a David-mentality in whose spirit there is no deceit.

Hands-on Discipleship

A group of four-year-olds from a Christian Day School were taken to a grocery store. This is just one of many ways to teach children about the world which surrounds them. One little fellow, knowing it was the day the group was to visit the store, walked through the door reflecting on a conversation he had probably had with his mother. He said, "If I touch anything in the store I will be told to keep "my hands to myself". Though I doubt he would have encountered any big reprimand, the home-side warning was effective. He kept his hands to himself. The Bible also has a number of warnings about our hands. It seems hands are a crucial part of the anatomy as far as the Scriptures are concerned. There must be some specific reasons. Hands symbolize work, by which we prove ourselves "doers and not hearers only". Hands emblemize helpfulness and fellowship without which we isolate ourselves and others. Hands gesture praise and worship. Hands warn. Hands heal. They provide a touch, which signals, "All is well". It is true that hands might get a four-year-old in trouble at the supermarket, but they can also get a well-motivated Christian into a lot of joy and fulfillment. What are your hands doing in the name of the Lord just now? Are they used for little else besides over-feeding your spiritual digestive tract? Put your hands into a place of Christian service… and do something to the glory of God!

Read: Titus 2: 1 - 14

To be busy for busyness sake is not a virtue. I know that, Lord, but laziness is not a virtue either. Give me holy unrest when my faith is just treading water and give me the discernment to recognize the difference between ministry and obligation.

A bumper sticker caught my eye the other day. It was the first time I had seen this particular one. The wording was "Love Thy Plumber". I am certain the people in the plumbing trade feel that message expresses their sentiment when they are pressed by construction deadlines, criticized for being unavailable the moment a distressed homeowner calls, or reprimanded by an irate customer who insists the repair bill is too high. But wait…most all of us think our particular group, vocation or profession deserves better understanding than it gets. If we put our feelings into "silkscreen and print", I suppose we would see bumper stickers bearing all kinds of pleas like, "Love they Hairdresser"…Love Thy Brick mason"…Love Thy Dentist"…"Love Thy Store Clerk"…"Love Thy Piano Teacher". It all goes to underline an underlying need in every life. We all want to be loved, understood and dealt with as individuals with personal worth and acceptance. Someone needs a word of encouragement from you today. Find that person and love on him for Jesus' sake. Who knows, your attentiveness may validate God's love for a sinner in need of a Savior.

Read: I Thessalonians 4: 1 - 12

Father, it really troubles me when I think of the opportunities I have missed being a validation of your love in the life of a neglected or hurting person. I need the prompting of your indwelling Spirit to make me an avenue, not an obstruction, to that love.

We are told the world's population figures have well exceeded the 6 billion mark. Despite the lowered birth rate in a few parts of the globe, there is still an increase in world population. The increase is not only due to the results of mathematical progression and to more births in Third World countries; it is due to the fact we are just living longer in countries like our own. Needless to say, with more mouths to feed and more live bodies to accommodate, we have our work cut out for us if we intend to be humane and civilized. Our work is cut out for us as mission-minded Christians, as well. With each succeeding day we lose ground with respect to the ratio of Christians to non-Christians in the world. That not only is a commentary on our effectiveness as witnesses of Christ, it serves notice to us regarding the decreased influence of Christian thinking in the world as well. I have lived long enough to see marked changes in how much less Christian values and motivations now affect our own society. Thank God, we still have many open doors to use in seeking to lead our friends to a vital relationship to Christ. To trifle with the opportunities we still have is a sin indeed! We cannot afford to be casual about international missions' responsibilities either. Our giving, our prayer lists, our readiness for short-term and career missionary service ought to clearly reflect our perceptiveness and a genuine sense of urgency. And while we are thinking about the task of reaching a lost world miles from us, we should always keep the spiritual survey of our own neighborhood up to date. Most of us live in the midst of an English-speaking, well lighted, curbed and guttered mission field ourselves!

Read: Acts 7: 1 – 5

Thank you, God, for putting me on a mission field. I realize that part of me is on every mission field where there are missionaries I pray for and support, but my two feet stand on a part of the world you've given me to personally lead to Jesus. I cannot trifle with that opportunity!

✣

Insights by way of the unexpected are always a delight to recall. Occasionally, one of these "accidental insights" comes through an unconscious misquotation. Such was the case in a Vacation Bible School Children's Department. The Bible study leader was recounting the details of the storm a sea as Mark records it in his fourth chapter. She graphically described the howling wind and the rolling sea, the excited disciples and the serene Christ, asleep in the hinder part of the ship. "The disciples awakened Jesus", she recalled. "They asked Him if He did not care if they perished in this storm. Then Jesus awoke.... and what did He say?" A bright seven-year old boy briskly answered, "He said, 'Please, be still'!" His was a misquotation, yes, but what an insight into every crisis as the Christian can see it! Christ is always in command of the situation. How frequently He must say to us, by way of gentle rebuke, if we will but listen, "Please, be still". David heard that Divine reminder log ago "Be still and know that I am God: I will be exalted..." (Psalm 46:10) Fellow Christians, we need to intensify our commitment to the sovereignty of God. We need to do less and let Him do more in us. The winds and storms of any life situation are no problem to Him. He may quiet the storm or He may quiet us amid the storm, but at His authority, there is peace and stillness. First, however, our trust must respond to His repeated reminder, "Please, be still".

Read: Isaiah 25: 1 – 5

It is hard for me to be still sometimes, Father; I just feel life is for me to handle all by myself. That kind of thinking gets me in trouble when I run into situations beyond my control. Teach me the grace of allowing you to do what I cannot do and to be still about it.

Love As Only He Can

A few years ago, I was speaking on the campus of a military prep school and was given the opportunity to have personal conferences with the students if they requested such a conference. One afternoon, a youngster, about fourteen years of age, met with me, saying he had a question he would like me to answer. He asked, "Can God help you with homesickness?" My heart went out to the young man because I knew how he felt, remembering my own experience of homesickness. At that same military academy, at the age of fourteen, I spent several of my first weeks there battling homesickness. In time, I found myself and a home for the next four years. Interesting enough, it was at that very school I found a personal relationship with Jesus and started a life with promise and meaning. I assured the boy that God could help with homesickness, because being homesick was actually the desire to be close to someone you love and who loves you. Indeed, God does love us and is always very close if we let Him be. God can help you with an ordinary problem of life, like homesickness or fear, or self pity if we will allow Him to love us as only He can.

Read: Psalm 68: 4 - 9

It is so reassuring to know, Lord, you know everything about me and every need I have. And when Satan would have me get discouraged or feel abandoned, I invite you to remind me how foolish I am to let him get by with it.

Certain hymns especially move me when I sing them. For me, the fourth stanza of "Have Thine Own Way" clearly articulates the relationship between Christ's Lordship and the Spirit's indwelling. The third stanza of "It Is Well With My Soul" is a great celebration of His complete forgiveness. When it comes to the subject of stewardship and the privilege we have of returning to the Lord from the abundance of what He has given us, I am unusually moved by the fourth stanza of "When I Survey The Wondrous Cross". "Were the whole realm of nature mine, That were a present far too small; Love so amazing so divine, Demands my soul, my life, my all." Once I heard of a Christian, traveling to Korea, who witnessed a strange sight. He saw a young man pulling a plow like a work animal while an older man guided the plow handles. The tourist took a snapshot of the scene and chuckled a bit. Perhaps he caught himself in his inappropriate laughter and he said, "I suppose these people are very poor". The missionary acknowledged that they were poor and added that they were Christians. The missionary went on to say that the two men had given their ox as a contribution to their church's building fund so they had to take turns pulling the plow themselves. The Christian tourist pondered, "That must have been a real sacrifice for them". The missionary replied, "They didn't call it that. They thought they were fortunate to have an ox to give."

Read: I Chronicles 29: 10 – 20

Heavenly Father, for me to speak of making sacrifices is presumptuous. There have been some people in my life who sacrificed for my benefit. Maybe I have made a few sacrifices for those I love. But you have sacrificed everything for me. Lead me to new levels of sacrifice as I offer thanks and praise to you.

The Best Use of Time

If there was a bank which credited your account each morning with $86,400, carried over no balance from day to day and every evening canceled whatever part of the money you failed to use, what would you do? To be sure, you would draw out every cent, every day! But we have just such a bank. It is called "Time". Every morning God credits your account with 86,400 seconds. There will be no balance to carry over the next day. Every second has to be spent today or it becomes canceled capital. Are you making the best of every moment in your life? The Bible says, "Teach us to number our days that we may apply our hearts to wisdom". (Psalm 90:12) The best use of this particular moment in time is to give Christ the control of your life. The best way to start your day is to ask the Lord to arrange your priorities. The best way to appreciate your day is to thank the Lord for His blessings as they take place. The best way to evaluate your day is to recount your encounters with the Lord and to thank Him for ministries He gave you to offer. The best approach to life is taking it one day at a time with gratitude for an eternity with Jesus.

Read: Ecclesiastes 3: 1 - 13

Help me, Lord to enjoy life with you at the center of it. Help me take time as the gift it is. Teach me to know how to use my time without getting stressed out and pressured. Show me how to rest without wasting my time. And keep me mindful that to be a workaholic is not your image of a "workman who needs not to be ashamed".

Let me call your attention to an intriguing passage of Old Testament Scripture, especially since it has a seasonal propriety. "His father had never checked him, all his life, by asking what he meant by his conduct. Also he was a very handsome fellow." (I Kings 1:6, Moffatt) Such is the description of Adonijah, the unruly fourth son of David. Obviously heavy responsibility for his son's undisciplined nature rested squarely upon David, a father who sought not to displease his child by firm expectations. This Biblical account has a way of probing into our own relationships and evaluations of fatherhood. It asks, first of all, if we are apprised of the conduct, attitudes and character of our own children. "In absentia fatherhood" is a label all to many wear these days and our cliché-like claims such as, "I know my own child", not withstanding we are all too unacquainted with our own children. And incidentally, sending children to church events while exercising the "parental privilege" of staying home", is hardly the best way to know about your child's actual spiritual development. It might be quite revealing to some of us parents if we were just "around" to observe the real attitudes and evaluations, which frequently emit from our children. Also it is very difficult to exercise the authority of fatherly discipline when, as men, we are undisciplined ourselves. Just how do we men think it possible to make children do that which we do not...or have not...or will not. There is a call...for Christian fathers...who care...who are first obedient to their Heavenly Father.

Read: Hebrews 12: 1 - 11

Heavenly Father, it is a privilege to be a parent. Though there are times when we are challenged to the hilt with the responsibility, we thank you for the opportunity of working with you in the making of adults. Keep reminding me that there are no days off from parenthood, but every day is an investment with dividends to come.

God and Father

꒳

Do you remember the first words your children said? I recall that the first word our oldest son learned to say was "moon". With two fingers pointed skyward, he would delight in saying over and over, "moon.... moon". But there can be no question that the most special word a child learns to say as far as a father is concerned is the word "Daddy". It is a special word because it speaks of closeness and warmth. The Bible tells us a Christian can experience a similar relationship to God. It says we can call God "father" with the same warmth a child says, "Dad". Of course, we cannot call God "Father" until we are His child and this is what the Bible says about that: "To all who invite Christ into their lives, God gives the right to be called His children" (John 1:12) True, God is to be treated with reverence and awe. After all, He is Sovereign, Judge of all the earth, holy and majestic. We are not to think of Him as just another person, albeit a perfect person. He is holy and eternal, yet the Scripture invites us to call Him "Abba" which is a warm and personal reference like our word, "Dad." If you are a Christian, you are in God's family with the privilege of a close, personal relationship to Him, all the while you hold Him in praiseworthy wonder.

Read: Galatians 4: 1 - 7

Father Dear, you are to be worshipped and exalted. Even now I offer to you my worship. You are my God and there is none other beside you and I adore you. Your only Son, Jesus, is my Savior and I am in your family. What a privilege it is to call you God and Father in the same breath.

The state capitol building was among our stops during a summer vacation. Our then seven-year-old had not seen this important landmark of the Old Dominion so we took a brief, self-guided tour for his continuing indoctrination as a Virginian. Standing at the gate to the Governor's Mansion, which is also in Capitol Square, Michael wanted to know if he could drop in for a visit. After all, before the Governor was elected and was living in our city, his youngest son and Michael attended the same kindergarten. This prior relationship seemed sufficient credential to Mike for a drop-by to the Governor's home. Of course, we had to explain to him that the situation was quite different now and such a casual visit was out of the question. It was then that the illustration struck me. Standing there at the entrance to the home of our state's first citizen, I again realized that acquaintance does not insure fellowship, nor is exposure the better part of a relationship. A strong vital Christian strengthens all who are in his company, that is true, but to possess lasting spiritual vitality, one must have his own set of inner resources. Too many of us travel through life leaning upon the relationships other people have with the Lord, leaving our own Bibles unstudied, our own quiet times unobserved, our own convictions unsettled and our own witness unoffered. That which makes others strong and vital in the Lord is also available to you and me. It is only as we develop our personal fellowship with the Lord, and lay possession to all He offers, that we have a relationship and strength to call our own.

Read: I John 5: 1 – 13, Romans 6: 16 - 17

Lord, it is so reassuring to read in your Word that we can know that we know you and that we are solidly in the family of God. You have helped me today to realize my relationship to you is not second handed, but that I am a joint heir with Christ and can inherit all that I need through that relationship.

Window Shopping

❧

Window-shopping is an integral part of most people's life-style. We browse and daydream while looking, knowing that there are just some things we cannot afford. We <u>wish</u> we could buy them. We even entertain the thought of how good it would be if someone else gave them to us. But most window shoppers resign themselves to the plight of wanting more than they can have. Perhaps it is the attitude of the window shopper which has overtaken all too many of us with respect to our commitment to Christ. We say, "It would be nice to be wholly committed to God, but that kind of thing is <u>just out of my class</u>. It's for those who can afford to go all the way with God. There may be a lot of things we cannot afford to buy, but tell me…who amongst us cannot afford to give himself to Christ? After all, He gave Himself to us. Actually it makes little sense to choose a half-hearted route to follow Jesus. The blessings He has for us are those experienced when we are close to Him. The Psalmist said it well, "Who shall ascend into the hill of the Lord? Or who shall stand in His holy place? He that has clean hands and a pure heart; who has not lifted up his soul to vanity nor sworn deceitfully. He shall receive the blessing from the Lord and righteousness from the God of his salvation." (Psalm 24: 3 – 5)

Read: Luke 11: 5 - 13

Lord, it is hard to realize that you have more to give me than I ask or think. It is even more difficult to confess that I have often chosen to walk at a distance from you and robbed myself of what I could have had. Right now, I want to draw closer to you and experience more than I can imagine.

Encouragers

꿀

"Edify one another".... So wrote Paul to the Thessalonian Christians. (I Thessalonians 5:11)   Have you ever confronted yourself with this question, "Am I a source of encouragement or discouragement to others?"   Our reliable presence Sunday by Sunday in the church hour is a cause for encouragement to a pastor or a teacher who has invested several hours in preparation.   By the same token, erratic, inconsistent attendance or perennial absences are culprits to sadden and discourage the same people.   Christians who are surrounded by a great host of fellow worshippers are impressed with being part of something strong and potent thus to experience a thrust of hope.   To be seated beside gaps and vacant spaces, reversely subtracts from that resource of encouragement God intended we have when He conceived of the gathered Church.   If we are forever delinquents, problem cases, burden makers, spiritual hypochondriacs, then we are draining other Christians dry of their energies, love, patience and hope.   And it does matter to God whether we are sources of encouragement or discouragement to our fellow Christians.   The Holy Spirit prompted Paul to admonish, "Quench not the Spirit".   (I Thessalonians 5:19)   Indeed, we quench the Spirit when we refuse to be a conscious instrument of hope to the other members of God's Family.

Read: I Corinthians 12: 12 - 27

Lord, I want to be part of the answer, not part of the problem.   Show me what part I have in the Body of Christ and help me to discover and use the gifts you have given me.   At this moment, I realize you did not come into my life for me to consume your blessings but to pass them on to others. Lord, make an encourager out of me.

Real Understanding

❧

There is no comment quite so empty as when someone says, "I know, I understand", when you know they couldn't possibly understand. And there is nothing so timely as the words, "I know, I understand", when you know the person does really understand. Two women met in a grocery store. They said nothing to each other, but they embraced and consoled one another. One woman had lost her husband two years before. The other had lost her husband just a week before. The widow of two years could offer the widow of a week a level of understanding all the talk in the world could not equal. That is why it means so much to know that Jesus Christ, the Son of God, was born, lived in a human body, and dwelt on earth years ago. It is like the Bible says, "He understands us because He was tested in all points like as we are." (Hebrews 4:15) Think of it, when you pray, telling God of your weariness, He understands. When you tell the Lord of your hurt from being betrayed, He has been there before you. When you struggle with temptation, you have a Savior who knows what it is like to do battle with Satan. As you pray, in celebration or in tears, hear Jesus speak to your heart, "I understand."

Read: Hebrews 2: 17 – 18, Hebrews 4: 14 - 16

Just to know, Lord, that you know life first hand, gives me even more reason to pray. And when I pray help me to remember that I can talk with you about every detail of my life. I trust you all the more because you know where I am coming from.

Worthy of Digestion

Let me share some thoughts I have gleaned from others. They are worthy to be digested.

All too often we 'chalk up' to circumstance or fortune the trials or the blessings of life, not seeking to know what instruction or encouragement the Lord had in mind for us through those experiences! This is not to equate healthy Christianity with paranoia. A paranoiac is one who is emotionally ill. He thinks that every thing which happens is somebody's way of liking him or despising him.

We know that God does not cause automobile accidents, nor does He indiscriminately knock planes out of the sky; He does not start wars, nor does He directly inject disease into our bodies. But God is Sovereign, so everything which happens to us as Christians is something which God wants to use to instruct us, discipline us, and shape us into the likeness of His Son.

Yes, God does instruct and discipline His children. He does permit life; its joys, its sorrows, its trials and triumphs to come upon us... but not that we might tremble with defeat or bloat with pride... rather that we might be altogether His!

Humility is to trust God so completely we will not insist upon our way over his way!

Read: Isaiah 55: 6 - 11

Dear God, forgive me for leaving you out of life's formulas. It is all too easy to get my world view from the world's view. You are not a merchant of chance, you are in ultimate control and your will is going to be done. I want my life to be in the center of that will.

Signs of Change

I once was driving through a city in the eastern part of our country and I saw a vivid reminder of a change that had taken place years ago. Along the side of the road was a fenced-in area behind which was an enormous stack of discarded outdoor signs. The signs were of various sizes and styles, but they were all three colors…. red, white and blue. And all the signs had the same letters printed on them…E-S-S-O. Seeing those dismantled signs reminded me that a change had been made. The Esso gas company had changed their name to Exxon, later to Exxon Mobil. They had put up new signs and the old signs had been taken out of circulation. The Bible says, "Therefore if any man be in Christ he is a new creature. Old things are passed away, all things are become new." (II Corinthians 5:17) The question for us is what signs are there in our behavior and outlook which reflect the change Jesus has made in us? In other words, what about us "advertises" the newness of life in Christ? Leaving up the signs of what we used to be sends mixed messages about God's power to change people.

Read: Colossians 3: 1 - 17

I don't want to be guilty of sending mixed messages, Lord. I want to be genuine evidence of the change you bring when you step into a life. I invited you to be my Savior and you did away with what I used to be. I truly want to give signs of the newness of life you have given me.

❦

"Trendy" things…are popular in America. There is something about our approach to life, which latches on to those things popularized by the "right" people. To wear the "right" labels, the "right" jeans, the "right" hairstyles, is like a mandate to the trendy thinker. Trendiness though, is not confined to wardrobes, vacation sites, hairstyles and music. The New Age Movement has been trendy for some. To be sure, there is nothing "new" about the movement's philosophy, for it is "old hat" as best. However, for the person who lives with a spiritual vacuum while insisting he will fill it himself, rather than allowing God of the Bible to do it, there is something infatuating about the self-disciplines and mystical pilgrimages, which make up the hodgepodge philosophy of something like the New Age movement. Like the head shops of the drug subculture, New Age bookstores have put in their appearance across the country. Their marketing style is to appeal to "thinkers" and searchers with "teachability", the trendy minded. New Age people, like the two who bolted in Eden's Garden, and those who built Babel's Tower, want God on their terms, not His. They want peace which they have achieved, not peace they have made with the Sovereign Lord. Beware of any so-called "faith", which centers itself upon the private claims of its disciples rather than the authentic truths of Divinely inspired Scripture.

Read: Ecclesiastes 3: 11 – 15

Praise you, Oh God, for your everlasting truth. You are forever the same, so your Word is forever. I do not want to have a trendy relationship with you. I want to square my life with the authority of your Word. I fix my mind on your changeless truth.

A study of crickets may see unrewarding at first suggestion, but when we realize there are hundreds of species of that one insect, we realize there is more to the insect world than meets the eye. A cricket is loaded with ability. His strong hind legs allow him to leap as much as 100 times his body length. It is told that a cricket can tell you what the temperature is provided it is around 40 or above. You count the number of chirps he makes in 15 seconds....add 37 and you have the temperature in degrees. Some think a cricket makes music by rubbing his front legs together, but a mother cricket makes no noises at all, she just listens. The Bible says God conceived the fish and fowl and everything that creeps on the earth. If He made such wonders out of insects, is it not foolish to live your whole life and never fulfill what God had in mind when He thought of you? And if God provides for insects, birds and plant life, isn't it foolish of us to resort to worry as our chosen response to uncertainty? The Psalmist says, happy is the person whose "heart is steadfast, trusting in the Lord", for he will not fear evil things. (Psalm 112: 7)

Read: Matthew 6: 25 - 34

Dear Lord, blind optimism is not what I seek; rather I need an increase in my faith. You are sufficient in all things. I just need to let myself in on that sufficiency.

❧

Consensus…is a perfectly good word, describing a desirable state of affairs for no small number of circumstances. On the other hand, it is a word, which, when applied to principles, values and absolutes, is fraught with danger. In circumstances of appropriate give-and-take, consensus is the route to coexistence. There are numerous negotiables in life, which suffer no great forfeiture when put through the mill of consensus. The Bible calls upon us to recognize the place of consensus, even deference in the name of unselfishness. "Be kindly affectioned one to another with brotherly love; in honor preferring one another." (Romans 12:10) We must recognize, however, there are certain non-negotiables in life, which ought not to be emasculated by consensus. There are not many ways to salvation; there is one – through Jesus Christ alone. There are not many Bibles; there is but one authentic, written revelation of God, uniquely given from the Mind of God to the pen of mortal men. There are not many versions of Christ likeness, for there is but one Christ to be like. I am fully aware that America is not a theocracy as was Biblical Israel. We are a democracy; hence we are a pluralistic society. But to stand down, and allow those who extol the virtues of morality by representation to jeopardize the country's future and is acquiescence Christians cannot afford. There are still some things, which are absolutely evil, and others which are absolutely good!

Read: Acts 4:12, I Timothy 2: 5 – 6

Father, compromise is all around me. If I stay by the absolutes of your Word, I will sooner or later be accused of narrow-mindedness, if not bigotry. Give me both the back bone and the grace to be faithful to you and gracious to those who find me a little too extreme.

Have you heard about the "Marathon to nowhere"? It seems there was a man who decided to undertake a challenge and establish a record, heretofore never done. He walked up an escalator for 14 consecutive hours! Now that is a strange undertaking! It would seem to me that if someone is going to walk for 14 hours he ought to have some progress to show for it. But we cannot be too critical because all too many of us have spent a good part of life going nowhere. Tell me, in what direction is your life going today? If you continue as you are now, will it really get you anywhere? The Bible tells us that Jesus once said, "I am the way, the truth and the life." If you want to make progress and have a future, take the Jesus "route" to life. Interesting enough, Jesus told us that the way to everlasting life starts out at the straight gate and follows the narrow way. In contrast, He said the way to destruction is through the wide gate and the broad way. The world sees it in the opposite direction. Whether it be when we are saved or as we live out our salvation, the Jesus route is the only way to have a fulfilling purpose in life and a lasting destiny in eternity.

Read: Matthew 19: 16 - 26

Lord Jesus, I remember you said you came so that we could have life and have it more abundantly. You are not a liar, you speak only with truth. So today, I willfully choose to walk with you and believe exactly what you tell me. I'm not interested in a walk on Satan's treadmill.

For the Lack of Light

❧

Have you changed a tire lately?..late at night… along a highway….
Alone? Neither had I until one Sunday night when I was driving back
home, savoring recollections of a good opening service of a revival
meeting. Suddenly my preoccupation was interrupted by that telltale
drone on the left rear side of the car. Sure enough, I had a flat tire in a
dark and distant spot along the highway. There was nothing else to do
but to swing into action like any red-blooded man should do. While I
was changing my tire, cars and trucks zoomed by on their well-inflated
wheels, none slowing down to help. What is essential to changing a
tire in such circumstances? …. A spare tire, of course… and a jack…a
lug wrench…. a pair of dirty hands, some sweat…and a cell phone to
call home explaining why you'll be late. There is one other extremely
helpful item for late night tire changing…. a flashlight. You guessed it.
I didn't have one to use in my escapade. Be all that as it may, I finally
got the job done. It would have been so much easier though, with
a flashlight. I learned something by way of this roadside dilemma:
Christians and churches can have the know-how and the equipment
and can work hard at our undertakings for God, but the light of His
wisdom and leadership would make the task so much simpler and
effective. In fact, without the light and purity of God's power, our
efforts are fumblings in the dark, met with questionable success.

Read: Mark 9: 14 – 29

*Heavenly Father, you have assured us in your Word that you have given
Believers in Christ everything that has to do with life and godliness. My
problem is that I try to live and seek righteousness with just my human
resources. Help me to remember you have the tools I need and you are
anxious to let me use them.*

Seventy Times Seven

It has been told that when Otto the Great was Kaiser of Germany he once attended worship services at a cathedral in Frankfort. As he entered the church, the Kaiser was confronted by an emaciated man, who fell at his feet and pled for mercy and attention. The Kaiser suddenly recognized the man was his own brother, Henry, who had done a very evil deed against him many years before. The Kaiser angrily pushed this former rebel aside with his foot and went into the church. The service had begun and the moment the Kaiser sat down he heard a portion of Matthew 18 being read: "How often shall I forgive my brother? Jesus said until seventy times seven times." Conviction so struck the Kaiser's heart, he left his seat to return to the place outside the church where he forgave his brother and made him a trusted government servant. Is there someone you need to forgive today? Equally important, have we sought to restore and accept those we have forgiven? To forgive while continuing to reject the person forgiven is not the Biblical interpretation of forgiveness. The apostle Paul, in writing his letter to the Galatians, said our style of forgiveness should include restoration and gentleness. Forgiveness is meant not only to relieve guilt but to establish hope.

Read: Colossians 3: 12 - 17

Thank you Lord Jesus, for showing us how God forgives. I have a lot to learn about the kind of forgiveness that goes all the way. Show me know ungrateful I am to accept your forgiveness while withholding mine from someone else.

A Friend Indeed

When Luke the physician, historian and New Testament writer, finished his Gospel, he sent it to a Roman nobleman by the name of Theophilus. What the relationship was between the two we are not certain. It would seem reasonable to assume Luke had attempted to witness to Theophilus concerning Christ and the Roman had shown enough interest that Luke wanted him to have a firsthand written account of Jesus' life and ministry. There is some indication that Theophilus at least responded favorably to Luke's witness if he had not become a Believer. Certainly the way in which Luke addressed him when he sent him the book of Acts would indicate a closer relationship had developed between them, or Theophilus had indeed, become a brother in Christ. Doubtless, there was another reason for sending these writings to a Roman nobleman. In a Roman-occupied world there would be little chance for Christian writings to get much distribution without the influence and backing of one who had the name and resources to accomplish such a thing. There is little doubt that Theophilus helped make possible the distribution of the third Gospel and the book of Acts, because of his influence and interest. One might say Theophilus truly proved to be a friend of the Bible, a friend of the ministry and a friend of the Church. Perhaps there was something even prophetic or providential about the man's name, Theophilus, for it means "friend of God". It is not difficult to follow through with an application of this interesting New Testament relationship…anyone who is a genuine friend of the Scriptures, a friend to the ministry and a friend of the Lord's church is proving himself to be a friend of God.

Read: James 2: 18 – 25

Of all the names I could be called as a Christian, I can't think of any more desirable than "friend of God". Lord, thank you for the privilege of being both your child and your friend. Today I want to evidence to the world just how much of a friend I am to you.

Years ago, a young man in California called himself the "credit card king". Walter Cavanaugh started a hobby of collecting credit cards from oil companies, department stores, discount houses, and wholesale firms. He said he had 204 such credit cards. According to this young bachelor hobbyist, however, he used very few of his credit cards to make any purchases. They just represented his buying-potential all across the country. Accumulating unused buying potential may be a delightful hobby, but it illustrates the way to an unfulfilling kind of life. God made promises to man that He intends for us to claim and use. He says, "Call unto me and I will answer." (Jeremiah 33:3) He says, "Come to me all you who labor and are heavy laden and I will give you rest." (Matthew 11: 28) He says, "Ask and it shall be given you, seek and you shall find." (Matthew 7: 7) He promised, "I will never leave you or forsake you. (Hebrews 13: 5) He said it to Joshua and it is also intended for us, "Do not tremble or be dismayed, for the Lord your God is with you wherever you go." (Joshua 1: 9)

Read: I Kings 8: 54 - 61

Lord, it is inexcusable for me to leave your promises unclaimed. So often I have struggled with matters as if I had no idea where to turn. There is no reason for me to live with distress when your promises are far ahead of me.

Ours is a restless world. To miss that fact one would have to refuse to watch television newscasts, bypass the front page of the newspaper and remain otherwise isolated for life. Most of us are informed of world events enough to be concerned and often outraged. However, concern and outrage are not adequate responses. These are days for God's people to do something positive. We are equipped and have instructions for just such times as these. And what can we do? **Be a prayerful people**. We certainly have the citizen-right to opinions about our national administration and policies, but we must not settle for just approval or disapproval. God has clearly instructed us to pray for those who are in places of governmental leadership. In fact, we ought to pray for government to be held accountable to God. **Be a missionary people.** There can be little question, as goes missions so goes world history. In the final analysis, the hope of world change rests upon the inward change of people. Missions is not just an assignment for zealous Christians, it is a vital force in world events. **Be a Biblical people**. The Scriptures not only teach us the way of daily living, they assure us concerning the ultimate outcome of human history. Our God is Sovereign. He made the world. It belongs to Him. He is the last word in human destiny and He has the final victory. That is why we will not despair, regardless what happens. Truly we have some timely responses for a restless world.

Read: Hebrews 11: 32 – 40

Give me courage, Lord, to speak up when pain and circumstances try to silence me. I realize being a Christian does not guarantee me immediate victories and solutions, but I am confident of the final outcome. The restless world needs to hear something positive from me.

❧

I read a figure of speech the other day that was new to me. It was called "the hummingbird horizon", and it refers to that breed of hummingbirds that are hatched and bred in the craters of extinct volcanoes. These volcano-bred hummingbirds never fly up and get a view of the open and free world above and outside them. Even when they are fully grown they remain in their limited world and breed other hummingbirds to be born and live, just as their parents. Sad, isn't it, to think of such a confined existence? But there are people who have little more than a "hummingbird Horizon" as far as their outlook on life is concerned. They have a capacity for fellowship with God. They could know the surrounding of living with Christ as Lord. But they are content to exist in the barren confines of indifference and unbelief. Open your eyes to Christ and get beyond "a hummingbird horizon". Rather than pertaining to the promise of heaven when we die, the following verses of Scripture apply to the way beyond an unfulfilled and unrealized Christian life and to do it here and now.

"Things which eye has not seen and ear has not heard and which have not entered the heart of man, all that God has prepared for those who love Him. For to us God revealed them through the Spirit; for the Spirit searches all things, even the depths of God." (I Corinthians 2: 9 – 11)

It really must hurt for you to see so many Christians who have never tasted all that is coming to us this side of heaven. I've already missed out on too much, I don't want to miss an earth side taste of heaven.

Hard Hats

Not long ago, I saw a sign at a local construction site. It bore these words: "Stop, Hard hats will be worn on this job by all trades... This Is Law..." In other words, no workman on that project was excused from the safety regulations imposed by the contractor. God has made some strong statements in the Bible, and they apply to everyone. There are no exceptions. For instance, he said, "Like sheep, all have gone astray." (Isaiah 53:6) He said, "Except you repent, you shall all likewise perish." (Luke 13:55) He said, "God is willing that all should come to repentance." (II Peter 3:7) No one is excluded. God seeks to forgive all who will accept his love by inviting Christ into their lives. You are not exempt, my friend. God has included you in His plans for love and forgiveness. Like the chorus says, "Oh how He loves you and me, Oh, how He loves you and me. He gave his life, what more could He give? Ho, how He loves you and me!" Remember God's Law includes His law of love.

Read: John 3: 16 - 21

When you say something, Lord, you mean it. Your promises and your expectations are meant for all of us, all of the time. I am disobedient when I ignore your love and when I refuse to pass it on. Help me prove my love for you by way of my obedience to you.

My Brother's Brother

꽃

A few years ago, I was packing the car trunk early one summer morning at a Georgia motel. We were about to leave on another leg of our vacation. A talkative little fellow, about eight or nine years of age, made his way over to me and started a conversation. "Are you leaving this morning?" he asked. I told him we were. "So are we", he countered. He went on to say, "We are going to see my daddy." Then I suppose he felt some explanation was due. After all, it seemed strange for youngster to be saying, "We are going to see my daddy." In a lower tone of voice he said, "We are divorced." Pondering that simple statement, I came to the conclusion the little fellow was more accurate than the legal document which stated his parents were divorced. A division in the family affects the whole family, not just those between whom a cleavage first appeared. Like a rock striking a windowpane, though the rock collides with but a single part of the glass, the whole pane is shattered. Applications of this truth are abundant. Indifference on the part of but one Christian affects the strength of every Christian. Love, caring, loyalty, enthusiasm, spiritual growth in the life of one part of the Body of Christ adds vitality to the whole Body. Being a Christian is a "we... us" affair.

Read: I Corinthians 12: 14 - 26

Lord, the Bible tells us you are the Head of the Church and we are parts of the Body. It stands to reason whatever body part I am is crucial to the health and function of every living Christian. I confess my self centeredness and though I am not my brother's keeper, I ask you to help me be my brother's brother.

Four hungry lepers said it first nearly three thousand years ago, but it is current for today. "... We do not well: this is a day of good tidings and we hold our peace... now therefore come, that we may go and tell the King's household." (II Kings 7:9) These men of old had been starving at death's door until they entered the hurriedly abandoned camp of the Syrians. There they found food and spoils in abundance. For awhile they could think of nothing else but their own proceeds and satisfaction. Then they felt the conviction which starving men have when they are fed... they remembered other starving men yet unfed! We who feed upon God's Daily Bread... we who feast on the affluence of His Grace... we "do not well" if we keep such good tidings to ourselves. The Gospel of Jesus is "good news". It is not meant to be a secret. It is not designed to be news clippings for our personal scrapbook. If it is good news, it is good news for everyone. (It is interesting to find that the original word in the New Testament translated, gospel, is strongly tied to the idea of being given broad exposure.} Fellow Christians, you are as responsible for spreading the good news as today's newspaper is for "freedom of the press".

Read: Romans 10: 5 - 15

Father, my tongue is all too ready to serve the gossip mill! There have been times I needed to tighten my loose lips. I ask forgiveness for all the ways my speech has failed you, but I want to claim my authority to be your witness to the "uttermost part of the earth".

Years ago, a controversy erupted over the then popular singers, The Beatles and Christ. It was short-lived but John Lennon and his shaggy friends did emerge temporary commercial beneficiaries over the matter. Such flash-in-the-pan issues, however, call attention to more enduring truths. Personally, I was encouraged that some folks had enough conscience about sacred things to challenge John Lennon's statement, "We are more popular than Christ." Of course, the truth of the matter is, Lennon really understated the facts. Jesus Himself said that the world, in general, actually hated Him. It is not a matter of competitive popularity at all; it is a matter of the spiritual conditions, which prevail. This brings to bear upon us some of the realities we too often ignore. We are so success-oriented and popularity-acclimated that we are inclined to feel these are the levels upon which we are to draw men to Christ and upon which we measure our Christian accomplishments. To be sure, there is a mystical strength, which comes to us when we are in the fellowship of large numbers of other Christians, but Christian discipleship never follows the path of social popularity. Popularity requires no enduring affections or unchanging allegiances. Someone can be the object of popularity today and scorn tomorrow. Christ wants men to love Him, not popularize Him. He seeks disciples, not fans. The Scriptures declare …"the world passeth away and the lust thereof, but he that doeth the will of God abideth forever." (I John 2:17)

Read: John 15: 18 - 27

I want to be happily serious as a disciple of yours, Lord. I want to be as serious as I am happy in my obedience to you. Courage is what I need to do these things. So, Lord, I ask for that courage this very day.

The Ringing of the Ropes

It seems like forever since I was a first-year cadet at Fork Union Military Academy. Memories of my four years at that school are abundant, and some are vivid and permanent. To this day, I can hear the ring of the hoisting ropes, banging against the tall, metal flagpole, mid campus, as Old Glory flapped in the wind. The old flagpole was considered the very center of the campus, located in what was called "The Circle". Every time I stepped on the cross walks of the Circle, like every other cadet, before or since, I saluted that ever-present flag. Regulations required that salute, but in time, it became second nature. In the course of four and a half years, that simple gesture of a salute became part of a healthy legacy. I have some perspective now and it causes me to cherish so much of my legacy. To honor my country's flag is as much a part of me as the hand which was taught to salute it. I fully understand that the flag is only cloth, sewn together in a combination of three colors. The nation's flag, however, gathers up our history, ideals, sentiments, hopes and heritage and weaves them into a pattern of red, white and blue. To salute that flag is not an act of blind allegiance, oblivious to the failures, woes and sins of the land. It is rather a grateful acknowledgment of all that is right about America. In the back of my mind I can still hear the distinct banging of the hoisting ropes against the old flagpole, where I first learned what it means to salute Old Glory.

Read: Psalm 33 (especially vs. 11 – 22)

God, you have blessed America! Without your blessing where would our nation be in the scheme of history? Because I love my country, I ask for your continued blessing upon us, not because we deserve it, but because we need it.

Responsible Liberty

Liberty is a cherished word on the lips of thinking Americans, especially when it is spoken or sung against the backdrop of patriotic sights and sounds. I **like** the emphasis. I **need** the emphasis. I take my liberty, as an American, too much for granted; hence, to have it extolled is a helpful antidote to my lethargy. The ancient Greeks had an advantage over us in their use of words. They used two particular words, both meaning "liberty"; yet those words stood far apart in their application. Interestingly enough, the two words were spelled exactly alike, except for one letter. That one letter's difference, however, makes a world of difference in the two words. One word translated "liberty" meant "relaxation" and became identified with indulgence. The other word translated "liberty' meant "release" and became identified with forgiveness. Neither of those two words is used in Galatians 5: 13 – 16, but the thrust of the distinction is there: "For brethren, ye have been called unto liberty; only use not liberty for an occasion to the flesh, but by love serve one another. For all the law is fulfilled in one word, even in this: Thou shalt love thy neighbor as thyself. But if ye bite and devour one another, take heed that ye be not consumed one of another. This I say then, Walk in the Spirit, and ye shall not fulfill the lust of the flesh." In Christ, we are free from sin's consequences, free to enjoy redemption's blessings, but not free to be irresponsible toward the protection and cultivation of freedom's atmosphere. To the contrary, to be free in Christ is to become concerned for each other's well being and to be obedient to the cadence of the Holy Spirit's stride!

Read: I Peter 2: 9 - 20

Your Word tells us that if the Son of Man makes you free you are free indeed. Thank you for that kind of liberty. Please keep me from being a slave to doubt, habits and temptations. But also I ask you to convict me when I exchange my freedom for irresponsibility.

Years and years ago there was a popular radio broadcast called "The Quiz Kids". It was a platform to display the mental capacities of brilliant children. On one broadcast, a 9-year-old genius was asked, "What do you believe is the most wonderful thing in the world?" After a long and thoughtful pause, the youngster answered, "I think the most wonderful thing in the world is redemption". The announcer and studio audience was astonished, for they anticipated the child's reference to some mechanical or scientific discovery or perhaps some basic emotion. The announcer then recovered to say, "I believe you are absolutely right. Redemption is the greatest thing in the world." Maybe we need that perspective in order to treasure all that is ours when we have Christ as our Savior. With Christ we are no longer lost, but redeemed. We are no longer guilt-ridden, but forgiven. We are no longer homeless, for heaven is our home. We are no longer without hope, but we have the Blessed hope. The hymn writer caught the truth of it all, "Redeemed, how I love to proclaim it! Redeemed by the blood of the Lamb!

Read: Psalm 107: 1 - 9

Father, you have spared nothing to redeem us from our folly and fallen nature. I need to remind myself of what you had to do to forgive and restore me. From the Depths of my heart I want to live out my gratitude for the world to see.

Make It Personal

❦

When Larry Brown, a former running back for the Washington Redskins, was given the award for being the Most Valuable Player in the National Football League, he was asked a natural question. "What one thing do you think has been the most important element in making you the football player you are?" was the question put to the then famous Number 43. Without a moment's hesitation, Larry Brown answered, "The most important thing which ever happened to me as a football player was a person... the late Coach Vince Lombardi. He taught me to play like a winner!" In the final analysis, the most important bearing upon anyone's life, football players, housewives, students, professional people...whoever... is made not by "something" but by "someone". For salvation to mean all that it should, a Christian needs to understand that his redemption is not based upon the event of his belief as much as it is upon his relationship to the Person, Jesus Christ. For church membership to be all that God intended, it must not so much rotate around church "events" but it must focus upon a relationship to the people who are the church. For the Holy Spirit to be all that He is, we must not first stress the evidences of His presence as much as the reality of His Personhood. Let us not miss all God has in store by missing the persons and personal relationships which He has given to us.

Read: John 10: 7 - 18

What a thrill it is to know you personally, Lord. And it is mind boggling to realize you know me by name. Yet that is the truth of the matter. I praise you as my Heavenly Father and delight for the world around me to know I am your child!

Not far from the walls to the old city of Jerusalem there is a sacred landmark called Gordon's Calvary. If you have visited the city of Jerusalem, you have doubtless seen that rugged hillside which bears an awesome resemblance to a human skull. This little hill is pointed out as the probably site of Jesus' crucifixion. The first time I saw Gordon's Calvary, I was deeply moved at the sight of this spot where the Son of God bore the guilt of my sin. Suddenly my thoughts were disrupted by the sound of air brakes. I looked down at the foot of the hill and saw a bus station. I thought, "How inappropriate! A bus station at the foot of sacred Calvary!" Then I thought again, it is appropriate. It symbolizes the truth of the cross...A bus station is where crowds of people gather and people are those for whom Christ died. All of us have sinned. All of us need a Savior. God loves all of us. Christ died so that all of us might have the chance to be saved. Then comes the sobering thought, all are lost until, or unless, they are saved. Sin and salvation are about us all, all of the time.

Read: Titus 3: 1 - 8

Sometimes, Lord, I see crowds but not people. I see people I care about and ignore those I don't know. Give me eyes to see hurting people, not just people. Help me see people for what they could be with Jesus living within them.

Like most "guerrilla gardeners", we have had some tomato plants in our backyard. A long look at tomato plants will teach one a great deal about health and fruitful Christian living. The Scriptures liken the Christian to the fruit-bearing branch and compares the Lord Jesus Christ to the life-giving vine. Jesus said so plainly, "As the branch cannot bear fruit of itself... no more can you except you abide in me." (John 15:4) I have seen highly potential branches bend and break until they no longer received any life supply from the vine. They soon wilted and thus became barren, incapable of carrying out the innate desire for fruitfulness. But thus far, we have only underscored a truth we already knew. Let me call to your attention a lesser-emphasized parallel to another spiritual truth. Tomato plants must be staked and tied, lest they easily break and lose their very life ties between the vine and branches. It is quite obvious that no man, regardless how "green" his thumb, can transmit the life giving juices of the vine to the branches. However, the gardener, regardless how ungifted he may be in the so-called knack for growing things can stake and tie tomato plants. He can provide support while resources beyond his own provide fruitfulness. The analogy is plain. Christians cannot make each other spiritually productive. That is the work of God's life-giving Spirit. However, it is in our capability to stand beside one another, binding the brokenness and weakness of some to the strength of others. Indeed, fruitfulness among Christians requires not only the life of the Vine, it requires the support of God's people bound with ties of caring.

Read: I Thessalonians 4: 9 – 12, 5: 8 - 11

What a promise you have given us! You said you would never leave us or forsake us. But you obviously want us to be part of that promise to other Believers. Send someone my way, Lord, whom I can "stake and tie".

One summer day, a couple of years ago, when the temperature was well into the high 80's, I was driving along one of our local streets and took note of an intriguing bumper sticker displayed on the car ahead of me. The bumper sticker bore a simple, two-word slogan. It said, "Think snow." I thought, "Think snow? On a hot day like this?" But I decided to give it a try. I mentally recalled the looks of a mid-winter snow along the road, ice formed around my windshield wipers and the heater battling the temperature inside the car. But try as I did, thoughts about snow brought no changes to a sweltering day of nearly 90 degrees. No amount of fantasizing can really change facts. Especially is that true with respect to God's eternal truths. The Bible says Christ is the way to God and heaven. The Word of God tells us that in Him is life, abundant life and the peace which defies understanding. It also says unless we repent we will all, likewise perish. Think differently if we chose, but it is far better if we agree with God and live like it.

Read: Acts 4: 5 - 12

The Bible tells us that, as a Christian, I have the mind of Christ. That is an awesome thought! Having the potential of thinking like Jesus, I want to begin by agreeing with what your word says. Surely that will go a long way in shaping my Christ likeness.

Pride is not a word to which we Christians often turn except to condemn it. That's certainly understandable because the Scriptures teach us: "Pride goes before destruction and a haughty spirit before a fall." (Proverbs 16:18) Webster defines pride first as "inordinate self-esteem, unreasonable conceit, manifesting itself in airs and contempt of others". But there follows a more desirable application of the word: "Generous elation of the heart; a noble esteem, arising from upright conduct, noble actions, or from an aversion to what is considered unworthy." In the latter sense of the word, I think God's people have a reason to take pride. I find myself on Independence Day, as other times when my patriotism is stirred, being very proud to be an American. When I hear my nation's heritage put to words or song, I feel a sense of rightful pride, which is not blind to our country's flaws, but is responsive to our country's virtues. There is a basic pride-factor, which I believe makes the difference in one's appearance, productivity, work habits and standards of life. I think there is nothing essentially wrong with a Christian taking a rightful pride about his church. It is a contagious excitement about one's church which extends its own built-in invitation to friends and neighbors to come, "taste and see" for themselves. Come to think about it, I guess pride stays "in bounds" as long as it is focused upon what God achieves around us even through us…. but never because of us.

Read: I Thessalonians 2: 13 – 20

There are faults in my life and in the lives of my fellow church members, Lord, so I don't want to overlook those things or indulge them. But you have chosen the Church to be your instrument to bless and serve the world. Help me to be a grateful encourager for those who are called The Church.

A Heart Problem

❧

The national crime rate continues to rise and sometimes to alarming proportions. What used to be primarily a problem of the big city, with its slums and ghettos, now has become a problem of the suburban and isolated rural areas, as well. Criminologists are baffled about the control of crime. It seems nothing really works. Crime is affected by the media, the time of year, the population, even the weather. But what <u>motivates</u> crime and <u>how</u> to <u>control</u> it is the question that stumps the experts. At this point the Bible has another of its plain-spoken insights: "The heart is deceitful above all things and desperately wicked. Who can understand it?" (Jeremiah 17:9) Whether it's crime, or selfishness, or greed, or anger, or jealousy, or lust.... our problem is first a <u>heart</u> problem. What will change those things is a change within us. That's the kind of change Jesus Christ makes when someone invites Him into his life. And it's the kind of change Believers in Christ are to exhibit in a world baffled about its crime problem. Let's be certain that people around us get the message that the difference in us is that we have had a change of heart.

Read: Psalm 51: 1 - 13

We hear a lot about change. Sometimes we are told we need to change our mind or change our direction or change our habits. Lord, the one change which can make the greatest difference in my life is a change of heart performed by you.

Beyond the Beginning

꧁

When our youngest son entered medical school, he borrowed a microscope from one of our physician friends. Such a loan was helpful, to say the least, during those four long years of preparation. I returned that microscope to our doctor friend, with appreciation. The occasion not only reminded me our son had finished medical school, it caused me to realize again that life marches on. Returning the microscope symbolized the progress and growth in a young man's life. He is no longer a medical student, though he will always study medicine. He once could borrow from someone else's store of medical instruments but the time came for him to have his own instruments. He will always need a microscope but surely, he sees more through one now than he did as a medical student. Returning the microscope underscored a lesson about Christian growth and maturity. It was like a commentary on a passage in the Bible: "Brethren, I count not myself to have apprehended, but this one thing I do, forgetting those things which are behind and reaching forth unto those things which are before, I press toward the mark for the prize of the high calling of God in Christ Jesus." (Philippians 3: 13-14) In any event, the insight is obvious. We who are the twice born are not to remain in spiritual infancy. For us to walk a treadmill in Christian growth and knowledge is a disobedient forfeiture of the goal of our salvation. We were taught the basics of repentance and faith not that we might dwell upon our beginnings in Christ, but that we might dwell upon the maturation that reflects Christ likeness.

Read: Hebrews 5: 11 – 6: 2

Father, Thank you for your patience. My immaturity, doubtless, has troubled you. You probably want to look me in the eye and say, "Grow Up!" Come to think of it that is what you have said to me through the Scriptures I have just read.

There is a term familiar to all racquetball players. It's known as "court-savvy". In other words, a good racquetball player has to think and plan ahead. Knowing where the ball is going to come he needs to be there when it arrives. Not to anticipate the action of a ball on the racquetball court is a sure way to lose. It's the same with life. If we are not prepared, in advance, for some of the adversities and conflicts we are going to face we will go under in defeat. This is what the Psalmist had in mind when he wrote these words: "You have dealt well with your servant, Oh Lord, according to your Word. Teach me good discernment and knowledge, for I believe in your commandments. Before I was afflicted when I went astray, but now I keep your Word. You are good and do good. Teach me your statutes." (Psalm 118: 65 – 68) If we want to survive and triumph we need to do more than just "show up" in life. Being Bible-savvy will make the difference in handling what comes our way.

Read: Psalm 119: 105 - 112

Father, it's almost impossible to anticipate what is coming our way. We have to accept the fact that we sometimes get hit from the blind side. But I'm asking you to lead me to those lessons in your Word which will make me durable and resilient.

Putting The Pieces Together

A puzzle piece.... was once handed to me by a Sunday School teacher. A schoolteacher as well as a Bible teacher, this Christian knew the effectiveness of using such objects to make a point. With each class member holding a puzzle piece, the teacher reminded them that one piece, by itself, makes no picture and seldom makes sense. But when all the pieces are fit together, the picture is complete. Just such an illustration conveys the truth of Roman 8:28: "And we know that all things work together for good to them that love God, to them who are the called according to His purposes." Everything that happens in a Christian life is not good. No one would are describe cancer as good, or a fatal accident, or birth deformities or an abrupt job loss. By themselves, like a lone puzzle piece, those things make little sense: they baffle and frustrate us. And Romans 8:28 does not suggest that all things are good, only that all things <u>work together</u> for good for the people of God. In other words, when life's experiences are put together by the Sovereign hand of God, they finally make sense and they have turned out to be good. Like separate puzzle pieces, Christians, though part of God's church-picture, cannot be alone what all of us are meant to be together. That speaks volumes about the importance of our consistent attentiveness to Bible Study and worship.... our agreement in prayer matters...our mutual responsibility as soul winners.... and our accountability to investing spiritual gifts. Disassembled puzzle pieces make no pictures; they just remain a puzzle. Individual Christians are indeed, people of God, but we remain a puzzle to the on-looking world until, or unless, we do together what the Lord designed and gifted us to do.

Read: I Peter 5: 6 – 14

Lord, I don't want to be the piece of the puzzle which is missing, or the one that just won't fit. I want to be a reason for others to believe your Word and be encouraged by it.

A preacher stopped at a turkey farm he had frequently passed in his travels. He asked the proprietor, "How many turkeys do you have here?" The farmer answered, "Oh about 6,000." The preacher had noticed the wire fence around the farm was only about 3 feet high, so he asked, "How do you keep all these turkeys inside the fence? How do you keep them from flying over the fence and running away?" The farmer's reply was revealing. He said, "We keep our birds well fed. As long as we feed them a balanced diet and give them all they can eat, they never attempt to leave." I think that provides insight for us about spiritual matters. As long as we are well fed on God's Book, the Bible, our minds will not easily wander and run away from a life lived close to Him. We often are reminded of the promise of Scriptures, "I will never leave you or forsake you". (Hebrews 13:5) WE take heart, and should, upon hearing those words. But the question arises, "Have we ever forsaken Him?" We have probably not renounced the Faith or openly denied Jesus, but we can wander from Him. We can also cave in to social pressure and distance ourselves from Him. Staying close to God's Word will fortify us from any proness to wander.

Read: Mark 8: 34 - 38

Sometimes, Lord, I am so disappointed with myself. I want to be faithful to you but I allow interruptions, social pressures and preoccupations to rob my loyalty to you. Stay after me, Lord, about my need to live in your Word.

Speak Up

❧

Thankfully, we in America are freedom conscious, freedom lovers and freedom seekers. One of our most cherished liberties is the freedom of speech. What meaning though, has freedom to speak if we have nothing to say? Or even worse, what meaning is there to freedom of speech if we refuse to speak. Christians in the world have something to say, something marvelous to declare. We call it our mission. It is ours to articulate the message that God was in Christ reconciling the world to Himself. What meaning though, has our mission if we refuse to perform it? Part of our failure as Christians, at least in America, is entwined in a paradox. We have a mission to perform and thankfully, we still have the freedom in which to do it but we too often appear to be people with neither mission nor freedom. Perhaps a Methodist pastor verbally sketched our situation: "The average Christian has little sense of individual mission in the world. If one were to ask him if he were a member of a 'chosen race, a royal priesthood, a holy nation', he would probably reply, "Why, no. I'm a member of Main Street Methodist Church". We need to awaken to our individual mission in the world. Let's not reserve our sense of mission to simply giving money to missions, but putting our mouth where our money is.

Read: I Timothy 4: 11 - 16

Too often, Lord, I am all too ready to talk, but not about things that really matter. I have opinions about numerous subjects but it's my personal relationship with you that I keep to myself. Increase my liberty and my courage so that I will be open about your place in my life.

A Christian once offered a gospel tract to a fellow traveler on an ocean liner. The man accepted the tract with a scowl and a grumble; then tore it into tiny pieces and threw the bits of paper into the ocean. The Christian was crushed with disappointment and walked away. The other man briskly walked to the ship's cocktail lounge. As he lifted drink to his lips he noticed two bits of paper clinging to his coat lapel. They were two tiny pieces of the gospel track he had torn to shreds and thrown overboard. He looked at the bits of paper. On one piece was just one word...."God". On the other piece, just one word...."Eternity". As the man sat there those two words bore into his heart. Eventually he reconsidered his relationship to God and became a Christian. What reconsiderations do you need to make in your relationship to the Lord? Is there a reconciliation needed in the amount of time you spend in God's Word and in prayer? What about a reconsideration of attitudes toward someone who has hurt your feelings? Can you let go of a grudge which is robbing you of your joy in the Lord?

Read: James 3: 13 - 18

Right now, Lord, I want to let go of anything I am holding on to which needs to be out of my life. Tell me what ought to be on my reconsideration list so I can be all you want to be.

It has been said.... some people ignore history, others repeat history, still others make history. Needless to say, such a statement is an oversimplification but there is enough truth in it to ponder its worth. There is still another way of stating the different ways people approach life's events and challenges: Some ignore things which happen; Some fear things will happen; Some prevent things from happening; Some wish things would happen; Some make things happen. To ignore history is folly. It is to invite the repetition of its mistakes and it is to forfeit the benefits of its encouragement. There is, however, an even clearer perspective for Christians on human events. Our God is Sovereign, meaning the ultimate outcome of all things is in His hands. This truth then should do wonders for our confidence.... our faith.... our initiative. Knowing that our God ultimately has history in His hands, how do we Christians go about influencing history? We have something to do with history's outcome by way of our prayer life. God has ordained that, as we pray, so human events are affected. Because we believe in the supernatural, we are convinced our prayers and Divine intervention are powerfully linked together. Follow the paths of world evangelization and it becomes obvious how history has been shaped. When we face undertakings, challenges, which fully press our capabilities, we are confident that we know something the natural world does not. We know that God makes the kind of history, which fatalists, cynics and the fearful assume is out of their hands. Our prayer life and our commitment to God's sovereignty have more to do with ultimate outcome of human events that the world's "movers and shaker" know.

Read: I Corinthians 3: 16 – 4: 5

Praise be to God for the assurance that you are judge of all the earth. And as your Word says, you will do what is right.

A group of people touring Yellowstone National Park watched a grizzly bear eating some food that had been put out for him by the attendants. Suddenly, a skunk appeared on the scene and boldly began stealing some of the bear's food. Since the sightseers knew how all the animals of the park are supposed to be afraid of the huge bears, they asked how this little skunk dared to get so close. Their guide explained the situation like this: "Oh, the bear is disturbed by it all right, and he would like to take out his vengeance on the impudent little skunk, but the bear knows the high cost of getting even with a skunk." The Bible says, "Vengeance is mine, I will repay, saith the Lord." (Romans 12: 19) Jealousy, envy, hatred and spite will soon consume you if you harbor tem long. Getting even serves pride and selfishness but it comes at a high price. More often than not getting even just escalates contention and there is no end to it all. The antidote to getting even is getting right with God and leaving judgment to Him.

Read: Romans 12: 14 - 21

Oh God, thank you for your forgiveness in my life. It has come by your grace not by my merit. Confront me with my selfish spirit when I delight in your forgiveness while withholding mine from others.

Pruning Job

Once we had someone trim the shrubbery across the front of our house. I had attended to the task many times across the years, but this time we needed a major pruning job requiring the kind of time, tools and tenacity I didn't have in ready supply. In order to justify the undertaking, the shrubs had to be radically pruned, so when the job was done, it looked as if we had an array of leafless, lifeless victims of some sort of plague planted in front of the house. For a few days it appeared we were making advance preparations for Halloween. In a matter of a couple of weeks though, new growth began to appear on those stark branches, and it was apparent a whole set of new limbs and a crop of new leaves were on the way. Needless to say, there is an obvious illustration in our shrubbery experience. The old habits, the attitudes and behavior that typified our lives before surrendering to Christ, must constantly be pruned back in order for the growth and vitality of our newness of life in Christ is to put in its appearance. To the natural eye such pruning seems too radical, painful and unnecessary but to the redeemed eye there is the capacity to see the delightful results. It is as John the Baptist said regarding his relationship to Jesus: "He must increase, I must decrease." (John 3:30) A close inspection of the verbs in that Scriptural sentence reveals they are agricultural words in their application. In order for Jesus Christ to "grow" and be "harvested" on the "limbs" of our being, we must prune back and plow under all that impedes that new life. Get out those spiritual pruning tools: your Bible, prayer, discomfort and obedience and allow the Lord to make room for some fresh, new, vital growth in your life.

Read: Ephesians 4: 11 – 16

If I am honest, Father, I have to admit I want to be a mature Christian with as little change and growing pain as possible. Keep convicting me of my need to grow and to do it your way.

A nurse in a settlement house asked a mother who lived in a metropolitan slum area which of her thirteen children she loved the most. The mother's answer was classic. She said, "I love the one who is sick the most, until he gets well, or the one who is away most until he gets home." Surely the mothers who are reading these lines can best understand what she meant. But more importantly, this mother of thirteen provides an insight into the loving attention of God. God loves all His children alike. There is no variation in the way He values Christian people. But there is a sense in which we can experience His special attention during times of difficulty. Instead of our problems causing us to fell neglected, we should realize just how near the Lord is. Perhaps you are in need of this encouragement right now. Or could it be you feel quite secure in God's hands but you k now someone who needs assurance. Make a phone call or write a note and make a difference in someone's life with the words, "God loves you and He always will."

Read: Psalm 31: 19 - 24

There are times, God, when I sense your nearness more than others. I know that feeling is planted in my head by the father of liars. At this moment I want to thank you for being there for me, come what may.

Old and oft-told stories are among the best to hear. Certainly they make their point regardless of their familiarity. That's why they are oft-told stories. A customer was car looking. Being interested in a luxury car, he asked a Rolls Royce salesman about the horsepower of a particular model. The salesman said he did not know but would ask the manager. The manager didn't have the answer, but he said he would find out. The sale seemed to hinge on the customer's satisfaction about the horsepower potential, so a message was sent to the car builders in England. When the reply was sent, answering the question about the car's horsepower, the message contained but one word, "Adequate". Whether the reply was convincing enough to land a car sale, I don't know, but the lesson is clear. The customer may have refused to take the word of the manufacturer but there was no question the manufacturer was confident he could deliver on his word. Perhaps there are those who look at God's claim in Philippians 4:19 as being broad, general, needing more specifics to be believable. Some would even say, "God made an encouraging promise, but He expected us to work out our own survival with a hard nose and a sharp pencil"! I believe there is more substance to God's promises than that! Basically, when Paul penned Philippians 4:19, he was writing a word from God. "Adequate." "But my God shall supply all your need according to His riches in glory by Christ Jesus." (Philippians 4:19) The long and the short of the matter is that we are privileged to base our confidence on the claims and promises of God.

Read: Philippians 4: 10 - 20

Lord Jesus, I realize where the hesitancy lies in my level of confidence. I just know myself too well to rely on my adequacy. I can depend on your sufficiency though, so keep me focused on you, not me.

Some years ago there was a popular craze called "Beach Mania". The "beach" mindset seemed to view anything couched in beach terminology as desirable. We saw T- shirts, posters, and the like, imprinted with the words: "Life's a Beach." No one enjoys the wonder and refreshment to be found oceanside more than I. But, whenever I am confronted with such a statement, my heart breaks just a little. I realize there are people who really believe that. They live from one excursion to another in the quest for happiness and fulfillment. To them, "Fun-n-frolic" on the beach is the epitome of life. But Jesus said, "I am.... the Life!" Not only that... He came that we might have life. Yes, Jesus is true Life. Therefore, life is Jesus. He fills life with joy and purpose. Life is not a beach, or a mountain, a lake, a hobby or a vacation. Life is what it is; work, school, paying bills, grocery shopping, maybe a Sunday afternoon nap. Through it all is life, and Jesus makes the difference in how we enjoy and endure that life.

Read: Luke 12: 13 - 21

Though I seem to forget sometimes, right now I am very much aware that your promise, "Fear not, I have overcome the world", is one of life's difference-makers. Keep me focused on you, Lord.

A Mind Made Up

⁊℮

A mythical group of sightseers, visiting some deep-South battlefields in mid-summer, listened to the comments of their native guide. He said, "Here a handful of Rebs routed 30,000 Yanks. And here two Virginia boys captured an entire regiment of Northerners." Soon enough one of the tourist spoke up with an obvious New England accent, "Didn't the North even win a single victory down here? The guide politely answered, "No, ma'am, and they probably never will as long as I am the guide around here!" Having your mind already made up, however, is not always so amusing. Have you made up your mind about what God is like and how He deals with hard-to-answer questions? Have you given yourself an honest opportunity to hear what He has to say in the Bible? If you have not, be honest enough to give the Lord a hearing. Satan wants to play with your mind and convince you that God is unfair or disinterested. Those conclusions are wrong and lead to defeat and anger. Turn a deaf ear to Satan and let God's Word speak to your heart. When you make up your mind about God be sure it's based on the Truth, not upon distortion.

Read: Psalm 27

Give me a heart for the truth, Dear God, so that I will not be easily misled by half-truths. Guide my eyes, Lord, to places in your Word where I can find authority to refute the lies and misinformation thrown into my path.

One of Great Britain's most embarrassing moments happened during the wedding of then Princess Elizabeth and the Duke of Edinburgh. Among the many dignitaries invited as guests of the royal family was the twelve-year-old king of Iraq. The young king wore no insignia of his throne when he sat among the honored guests who watched the wedding procession along the streets of London. Impulsively, the young king left his seat ad pushed his way through the crowd to get a better look at the beautiful royal horses. As a result, he was rudely handled by some police officers. When it was discovered who he was apologies abounded. The newspapers said, "If we had only known who he was." Jesus Christ is the Son of God. Let us not fail to show Him today all the honor and love He deserves. And remember, those who do not know Jesus as Savior will more likely want to know Him when they see us reverence Him and obey Him.

Read: Matthew 16: 13 - 17

Sometimes, Lord, we hear it said that we should not wear our religion on our sleeves. I'm not too sure just what that means, but I know that when we obey you we prove our love for you. That is the best way to identify who we are and who you are.

Something fresh does not always have to be something new. This is an insight, which could help some who are ever looking for the novel in their Christian experience. Too many well-meaning Christians in evangelical circles today are inclined to seek that which is novel more than that which is continually fresh. Such an approach to Christian living is more likely to lead to spiritual faddism than to spiritual growth. Someone who is only causally perceptive can see the "fad-cycles" which seem to attract certain kinds of Christians. To be sure, there are many facets of responsibility and interest in the life of a Christian disciple, too many to be considered and digested at once. Hence, it is only natural that we deal with these things separately so long as we do not deem the newest aspect of the Christian life the only exciting aspect. To focus on novel discoveries to the neglect of changeless truth is to pave the way for an erratic walk with God. Keep it simple, keep it fresh. Focus on the authority of Scripture, on the Lordship of Christ and on the discipline of obedience.

Read: Hebrews 12: 1 - 14

Dear Heavenly Father, what a privilege it is to call you Father. Teach me there are no shortcuts to Christian maturity. Remind me that you have disciplines in place because you love us. And whet my hunger for righteousness not excitement.

The Greatest Moment

Paul Anderson was once called the world's strongest human. I would hardly argue the point. Paul, in one lift, raised over six thousand pounds off the ground. I once sat next to Paul at a dinner meeting and heard him say that the great moment in his athletic career was in the former Soviet Union when he won the weight lifting event, which accorded him the title, the World's Strongest Human. But then Paul said, "That was the greatest moment in my athletic career. The greatest moment in my life is when I asked Jesus Christ to come and live within me. That is the greatest moment in anyone's life whether he is an Olympic athlete, a housewife, a business executive, a brick mason, a student or an office secretary. Have you had your greatest moment? If you have, are you still rejoicing in it? Whatever your title, or your role in live, nothing compares to the simple recognition that you are a Christian. The title is not an achievement, it is a gift; a gift to be borne with gratitude and accountability.

Read: Philippians 3: 4 - 14

Think of it! There is no name which is above every other name but the name of Jesus. And as a Believer in Christ, I bear that name. I want to protect the reputation of your name. Lord, I ask you to help me to do just that.

There is a story about an ancient heathen ruler who devised a treacherous way to eliminate those he disliked. He fashioned a beautiful goblet in which he molded the form of a poisonous snake at the bottom of the cup. The model of the snake was that of a coiled serpent, fangs showing, and ready to strike. The ruler would invite his unsuspecting victim to a feast. He then would have his guest served a poisonous drink from the beautiful goblet. When the victim had finished his drink, he would see the coiled model of the snake in the bottom of the cup. He immediately knew he had been deceived and poisoned! The Bible says that sin is like the goblet... sin's consequences lurk at the bottom of sin's momentary pleasure! Satan designs sin to be enticing, even irresistible but his goal is not deception; his goal is destruction.

Read: John 10: 7 – 10, I Peter 5: 8

I am no match for Satan, Father, neither am I perceptive enough to withstand his underhanded ways. Help me recognize sin's camouflage when I see it.

❦

It was the famous preacher, Charles Spurgeon, who used to tell this story in his sermons. A certain duke once boarded a galley ship. As he passed among the crew of slaves, he asked what their offences were. In each case they insisted they were innocent and placed the blame on someone else. One young galley slave, however, said, "Sir, I am guilty, I deserve to be here. I am a thief. No one is at fault but me!" At that, the duke seized the young man by the arm and shouted, "You scoundrel, what are you doing here with all these innocent and honest men? Get out of their company at once!" Thus the one honest slave was set free from his heavy oars. You see, the first key to freedom from guilt is admission of guilt. God says He resists the proud, but gives His grace to those humble enough to be honest about themselves. Simply stated, to confess our sins is to agree with God's opinion. Then, maybe another way to define confession of sin is to call our sins by their right name.

Read: James 4: 4 - 10

My sin cannot be hidden from you, Oh God, so it is pointless to deny my guilt. At this very moment, I acknowledge my sins and I ask for your forgiveness. And I rejoice in the assurance that you honor humility and honesty.

Human Nature

🙌

It is a sad commentary on human nature that when all is well, comfortable and successful, we generally are known for spiritual indifference. It is when we are in some state of brokenness; we readily shed our pride and realize God's ways are the ones which really make sense. That's why a person... must realize he is lost, without Jesus, before he can be saved; must sense guilt before he repents; must know the frailty of life before treasuring eternity. The good news is you don't have to be down-and-out, or on the brink of disaster, to turn to Jesus. It's not the degree or type of sin which puts us in need of a Savior, it is the sin nature which needs to be reconciled to God. It's not that some people need to be saved more than others. We all have sinned and fallen short of God's perfect standards. And he is not willing that any of us perish but all to come to repentance. Once we have a Savior, He becomes not only our Adequacy to forgive sin but He is our Sufficiency in every day we live, the good days and the hard ones.

Read: I Corinthians 10: 13, Philippians 4: 10 - 12

Without your forgiveness, Lord, my life and my eternity are hopeless. Praise God, that to have Jesus as my Savior is to have heavenly hope and to have His sufficiency for all my earth side needs. Hallelujah!

Hypochondriacs enjoy poor health. They so thrive upon problems that it is expedient for them to have problems...even if they must be manufactured. Genuine illness is no pathetic matter though it is cause for concern. Someone has said that much of what ails the church today should be categorized as hypochondria. Upon reading what so many church analysts are saying nowadays, I am convinced that some of them are "enjoying our poor health". Let's state it another way. Today's churches have some bona fide illnesses. These are infections needing treatment. Just treating apparent symptoms can perpetuate the bogus illness, for it implies its reality. Band-Aids on uncut fingers may attract sympathy but they do little for the unacknowledged and well-hidden internal infections. Carnality among Christians is an infection, which makes for real ill health in the Body of Christ. Carnal Christians are saved, but they are unsurrendered to the control of Christ. In some cases they are dedicated people...dedicated to the work of the flesh... and that can be spiritually unhealthy. A prescription of confession, repentance, integrity and commitment is God's medicine and our hope for good health.

Read: Romans 8: 1 - 11

The closer I stay to you, Oh God, the healthier I am. To live in your strength is the answer to my weakness. Give me holy unrest when I live by unholy habits. Urge me by your Spirit to hunger and thirst for the righteousness which makes for a wholesome health picture.

Free To Be Me

❧

Tell me, when is a person *really* free? Is it when there are no restraints? And when there is no control? It might seem that freedom is the absence of control until you investigate beyond the surface. For instance, let us say we are observing two sail boats on a bay of water. One sailboat has both a rudder and a helmsman, but the other boat has neither. The sails are hoisted on both boats and the wind begins to blow. Now which of the sailboats is free? Is the one without a rudder and a helmsman free or is it only the <u>slave</u> to every gust of wind and roll of the waves? You see, real freedom is found in direction, purpose and control. By the same token, life is not free when it is aimless and uncommitted. When Christ is at the controls of your life, you are really free to live! Freedom is a precious commodity, too precious to be exchanged for indulgence or irresponsibility. Place your tongue under the Lordship of Christ and your speech will be clean and truthful. Submit your thought-life to the Mind of Christ and you can trust impulses and judgment. Then you can say, "I'm free to be me!"

Read: John 8: 31 – 36

Thank you, Lord, for conscience. Yet by itself, conscience can be overruled by temptation and sin. I need you at the controls of my inmost life so I can get beyond living by the rules and enjoy living in your will.

Loving Those God Loves

❧

A pastor friend shared with me this letter sent to him by a nine-year-old girl who came to the church by way of their modest bus ministry: "Dear Preacher, I like church. Is better than my house. I like your talks too. I wish I knew somebody at the church. I only know you and God. Love, Angie P.S. I know the bus driver." Sometimes we unconsciously build walls between ourselves and those beside whom we sit in church gatherings. We can be so occupied with just "being there" and "doing our worship" that we fail to sense the loneliness, the pain, and the hunger for belonging, which prevails in a fellow worshipper nearby. Church is not a place where we go to behave ourselves for an hour or so each week. It is a family of Christians who get together because they need each other. To be all that we ought to be and can be to one another, there must be an awareness and response between us. Worship is not only loving God, it is loving those whom God loves.

Read: I Peter 1: 22 - 25

Father, when I think through the list of people I love, I conclude that I mostly love those who love me. I need a list longer than that. According to your Word, I am even to love my enemies. Fulfilling that expectation, I need to love more like you and less like me.

❧

Have you ever driven your car into an intersection wherein you had the right of way, and suddenly someone sped across your path, causing you to slam on the brakes? Certainly you have. Perhaps the more embarrassing question is, have you and I ever been the driver to violate someone else's right of way? Of course we have. So often though, when someone makes such a mistake in driving, it seems their way of handling their guilt is to look the other way so as to pretend the other car was not there. Looking away from reality is no way to handle driving mistakes nor is it any way to approach life. The Bible says, "The Lord is nigh unto them that are of a broken heart; and saves such as be of a contrite spirit." (Psalm 34: 18) Don't look the other way, Christ is right there where you are.... loving you...wanting to forgive and restore you. With that truth in mind why would we ever want to ignore our sin? To ignore our sin is, in fact, to look away from a gracious God.

Read: II Corinthians 7: 9 - 10

I acknowledge my sin, Oh God, even sin I have long since dismissed from my mind. I truly want a clean record with you and I k now to act innocent is not the way to do it. Just now, my spirit is that of the publican, Be merciful to me, Oh God, for I am a sinner.

It is amazing.... how many sermons there are to be heard and seen in everyday sights and sounds. I "saw" a sermon one afternoon not long ago. Evidently, school was out for the day. Two boys were walking home. When I drove by them, I noticed they were stepping at a fast pace, almost marching. Then I realized why. Each of them was carrying a set of drumsticks, which I guess he had used that day at band practice. So, there they were, marching down the sidewalk, in step, beating their drums...except there were no drums. Theirs was an imaginary march to the cadence of imaginary drums. That's all right for schoolboys.... after band practice. It's even a creative way to walk home after school. For a Christian though, to march through life, beating away on unheard drums, is not nearly so understandable. We Christians have the "drums".... They are the truths of the Gospel. For us to pound away with the drumsticks of a busy life, a set of enviable achievements, an appropriate affiliation with a church and an acceptable reputation, while bearing no distinct, specific witness of Jesus to others, is to beat drums, which have no precise sounds. On the other hand, to have the "drums", and never to use our drumsticks, produces the same effect. We have the drumsticks.... lips which can form the words, a mind which can apply the truths, a set of constant opportunities we can seize whereby we literally tell friends about Jesus. Obviously, the object for us is to bring the drums and our drumsticks together, sounding a clear witness to our relationship with Christ. After all, there may be benefits to being a member of the band, even a bit of pride in belonging, but what's the point of being a drummer who makes no certain sounds? Be one of God's drummers.

Read: Romans 10: 14 – 16

Lord Jesus, I need courage to speak up for you. Too often I have marched to the beat of intimidation and kept my relationship to Jesus to myself. Help me to seize an opportunity today to say a word for Jesus.

Fasten Your Seat Belts

❧

Have you ever been a passenger on an airplane and heard the captain say something like this over the public address system: "Ladies and Gentleman, we do not anticipate any turbulence in flight today but just in case we do, we ask that you keep your seat belts fastened while you are in your seats." I other words, the best way to handle the turbulence is not last minute reaction but proper advance preparation. So it is with life. To be sure, God responds to the call of His people when they seek His help in trouble, but it is far better for us to maintain a daily up-to-date relationship to Him. That is where the best security lies in case unexpected trouble arises. That is what the Bible is talking about, in effect, when it says: "Rejoice evermore, and pray without ceasing". (I Thessalonians 5: 16 – 17) In other words, keep up-to-date with God so come what may, you will have what it takes to be an over comer and the lord will have an opportunity to show the world He is the difference maker!

Read: I Thessalonians 5: 12 - 23

Right now, Dear Lord, I have no idea what awaits me today or tomorrow. I know I have the responsibility to avoid ma king trouble for myself but only you know the unknown. So I'm fixing my eyes on you come what may.

Sensitive Enough To Serve

❧

More recently…than in a long while, I have become aware of two well-documented truths. First, more people bear burdens and wounds than we can possibly imagine. Second, the happiest Christians are those devoted to helping others bear those burdens. Anyone who possesses the quality of sensitivity will become aware of the hurts and needs which are constantly around us. That observation offers some commentary to the situation wherein a Christian is not particularly aware of such needs. It is a paradox, if not a travesty, that some Christians are zealous on issues and debates but are oblivious to persons who languish in the midst of those very issues and debates. Still another mystery is found among those Believers who are enthusiastic on the subjects and principles of "successful" Christianity and they dress, drive and live the part. However, they are apparently unaware that the Gospel also has something to offer to those not numbered among "the beautiful people". Not all Christians have children who make the Dean's List. Some Christians have rebellious sons and daughters. Some Christians don't have much self-esteem and some are still looking for a job. There are some Christians who have sick and aging parents. Other Christians struggle to honor God with a marriage that started on the wrong foot. There are Christians with heart disease and learning disabilities and there are some who are widowed and lonely. Somehow, bright, crisp success slogans offer very little help to those who are living on the edge of personal pain. Thank God for those Christians who are in touch with enough reality that they can sense needs in others and who believe it is far more Christian to serve than to succeed!

Read: Matthew 20: 20 – 28

Forgive me, lord, for being so focused on my success or failure as a Christian that I forget my role of being a servant. The goal of my life should be Christ likeness and that means being a servant not a braggart.

Vengeance Is Not Ours

There once was a farmer who was weary of the destruction being done to his farm by a pesky hawk. To the disapproval of an animal rights activist, the farmer decided he would put an end to his problem by trapping the bird. But he was not fully satisfied with only trapping his adversary. So he decided to tie some firecrackers onto the feet of the bird, light the fuse and watch the hawk go out of his mind with all this noise tied to him. To the chagrin of the farmer, however, the bird flew into an open door of the barn. Soon the barn was burning to the ground, a witness to the folly of the farmer's vengeance. The Bible tells us that the tongue is an unruly evil, can set afire the course of nature and that no man can tame the tongue, only God can. Left to ourselves and our inclination to even the score, we can make life miserable for ourselves. We need Christ within to control our mind, tongue and life. Such requires that we willfully commit retribution and judgment to the Lord. Evening the score oversteps our boundaries and runs the risk of a serious backfire.

Read: Romans 12: 9 - 21

Nothing escapes you, Lord, and I don't have to worry about your capability to set the record straight. Give me the peace needed to rise above resentment. Scorekeeping is your job not mine.

❧

Not all "gator-aid" comes in a bottle. At a Florida G.I. training camp, part of the daily routine was to run through an obstacle course. On the final stretch of the course the men had to grab a rope and swing across a pond of water. Under the hot Florida son, the water looked so inviting the men could not resist the temptation to let go of the rope half way across the pond. They would splash into the water and relieve their hot and sweaty bodies....that is, until an enterprising lieutenant figured how to break this refreshing habit. He made the pond a new home for a full-grown alligator. After that, the men easily cleared the pond when they swung across. The moral of the story? Staying away from the places where Satan can attack you is the better part of avoiding sin. We are told Christians can resist the Devil, not in our strength, but in the strength of Christ. If we, by His strength, can resist the devil, we can resist the enticements and environment which spawn temptation and sin. Too long and too often, we have bought the lie, "I can't help myself, I'm just weak." We are no weaker that Christ is strong! So send Satan packing!

Read: II Timothy 2: 20 - 22

Heavenly Father, you know everything about me. So I ask you to reveal to me when I am being influenced by whatever capitalizes on my weakness. And help me in the choice of friends. Send friends my way who know sin's pitfalls when they see them. It is their influence I seek and their acceptance.

The Wristwatch

❦

A missionary in India was showing her wristwatch to an elderly lady who had lived her life in virtual poverty. As the elderly national listened to the ticking of the missionary's watch, she seemed amazed. In her excitement she said, "It is a little machine that keeps saying, 'Quick, quick, quick'…" As I understand it, the Tamil word for quick is a word that sounds very much like the rapid tick of a clock or watch. The missionary immediately seized her opportunity and said, "Yes, it does make a sound like 'quick, quick, quick' …and it always reminds us that time is hurrying by. So we must not waste a single moment by failing to give the rest of our days to Jesus Christ"! Take a moment to look at your watch, or glance at a nearby clock. As you watch the seconds click by realize those seconds will never be available to you again. It's not a study to motivate being busy for busyness sake. It is, however, a reason to cherish every moment of life and the accountability involved in every 24/7.

Read: Psalm 90: 1 - 12

Thank you for every day you give me, Father, for I realize it is a gift from you. You have meant some of that time for work, some for relaxation, and some for family and remind me you give us quality time to be spent with you every day.

A Study in Happiness

While waiting in my car in a shopping center parking lot, I learned a lesson. In a matter of minutes, three different cars parked in nearby spaces. After the first car left, an older two-door sedan pulled into its place. I watched the three occupants leave it. A woman and a teenager were first to get out. Moving to the trunk of the car they took out a wheelchair and rolled it to the driver's side of the car. I then heard laughter and watched the happy exchange of what apparently was a mother, son and handicapped father as they worked together to slip him into the wheelchair and made their way into a department store. No more than five minutes passed and another car, a small car of newer vintage pulled into a space opposite the one where I had parked. Three people got out of that car as well. Interestingly enough, the driver was also handicapped and a wheelchair was taken from the trunk to transport her into the department store, as well. Again I was struck by the laughter and relaxed relationship, which was shared by the three adults who had gotten out of that car. Then a car pulled right next to mine. The car and its four passengers immediately caught my attention. I would have remembered the car just by the sight of it alone. Being a late-model luxury car, it announced its own arrival. However, this two-tone convertible with chrome-wire wheel covers was occupied by four of the unhappiest looking, well-dressed people I ever saw. They got out of the car on healthy legs, having a full-blown argument while they walked toward a department store. All of which says not all happiness comes by way of late model cars, unencumbered health and fashionable clothes.

Read: James 5: 1 – 11

A sense of humor is not the same as happiness, Lord. I know that and I know happiness is not the result of a shopping spree. So I want to come closer to you today and find the peace and joy awaiting me.

٭

One of our stopovers on a family vacation was the pre-season training camp of a professional football team. After watching the team's morning workout, we stood at an exit gate near the dressing rooms so our younger sons could meet some of the players. As the first players began leaving, our boys started autograph hunting. They met one well known but lesser publicized veteran player, who smiled and said, "Don't bother with me boys, the superstars are coming." He then proceeded to give them and autograph. The player's remark about the super stars reminded me of something John the Baptist said long ago about the Lord Jesus Christ: "He must increase, but I must decrease." (John 3: 30) What John said about Jesus and himself not only tells us about John's humility and ministry, it gives us an insight about how we grow in Christ likeness. To the proportion we elevate the importance of Jesus' place in our lives, we are more Christ like. Reversely, as we insist on having things our way, we are less Christ like. If he is to increase in importance, we must decrease in our self centeredness.

Read: John 1: 26 - 34

Father, I think I am learning more and more about the Lordship of Jesus. As long as I am self centered and strong willed in my relationship to Him I will never experience all that is coming to me as a Christian. Help me, Lord, learn how to "decrease".

The statistics are still going the wrong direction for a healthy, promising home life in America. The challenge is bigger than ever for Christians to provide examples of wholesome, enduring family living for others to see. It seems to me there are some key words which, if given full expression in our marriages and homes, can go a long way toward putting family life into focus for us and those who observe us. <u>There is commitment</u>. Long-term commitments are hard to come by in most any area of life today, but the inability to stay by a commitment is disastrous to a family! We need to stress over and over that while society may assume that "falling in love" is the basis for a marriage, the Bible tells us that it is the commitment of Love which assures a lasting marriage. <u>There is gratitude</u>. To lose one's ability to say "thank you" is sad for that person, but to cease to express appreciation within a family is like giving a license to Satan to destroy the joy of living together. Forgrantedness is a dread disease for a marriage. Gratitude is the cure. <u>There is forgiveness</u>. If to say "thank you" is vital to a marriage, so is the ability to say, "I was wrong and "I forgive you". No home can long stand the pressures of defensiveness, pouting and evening the score. There are still other words, which are indispensable to wholesome home-life: time, communication, sharing and what about prayer? There are no meals so irresistible and no schedule so hurried that warrant a prayer less household.

Read: Deuteronomy 6: 1 – 9

Thank you, Father, for the reminder that you conceived marriage and the family before any other institution. Obviously you meant for the home to be the place we first learn about you. I recommit myself to honor you by nurturing and protecting my own family.

Pumping Iron

When weight lifters press and lift the weights, they call it "pumping iron". It's astounding how strong some people become by lifting weights over a long period of time. But it's sad when people are strong in so many areas of life and weak in their spirit. Some have strong minds.... strong bodies.... others have strong personalities, but they have weak convictions.... weak standards.... weak commitments. The Bible says, "Be strong in the Lord and the power of His might." The Bible says those who are strong in he Word of God can overcome the wicked one. (When you realize you are weak without Christ, that's when you start getting strong.) "Pumping iron" for a Christian is to read and study God's Word. It is to maintain a consistent prayer life. It is to be surrounded by encouragers who also hold us accountable. But there is still another influence on the development of our strength. It is to realize when and where we are weak and to allow the Lord to be our strength in those moments. It is then that our strength is perfected in our weakness.

Read: I Corinthians 12: 1 - 10

Help me, Dear Lord, to be responsible for those things I can do to strengthen my Christian life. I need to remember you will not do for us what you intended for us to do ourselves. Also I need to be reminded there are some things only you can do and I need to allow you to do them.

A Time To Lead

There are times for Christians to lead and not be led. Of course, there is never a time when Christians should not assert their influence in the world. There are however, circumstances today, which call for a specific kind of influence to be exerted by God's people. Someone has said that we are living amid a "crisis of confidence". The energy picture is far from bright. Efforts to check the fluctuation of the economy have been less than effective. If we listen to many of the analysts and commentators of our day, we can easily become disciples of despair. That is where Christians need to lead and not be led. It is not a question of realism or being practical. It is rather a mater of the Object of one's hope, one's faith and one's confidence. If we Christians are convinced that our Lord is the Sovereign-Owner-Judge of all the earth then there is every reason for us to: believe when others doubt; act when others fear and hope when others despair. It is not just a matter of "Positive Thinking" or "Possibility Thinking". It is a matter of the very nature of God, the promise of Scripture and the strength of faith. David wrote of it in his 108th Psalm: "Give us help from trouble: for vain is the help of man. Through God we shall do valiantly, for He it is that shall tread down our enemies." (vs. 12 – 13) It is time for us to lead, not to be led.

Read: Psalm 27

It is not a matter of being boastful or unrealistic, Lord. I understand that. But I want to live above pessimism and fear. I want to be a reason for the world around me to take heart. Increase my faith in your Sovereignty.

Out of the Vietnam War, in the 1960's, the story about a Colonel John Dramesi who passed some of his time in a P.O.W. camp by hand-making an American flag from scraps of cloth. That Flag symbolized a liberty for which Colonel Dramesi hope and dreamed, but it could not actually give him his freedom. When his country negotiated his freedom, his hand-made flag ceased to represent hope but it represented reality. The Bible says, "If the Son of man makes you free, you are free indeed." That is God's promise and man's greatest hope. But it remains only a promise until we invite Christ into our lives. Then it becomes a reality! In Christ we can live with the assurance that the consequence of our sin has been completely dealt with! With the Spirit of Christ within us we are free to resist temptation, for it no longer has mastery over us. In Christ we are free of the notion that our salvation has to be earned through self effort. With Jesus as our Savior we are free indeed!

Read: Galatians 5: 1 - 6

Dear God, give me deaf ears when Satan tries to peddle his wares. I am not earning my salvation, I am living my salvation. Yes, I am capable of sin, although a Christian, but I don't have to sin! Praise God, I am free from the guilt of sin and free to pursue the likeness of Jesus.

August Grass

Along in mid-August, there is a certain smell to freshly mown grass known to everyone who has played the game of football. You see, the odor of August grass means it's "that time" again. It's time for sweltering two-a-day practice sessions; time for the sound of coaches whistles; time for laps, wind sprints, two-on-one sessions for linemen and pass patterns, run over, and over, and over. To football players, August means sweat, whirlpools, donning wet pads in the afternoon and facing indescribable dressing room odors in the morning. It means weight loss regained by an unbelievable thirst for Vitamin Water or Gatorade. It means to fight to keep your position or to take one from somebody else. August for a football player, is when you hope for an afternoon breeze or maybe a downpour, and a no-pads practice session indoors. It means it's time to push yourself to the limit, to hit full speed because, if you don't, it's not the other guy who gets hurt. And August is that time of year when football players second-guess themselves while they watch others apparently enjoying those last few weeks of a carefree summer. So why do football players endure all those demands that go with such preseason rigor? Because they know there are no shortcuts to game days, winning seasons, or the personal achievement of having a jersey number all you own. I guess it's a lot like being happily serious about your Christian life. There are no real celebrations of great spiritual victory until there is the investment of putting all your heart, soul and mind into a discipleship which is all your own.

Read: II Timothy 2: 1 – 13

Sports have their seasons but to be a disciple of Jesus is a year round proposition. That's what I want to be, Lord, a daily disciple, year in and year out, giving it my all.

Sometime ago I woke at the wee hour of two in the morning. It is true, I did not stay awake long, for I have little trouble sleeping soundly. But in the few minutes I lay awake, I realized how many strange noises one hears at such an hour of the night. There are creaks and squeaks, the fluttering of window shades, the distant barks of dogs, which cause your dog to growl. As I lay there, I thought how easy it is for someone to let his imagination run wild about such noises to the point of unwarranted fear. Then I remembered a passage in the Bible that can help people who will completely trust the Lord with their lives. The Bible says the God who keeps His people "never slumbers and never sleeps." (Psalm 121:4) All too seldom do we remember that our Lord prays for us. He even contends with Satan in our behalf when the Adversary lies to God about us. Daylight or dark, whether or not we realize the seriousness of our circumstances, our God is with us. So sleep well, Christian, your Lord is always awake!

Read: II Chronicles 20: 5 - 15

What a promise! Lord, you not only said you would never leave us or forsake us, you said you would never go to sleep on us! I want to claim that promise and take it to bed with me tonight.

My three sons grew up with all the sights and sounds of church life. They realized they were, by virtue of who they were, under constant surveillance. But they also added some observations of their own. These sons never permitted me to become but so impressed with the effectiveness of my own preaching. In addition to commenting on my pulpiteering, which went overtime, they reminded me of the various stages of sleep they noticed in the congregation... during sermon time. So long had they watched the antics of church sleepers, they had even categorized them with their own descriptive labels. "Nodders"... Those who fight sleep with continuously bobbing head. "Meditators"... Those who took their snooze with a reflective look. "Z-cutters"... Those who are soundly detached from the realm of the conscious. "Eye-fiddlers"... Those who keep their eyes open by repeated discoveries of foreign matter in them. Most any Sunday I expected to hear some fresh label applied to a newly discovered style of church sleeper. It just served as a reminder... someone is always looking. We are forever under observation and not just while we occupy space on a Sunday pew. Like Paul, the apostle said, "We are an epistle known and read of all men." So it is true, there is a gospel according to you... and me.

Read: Luke 11: 33 - 36

There is a certain amount of pressure to it, Lord, but I count it a privilege to represent you to the world around me. Help me to remember that your reputation is at stake when my behavior is being observed.

232

Never Give Up

❧

A Christian by the name of George Smith once went to a part of Africa as a missionary. He actually stayed on the mission field only a short while because opposition eventually drove him out. In the brief time he was in his assigned place, he led only one person to Christ. That person was a modest, uninfluential woman. George Smith died just a few months after he left Africa, doubtless considering his ministry a failure. Years later, other missionaries providentially discovered the place where George Smith had served. They found a Bible he had left behind. They found that a church had been started. From that foundation, new missionaries went to work and years later it was reported that a total of several thousand people in that area had become Christians. Don't give up, my friend; you never know what God can do with your life, now or later! It is not success which God expects of us, it is faithfulness. We are not solely responsible for the work of the Lord, we are part of the multiplied witness of His Church. Only in eternity will we learn the impact of our testimony.

Read: I Corinthians 3: 5 - 9

Sometimes, Lord, I need to think beyond the moment. My witness as a Christian is not solely measured by its immediate results. Who I am and what I do in the name of Jesus will continue and multiply until the Lord returns and judges our faithfulness. I want to be found faithful both now and when you measure my days.

Love and Obedience

Boyhood memories bring to mind the picture of our home when I was a venturesome eight-year-old. We lived in Miami, Florida where my father was employed by the telephone company. Our home was in a residential neighborhood, but not far from our house there was a quarry. The water was deep, thus dangerous, but it was also very inviting to boys my age and older. It was not uncommon to see bicycles parked all about the quarry on Saturday and Sunday afternoons while their riders swam in the cool, green water. Parents in the area became apprehensive though, after a drowning or two... and I can hear, even now the frequent warning of my mother, "Son, I don't want you to go anywhere near that quarry." Repeatedly my mother would conclude her warning with this simple admonition, "Son, if you love me you will obey me." Many times I have been reminded of that motherly advice upon reading Jesus' statement, "If ye love me, ye will keep my commandments." (John 14:15) There is an inseparable relationship between love and obedience. So it is in the home... where love prevails, respect for one another's wishes and well-being also prevails. So it is in a church family... where love permeates, mutual respect dominates. So it is in our relationship to Christ... where love for Him grows, there obedience to Him shows.

Read: II John 1: 1 - 6

Lord, I want to match my actions with my words. Along with others, I have said that I love you, but too often my actions fail to prove it. I seek your strength right now to be your obedient and proven disciple.

Beach Stroll

❧

The story is told that Oliver Wendell Holmes once met a little girl while he was taking a stroll along a beach. After they had walked and talked a short while, the little girl said, "I have to go home now so my mother won't worry about me." To that Holmes said, "If your mother asks where you have been, just tell her you have been walking with Oliver Wendell Holmes." With a sweet and naïve kind of innocence, the little girl replied, "And if somebody asks you where you have been, just tell them you have been walking with Susanna Brown!" Unknowingly, the little girl caught the spirit of God's love toward all of us. The Bible says that with God there is neither Jew nor Greek, male or female, bond or free. He loves all of us.... just alike...and Jesus died for us.... just alike. Most of us have had to do battle with some measure of prejudice or bias. Sometimes we make lasting impressions out of first impressions, with little opportunity for change. To be sure, we need to carefully choose our friends and being gullible is no place to start. The place to start is where Jesus begins, the place of human worth.

Read: Matthew 9: 36 - 37

Father, you see us not only as we really are, you see us as what you can make us become. That's the perception I need in order to love the lost and to love my enemies.

The Real Secret

❧

A life of shallow spirituality can appear most acceptable by some prevalent religious standards. However such an existence does little more than to weave a virtual net about the Believer, making him impotent, powerless to be what he could be. Satan, the user of uncanny skill, can entwine the professing Christian in the cords of church-related going and coming until the churchman becomes exhausted through trying to escape this net of obligation. The problem lies back of the net, back of the hurried going and coming, back of the church program, it lies within the soul of the individual. You see, we have unconsciously come to the place that we measure our own spiritual status and that of others by how much is DONE, if even only mechanically. This is certainly not to say that nothing needs to be DONE but it is to pry deeply into the matter of motivations. Do we turn the crank of our religious machinery, working ourselves into a weariness of "well-doing"? Much to our dismay, working harder at the church "business" does not necessarily sweeten nor vitalize our motives. The real secret to Christian life is not work but surrender. How close do we live to the source of Divine Energy? How thoroughly saturated with His power have we become? Don't be aloof and skeptical at this juncture, for I speak not of dangerous fanaticism, rather I speak of the GENUINE need of one who wants to lead a joyous, reasonable and productive Christian life! Live close to the Word, near unto prayer and to control of the Spirit.

Read: Galatians 3: 1 - 14

It is an eye opener for many to discover that working hard at doing good is not the route to a fulfilling Christian life. Forgive me, Lord, for trying to serve you in my own energy. I want to allow you to energize me with your indwelling Spirit. Then I will have a lot more to show for it.

Get With It

❧

"Go to now"... Is the way the Bible's Epistle of James puts it. In today's language we would say... "Face facts!" .... Or "Get with it!" This phrase is designed to awaken the reader to the truth which follows it: "Get with it... you do not know what your life will be like tomorrow. You are just a vapor that appears for a little while and then vanishes away. (James 4:14) Therefore, to one who knows the right thing to do and does not do it, to him it is sin." (James 4: 17) Life is all too brief and unpredictable for us to be careless about its use. We all have something we need to let the Lord do in us or through us. We had better "get with it", while there is time: ... time to witness... time to teach... time to give thanks... time to love... time to pray... time to let God make us over in His image. Though our god is eternal and not limited by time, He works with us in the framework of time. We are the ones for whom time has its limits. We are also the ones for whom time has its earth side rewards as well as eternal dividends. We have no more time, or less than others do, but we have choices to make and then, to get on with it!

Read: Colossians 4: 2 - 6

Eternal Father, I praise and exalt you, for you are forever the same! Thank you for understanding time and life as you lived it in the lord Jesus. I bring to you this day and ask that you guide me through it. I really want you to be pleased with how I spend it.

It was a late August evening, suppertime. Along with thirty other freshmen, I had drawn equipment that day to start pre-season football practice. Having gone through the cafeteria line, I picked out a place to set and settled in beside another freshman. We had a one-word exchange. "Hi." Our conversation then broadened to a tw0-word exchange. "I'm Jim." "I'm Charlie." Then I bowed my head to thank the Lord for my meal. Momentarily, I felt a jab in my ribs. "You got a headache?" Jim asked. "No, I was just praying for a minute." Jim chuckled and, in that unforgettable Pennsylvania accent of his, he said, "Say one for me". Though we were never close friends, we had a cordial relationship. I'd like to know how many times across our college days, Jim jibbed me with "Don't forget, say one for me". A couple of times, Jim and I had a serious conversation about what it means to know the Lord and to be able to "say your own". I recall on one occasion I said "Jim I do pray for you from time to time but I can't say to God what you can only say for yourself". Jim got serious on the subject for a few minutes. "I get it. It's like my assignment on a pass play. You can protect the quarterback for me, but I have to catch the pass for myself." Where Jim is today, I don't know. I hope he now has a relationship to the Lord whereby he talks to Him on his own. One thing is for sure, Jim gave me an insight about individual accountability to the Lord. Just as no Christian can assume another believer's prayer life, no one can enjoy the Lord for someone else.

Read: Matthew 16: 13 – 19

Lord, I thank you for the ways other Christians bless and strengthen my life. I want to be a source of encouragement to other Believers myself. Yet I pray that I will never forfeit what you have in mind for me by failing to keep my relationship to you up close and personal.

National Debt

❧

The national debt is somewhere in the trillions of dollars. Those figures are so huge I cannot begin to conceive how much it really is. Some enterprising citizen tried to illustrate the national debt at that moment by saying it is the equivalent of a freight train, 36 miles long, with 3,456 box cars, each stuffed with stacks of dollar bills. Or it is equal to a ribbon of dollar bills, going around the earth at the equator, 160 times. Even with such graphic descriptions, I cannot imagine how much the national debt is. Then I think of my debt to God. I think of my anger, my jealousy, selfishness, pride, lust, lies.... multiplied thousands of times and I wonder how God could love me and want to forgive me! And yet that is what Jesus Christ came years ago to tell us. Just to read His three-part story of the lost sheep, the lost coin and the prodigal son, is to be overwhelmed with the greatness of God's love for us all. Isaac Watts, the hymn writer, was overwhelmed with the thought of God's grace and forgiveness when he wrote the words, "Were the whole realm of nature mine, that were a present too small; love so amazing, so divine, demands my soul, my life, my all!"

Read: Psalm 130

Your grace is amazing, Father. Forgive me for ever taking your love and forgiveness for granted. May your patience and compassion toward me be a source of both humility and hope.

The Message of Choice

The power of choice is indeed a power. Inherent in choice is the awesome power of determining our salvation. God provided the basis of our redemption through Grace, but the condition of our redemption lies in our choice of Christ as Savior. But even after becoming a Christian, the potency of our choice continues. Daily, and repeatedly each day, we have opportunity to make choices between that which will more clearly identify us with the Lord and that which distances us from Him. By that which we choose to do or choose to be we openly declare our relationship to our Lord. Somehow I feel the need for a renewed emphasis on choice as a method for Christian witnessing. If only we preferred the risk of a little ridicule to the guilt of a lot of spiritual cowardice. If only we chose to be in the house of God on a consistent basis. If only we chose prayer meetings in preference to club meetings. If only we chose a love for Bible study more than a love for the shopping mall. If only we chose sacrifice rather than obligation as our incentive to give. Such choices would speak volumes about the reality of our walk with Jesus.

Read: James 1: 21 - 25

Dear Lord, help me in making the kind of choices which will be testimonies of my devotion to you. Especially do I pray for your strength in choosing a time every day to spend with you in prayer and your Word.

Starvation

❧

Did you know that hundreds of people in the world die every hour from malnutrition? By the time we sit down to our supper table tonight, over 2,000 people will have died for the lack of food. We say, "That is terrible!" And we are right. It is terrible. We must find some way to better distribute the world's plenty. By the same token, there are millions who are starving for the spiritual nourishment of God's message. There are people sharing earth with us who have never even heard that God loves them and Jesus came to die on the cross for them. Even more tragic is it for someone to have food but refuses to eat it. Think of the spiritual feast which surrounds you: Bibles, churches, books, telecasts, radio messages, tapes and CD's all about you. There is no excuse for people on this earth to starve for the lack of the gospel. It is a matter of the "haves" getting to the "have nots" and sharing. It is so less inexcusable for Christians to go undernourished while the Bread of Life is offered to us at every hand.

Read: John 6: 26 - 35

Keep reminding me, Lord, that your Word is not only truth, it is nourishment. I know you will feed my soul if I will only go to where the food source is. I pray for a hunger and a thirst for righteousness.

❦

Jesus is the Vine, we are the branches. Because life, strength and productivity are in the Vine, the branch cannot bear fruit, lest it abide, or be attached in the Vine. Our fruitlessness, then, is not always due to inactivity, but more often than we would like to admit, to our detachment from the life giving sources of the Vine. The branch exists to convey the life of the Vine and to bear fruit that others may eat and live thereby. A Christian then, like a branch, clustered with fruit, becomes a "tree of life" from which others can be fed and refreshed. As Andrew Murray has aid, the Christian is "a center of life and blessing and that simply because he abides in Christ and receives from Him the Spirit and the life of which he can impart to others." Our fruitfulness is not solely for us, it is for those who would take it from us and feed upon it. There is no place, then for the unfruitful Christian nor is there a place for the idle Christian. What of your neighbor and what of the folks at the office? Do they wait, even unconsciously, upon your fruitfulness? If our branches are fruitless it is due to detachment or idleness. In either case, the life of the Vine is quenched and the unfed remain unfed. We simply cannot have fruit to share and allow it to die on the vine!

Read: Jeremiah 17: 7 - 8

It is all too easy, Lord, to presume that your fruit is ours to consume. I realize, in this moment, your produce is not ours to consume but ours to share. May my attachment to your vine grow stronger and my branch bear much fruit.

Time Magazine once pointed out that successful advertisers have learned how to cash in on certain popular phrases that have caught on with the public. These so-called "in" words convey, in concise language, an explanation which otherwise would be long and drawn out. Some advertised items are referred to as "out of sight" or able to help us "do our thing". There is one such expression that really says a mouthful. It is the simple, four-word, speech-figure: "getting it all together". That is precisely what God does for someone's life when that person makes Jesus Christ his Savior and Lord. God is able to "get it all together" for us. Life makes sense; has purpose; heaven follows life; sins are forgiven. Yes, inviting Christ into your life is really "getting it all together." But, just as important, it is Christ who "keeps it all together". We must remember the Bible tells us that only Jesus saves and it is He who keeps us saved. We are not saved by good works; neither are we secured and sanctified by self effort. Our good works are the evidence that Jesus has "gotten it together" in us.

Read: Titus 2: 11 – 3: 3

Lord Jesus, I want to be known as a Christian. I don't want people to think I have earned the title, for that would misrepresent the facts. Help me to so focus on Christ likeness that His presence in me will be unmistakable.

I once overheard a man and his wife debating whether they ought to buy some small pepper plants for their garden. As they looked over the plants, the husband said, "Why those plants look sick." His wife responded, "No they aren't sick, they just haven't grown much." The husband said, "That is what I mean. They are sick, that's why they haven't grown much!" When a person becomes a Christian it is like starting life all over again. The Bible calls it new birth. And as babes of Christ, it is normal for Christians to grow, to mature. If we do not grow, we are less than normal. Listen to this Bible verse: "As newborn babes, desire the sincere milk of God's Word that you may grow thereby". (I Peter 2:2) God's Word goes on to say that we should grow beyond the regimen of milk and add meat to our diet. As the writer of the book of Hebrews said it, "Solid food is for the mature". (Hebrews 5:14) To be sure, Christians begin with new birth, but we are born again not to stay in infancy but to grow into the "stature of the fullness of Christ". (Ephesians 4:13)

Read: Hebrews 5: 12 - 14

It is my heart's desire to grow as a Believer in Christ. But, Lord, I need for you to convict me of my childish attitude and my self-centeredness. Let me begin, right now, by facing the selfishness which spoils my spirit.

Mixed emotions go with this time of the year. Summer's end means schools begin. College freshmen are as excited as they are apprehensive. Their parents are as apprehensive as they are anything else. It's time for it all to happen…. It needs to happen… Yet with this kind of progress there is some pain. A mixture of pain and pride belong to the faces of young parents as school buses pull away with their loads of human treasure. Giggles and trusting eyes cover the bewilderment of the school's little people… but with this kind of progress there has to be a little pain. Groans of complaint are a teenager's predictable response when reminded it is the end of August. Yet there is among most of them, an anticipation of the new, and the unexpected the unknown. They will have some hurts during the next nine months and they will inflict some… but with this kind of progress there is some pain. Teachers… notoriously under compensated… still return to their class rooms, quite realistic about today's educational problems, still optimistic about youth's potential and rewarded by that occasional student who makes it worth it all. Yet with this kind of progress there is some pain. There is bound to be a lesson for all of us who are "enrolled" in Christian discipleship… learning life… learning love… learning the Spirit… the Book… the Lord. With this kind of progress there is joy and… some pain. It is worth it all. Ask the student. Ask the parent. Ask the teacher. Ask the growing Christian. Ask the Master Teacher.

Read: Romans 5: 1 - 5

Father, we seem to understand that growing pains are part of life. Somehow, though, we don't want the pain that foes with Christian growth. Teach me that with Bible study there is discipline; with forgiveness there is repentance; with prayer there is endurance; and it is worth it all.

Good To Give Thanks

Ingratitude is epitomized in this little story I picked up some years ago. Having just been given an apple by a neighbor, a surly youngster was coaxed by his courtesy-minded mother. "Now what do you say to the nice lady for giving you the apple?" The shocking reply left both the mother and donor speechless. "Peel it for me," responded the ungrateful youngster. Such an attitude displayed in a child prompts all kinds of thoughts within us as to how we could remedy the situation not the least of which would be a good "act of discipline". Such an unthankful spirit is ugly when observed in a child, but ingratitude displayed by a Christian adult or young person is worse than ugly; it is as ugly as sin! The Bible tells us that unthankfulness is the hallmark of unbelief just as thanksgiving is evidence of living in the center of God's will. Knowing that you and your family have received blessings.... experiences... answers to prayer... from God, I encourage you to <u>openly</u> express your thanks unto the Lord! "It is a good thing to give thanks," says the Scripture... good for us... good for others... good for God.

Read: Psalm 103

How often, Dear God, I come to you in prayer with a barrage of requests. When I think of it, it is embarrassing. How can I bypass thanksgiving and praise enroute to you with my petitions? In this moment I simply want to praise and thank you for all you are.

A Dime's Worth

You never know when someone is watching to see if you are for real. An evangelist once zealously preached a sermon on the text, "Thou shalt not steal." The next morning he boarded a city bus, giving the driver a five-dollar bill for the fare. As the preacher took his seat, he counted his change and found he had been given a dime too much. He returned the dime to the driver explaining that he had given him too much change. The driver answered, "Yes, I know. I did it on purpose. I heard your sermon last night about honesty. I just had to find out if you were for real. I said to myself, "If he practices what he preaches, I'll go back to hear him again"! Think about it. We can gain or lose someone's confidence and our integrity for a dime…or even less. For that matter, we can forfeit our influence with a sudden outburst of temper or a profane word. A lie does not have to be but so big for us to be known as a liar. We may not be in control of the circumstances of life which surround us but we can by God's grace, be in control of how we represent our Lord through it all.

Read: Psalm: 15 – 1 - 5

Lord, I need to be reminded that your integrity is at stake with how well I represent you. Strengthen me amid moments of secrecy and peer pressure to be found faithful.

SEPTEMBER 4   *Out-Believing Your Opponents*

❦

Prior to a football game between the University of Richmond and Villanova University, I sat in on a brief talk by one of the Richmond Assistant coaches. The coach reminded the team it had been two weeks since they played, having had an open date following their victory against Boston University and the clinching of the Conference title. He warned them about the difficulty of getting "up" for a game under such circumstances. Then the coach said, "Let me tell you how we will win this game tomorrow. We don't **outweigh** them; we probably will not **out coach** them. We might **out-quick** them. But we will not **outmuscle** them. All that doesn't matter because those are not the things that will determine our victory. There are three ingredients, which will figure into a win for us tomorrow. We must out-**tough** them. We must **outlast** them. We must **out believe** them." As I watched the game the next afternoon, I saw the coach's prophecy fulfilled between the sidelines. The lead had changed hands five times… The clock was ticking out the final seconds… with 25 seconds to go and only a fourth down as a remaining opportunity to score; the time had come for one group of young men to out believe another. The play was called, a pass was thrown and a catch was made deep in the end zone. Richmond had won 38-35. And while one group of young men stood in **disbelief**, another group leaped and shouted their "**out belief**". There is a whole series of sermons in that gridiron incident based on the text: "I can do all things through Christ who strengthens me." (Philippians 4:13)

Read: II Timothy 1: 6 - 14

Dear God, the greatest thing I have going for me is that you are greater than any enemy or obstacle coming my way. I choose to believe that and thank you in advance for your victory.

Going Public

❧

Once a little girl asked her Christian mother "Do you love Jesus?" ... the mother's answer rebounded. "Why certainly dear, why do you ask such a thing?" The child said, "well, you talk about Granddaddy and Grandma…and Uncle Frank and Aunt Frances…. but I don't ever hear you talk about Jesus. I thought if you loved Jesus you'd talk about Him too." The mother was genuinely touched by the child's simple observation and determined in her heart she would talk more freely about Christ as one she truly loved. And that is as it should be. The Bible says, "Let the redeemed of the Lord say so." (Psalm 107: 2) Today there is still time and opportunity to mention Christ's name in a conversation with someone. Who knows, if you mention Jesus, maybe someone else will be encouraged to do it too. That is the beauty about "going public" with Jesus. Just a simple thing like quietly expressing thanks to the Lord in a public restaurant reinforces others who want to do the same. It is not a matter of "wearing your religion on your sleeves", it is a matter of "putting your mouth where your heart is".

Read: Luke 9: 23 - 26

Lord Jesus, thank you for identifying yourself with the likes of me. When you were here on earth, you were criticized for spending time with ordinary folks and sinners. You wanted people to know you loved them. I want you to know I love you. So I will not keep it a secret.

From my hotel room I could see a large banner displayed across the rooftop of a nearby building during an out-of-town trip some years ago. The local Y.M.C.A. was having a membership drive and the sign was there to help them publicize their offers: "MEMBERSHIP SALE NOW!" I presume a membership sale at a Y.M.C.A. would offer things like full benefits at a reduced rate. That is a legitimate offer and quite appropriate for enlarging the membership of a "Y", but it would certainly be out of place for enlarging the membership in the Body of Christ. More so now than ever in the history of American Christianity is there a need for Christians to pay whatever price is necessary to grow churches with worthy expectations of their members. To be sure, we will always be imperfect, even at our best, but we can never afford to lower the standards of quality Christianity. To make the witness of Christ believable, it will always be at the price of moral consistency, financial integrity, ethical reliability, conversational purity, spiritual maturity and personal fidelity. Some critics of evangelical Christianity will always seize the opportunity to demean us, especially when we provide the proof for their arguments. We hardly have room to complain when we are "done in" by our own.

Read: I John 2: 3 - 6

If I know my heart, Lord, I want to be one of the reasons unbelievers would give the Gospel a hearing. I realize people are not saved by following another person's example, but a good example silences a lot of arguments for unbelief.

Perhaps you were raised as I was on a phrase you remember to this day. "If a thing is worth doing, it is worth doing right." That is refreshing advice for the carelessness, which often typifies our day. There was a young stonework apprentice who was given the job of carving an intricate ornament. As a Christian, he felt that his handwork ought to reflect care and honest labor. He had no idea where the ornament was to be used, but he put much careful labor into it. Months later, he was strolling through an art gallery which had just been opened to the public. To his surprise, there he saw his ornament, which had worked into the building décor. He said to himself, "A good job shows up after all!!" The Bible says, "Whatsoever thy hand findeth to do, do it with all thy might!" (Ecclesiastes 9: 10) The Bible is quite clear about the place our works have with respect to our salvation. We are not saved by good works, but by God's grace through faith. Yet the Scripture tells us that we are recreated so that our good works would be the result. And we are told to allow our salvation to work its way out evidencing God is at work in us. As we allow God to work a good work in us we can say with the stone mason, "A good work shows up after all."

Read: Philippians 2: 12 - 18

You saved me, Lord, so that you could do your work in me and through me. That's what I want to happen; that I will unmistakably be a workmanship which can be explained only in that God did it.

SEPTEMBER 8   *Elbow Grease*

❧

The first game of the season was coming up. So it was football helmet cleaning time…and our then nine year old had gotten out the Big Wally and Comet cleanser to apply to the grime and smudges on his gridiron hard-hat. Most of the dirt wiped away with relative ease, but some refused to yield even to second effort. Determined to do the job just like his coach had instructed, our sandlotter asked his mother, "Mom, do you have any elbow grease?" Her reply was natural: "Do I have any <u>what</u>? The coach told us to use elbow grease on our helmets to get them clean." A motherly chuckle was the first response; then came an explanation to our fourth grader who was more familiar with modern speech figures like "cool" and than with timeless terms like "Elbow grease." "Son, elbow grease means real effort or hard work." So back to the helmet our youngster went reapplying cleanser, but this time mixed with "elbow grease." And it worked. All the elbow grease a Christian can muster will not accomplish some kinds of spiritual productivity. But there are some things in the Christian life which are primarily achieved by "elbow grease", like: Practicing mutual respect in the home by listening; by commending and acknowledging worth; Learning to speak the various languages of love; Cultivating a love for worship through a careful maintenance of daily family prayer time. See if you have some "elbow grease" which you could put to use just now in your Christian family life.

Read: I John 2: 12 - 17

Heavenly Father, to exalt you in the home and to learn the Word of God in the surroundings of family is truly one of life's highest callings. I want to be found faithful as a homebuilder with your blueprints on hand.

A New Wardrobe

When our sons were growing up, they liked borrowing my clothes to wear. One morning one of them asked if he could wear one of my shirts. He had borrowed another shirt of mine the day before. I told him he could use the shirt but I asked, "Son, why don't you wear one of your own shirts today?" His answer was symbolic. He said, "Dad, I could wear one of mine, but it is more fun to wear something different than what you have gotten tired of! Have you gotten tired of seeing yourself act like a dull, unhappy, bored, critical somebody? Would you not like to look and be different? God has a whole new wardrobe of life to give you. The Bible says tells us when someone becomes a Christian he becomes a brand new person inside. He is not the same anymore. A new life has begun. So for a Christian to act as if there has been no change within is a strange form of hypocrisy. Jesus had some strong things to say about Believers denying Him before other people. What an opportunity we have to witness to the world around us by allowing the change He has made in us to be portrayed by us.

Read: Colossians 3: 5 - 17

Lord, to have a whole new wardrobe and to continue wearing old clothes doesn't make since. Thank you for my wardrobe of Christ like behavior. I intend to wear more of it.

God's Road Map

There are numerous routes which can be taken as you travel from place to place. Some highways are more direct; some are more scenic, while others provide more benefits. These various routes have different conditions involved in their use. Some permit speeds of 70 miles per hour while others permit only lower speeds. It all has something to say about the "routes" we select in "traveling" through this Christian life. Some of us choose, at times, the shorter routes in living for Christ. In such instances, we do not involve ourselves in so much time spent upon the journey, but time saved means the loss of so much beautiful "scenery": prayer, Bible study, a word fittingly spoken for our Lord to one not even traveling the road. Of course, one can become so impressed with his satisfaction about the scenery that he forgets that there is a destination to be reached. Often we encounter the individual who is so engrossed in how the scenery of some spiritual activity has engaged him, that he stops traveling altogether, not realizing there are other more lovely sights to see further on. The analogy is clear. How much wiser is it for us to travel God's "road map", doing things His way and with His goals in mind. Oh yes, there appears to be profitable short cuts available to us, but they by-pass so much God intends for us to see. Besides, "engine trouble" on a lonely short cut is so unnecessarily time consuming and can leave your quite stranded! It is not only safer, but so much more promising to follow God's way. We cannot afford to "travel" otherwise.

Read: Matthew 7: 13 – 14, Hebrews 12: 1 - 3

Lord Jesus, you have not only made a way for us to heaven, you are the way to life eternal and to a life worth living. Your way is the only way for me and I commit my travel plans to your road map.

Choices

Choice is a delightful privilege, but it is also an awesome responsibility. Periodically, we go to the polls to make political choices. But there is a realm of choice, which is even more exciting and awesome than that of a political election. It is the choice we make about God. Many years ago a great political leader of the Bible made a speech to his nation. In that speech he said, "Choose you this day whom you will serve"...but as for me and my family, we will serve the Lord!" (Joshua 24:15) Maybe you have voted many times, or you will, but remember there is no choice you will make more important than the ones regarding Christ's place in our life. No decision you make equals the one you make for Jesus as your personal Savior. After that decision you are not finished with decision-making in His regard. You make a daily decision to have Him as Lord of your life and that decision is tantamount to being filled with His Spirit. We choose not to sin by way of His strength. We choose to give time in our daily routine to Bible reading and prayer. We choose to do the right thing just because it is right. The power of choice is a God-given privilege but it also is a precursor of the life that follows.

Read: Proverbs 16: 1 - 11

Help me, Oh God, to make responsible choices. Give me unrest when I am about to make wrong decisions and give me great peace when I make good ones.

Broken But Blessed

❧

"But we have this treasure in earthen vessels..." (II Corinthians 4:7) The more I consider it the more astounding it becomes. As a Christian I am a container in whom God has deposited a knowledge of His Truth. More importantly, as a Christian, I am an ordinary residence in whom the Holy Spirit of God actually dwells. And fellow Christian, you too are just such a residence. Think of it....all the life... the power.... the peace... we so often say we seek is within us. We need not be looking, groping for these things "out yonder somewhere"; they are residing within us, waiting to burst through and fill our being as the shells of our will are broken and yielded. A confession is in order at this point, however. You and I must admit that we want the results of a Spirit-flooding, but all too seldom do we want the process by which such an internal flood takes place. Borrowing Watchman Nee's term of "being broken"...perhaps our greatest need, man-for-man, is to pray for the willingness to be broken rather than praying only for "results-without-price". B.B.McKinney wrote it well in one of his hymns: "Holy Spirit, breathe on me, my stubborn will subdue..." Many Christians have had to walk the rough roads of adversity and wade in the deep waters of difficulty. Some have been hit from the blind side by an unexpected blow. Needless to say such painful encounters are unwanted and sometimes we wonder why they have to come at all. Yet, it is through such trials, anxiety, and anguish that we become broken enough to become dependent upon the Lord and obedient to Him. I once heard it said, "God cannot use someone greatly until he has suffered much."

Read: Matthew 11: 28 – 30, II Corinthians 4: 16 - 18

Father, there are times when I feel I have tasted of suffering, then I look at others who have endured far more than I. Help me to remember it is not the amount of difficulty we encounter, it is the growth we experience in it.

The Valedictorian

Many years ago, a college student at Amherst placed a letter from the alphabet on the door of his dormitory room. It was the letter "V" and it remained on his door throughout the four years he was a student. His follow students often wondered what the letter "V" represented, but it remained a mystery until he graduated. The student finished at the top of his graduating class, thus was the valedictorian. The "V" on his door for four years represented the goal he had set for himself. What letter of the alphabet best represents your life's goals? "M" for money? "F" for fame? "S" for self? Why not a "C" for Christ? Then you could say with Paul, the first century Christian, "For me to live is Christ." (Philippians 1: 21) The rest of that Scripture verse, "and to die is gain", should be thought of in the same breath. The whole verse of Scripture makes for a great life goal. Whether in life or in eternity Christ makes the difference!

Read: Mark 8: 34 - 38

Dear God, the longer I live the more I realize one's world view is the difference-maker. I want to see things in the way you see them and not waste my time focused on things which hardly deserve a glance.

No Mixed Signals

I was eight…and had just been told "no" by my parents. It seemed they always said, "no". As I saw it, I was a prisoner, fettered to the strictest set of parents in the neighborhood. There seemed only one thing to do…escape…. and do it on my bicycle. I had not gotten far when I sensed the family car had pulled along side me. My dad was driving and had the presence of mind to raise his voice only loud enough to be heard over the drone of the car motor. "Turn your bike around and get yourself home. I expect you there in the next ten minutes." Have you ever tried to stretch a five-minute bike ride into one lasting ten minutes? You can do it if your goal is to delay the inevitable. My dad disciplined me and I vividly remember how it felt. I have another vivid memory about that ordeal though. I remember after my well-deserved discipline, my dad picked me up, placed me in his lap and hugged me. What he said was brief but spoke volumes to me about what parental love is all about… In the process, my dad taught me a lot about the nature of God's love. Maybe some child behaviorist would criticize such a scene, insisting it produced mixed signals. I know differently, though. The signals were not mixed; they were very clear. My dad loved me, come what may. Not many weeks after the bicycle episode, my dad slipped into eternity. He taught me a lot in eight short years… not the least of which was a rich illustration of what the Bible means when it says, "Love never fails." (I Corinthians 13: 8)

Read: Psalm 89: 28 - 34

Thank you, Heavenly Father, for your everlasting love. I cannot explain it and I certainly do not deserve it, but because of Christ, I have it. Even when I feel your discipline in the midst of my failure, I will remember that your love never fails.

Early Impressions

Growing up in the home of an aunt and uncle, I was introduced to a set of memories, which increase in their significance the longer I live. There are memories related to our two family radio sets. One set was in the living room and the other sat beside my uncle's bed. It seemed to me as a boy, every Friday night about ten o'clock I would hear the sound of an announcer's voice over my uncle's radio saying, "The winner and still heavyweight champion of the world, Joe Louis". Though it really wasn't every Friday night that I heard the distant voice of a radio ring announcer, every Sunday afternoon about four, I heard the sounds of Rudy Atwood at the piano playing the theme song of the Old Fashioned Revival Hour, "Heavenly Sunlight". Another memory I have from boyhood days is the sight of the church's offering being counted on our dining room table after Sunday dinner. My aunt was the church Treasurer and her job included counting the offering with the help of two or three church members who dropped by to lend a hand. It wasn't just the procedure of counting the church offering to which I was exposed; it was the emphasis upon giving to the church, which made a deep impression on me. My folks were tithers and they talked about it openly. I couldn't know how to appreciate the influence made on me back then, but I see how much a part of me they are now. When your children look back over the years, what will they remember they were taught about giving to the Lord?

Read: Proverbs 3: 1 – 12

Thank you, Lord, for those who impacted my life more than they could know. Use me, in some way, to influence those who are watching me, because someone always is.

The word "P.O.S.H" has an interesting history. Originally it was an abbreviation placed on British boat tickets for first class passengers. Assuming the ship would travel south from England and would return to England traveling north, first class passengers were given cabins on the side of the ship away from the sun. P.O.S.H. meant "Portside Outbound, Starboard Side Homebound." P.O.S.H. then, became a word to describe luxury. Becoming a Christian is not like securing a ticket to life on which God has stamped "P.O.S.H." Christians, like anyone else, encounter difficulties. What good is it then to be a Christian in this world? Because Jesus experienced life and conquered all its enemies, we who follow Him are assured that no enemy of life can have lasting victory over us. Being a Christian is not to have an exemption from life's difficulties; rather it is to have the assurance of an over-comer and the expectation of a conqueror. In fact, Romans 8: 37 tells us, "We are more than conquerors through Him who loved us."

Read: John 16: 29 - 33

Praise God! Even when I am weary of difficulties and apparent defeat, I can h old my head high, knowing help is on the way. I may not always feel like a winner but your Word tells me when I am on your side I am more than just a winner.

A Matter of Minutes

❧

It's been a lot of years since I wore a football helmet but not so long ago that I don't remember that football is a game of inches. If football is a game of inches, life is a matter of minutes. Time is something we all have, rich and poor alike. It's how we use our time that makes the difference. A minute here and another there, and a day has suddenly gone away from us. It is like the Bible says, "Go to now you who say, today, or tomorrow, we will go into such a city and continue there a year, and buy and sell... You know not what shall be on the morrow. For what is your life? It is even a vapor that appears a little time and then vanishes away." (James 4:14) God wants us to experience the most important of all life's moments... inviting Jesus Christ to be our Savior and allowing Him to be our Lord. And then, there are those added moments and days to enthrone Jesus as our Lord.

Read: Psalm 31: 15 - 24

Dear Lord, I have today and the guarantee of no more. In fact, I have this moment and possibly no more. So I give you my time and I take what you have promised, "Be strong and let your heart take courage." (Psalm 31:24)

Daytime television talk shows are not my favorite attractions but I recall seeing one some years ago which features a subject other than the fare I would have expected. The main guests were a mother-in-law, two daughters-in-law and a psychologist who were to give insights into the legendary struggles between in-law mothers and daughters. Central to the discussion were the conflict and tension between an in-law mother and daughter on stage, which had reached the eruption level over seating arrangements at a family dinner, the daughter-in-law had hosted. I found it difficult to believe that so much of an hour on national television could center on such a controversy. What added even more bewilderment to the situation was that the dinner in question was actually a Seder, a Jewish religious celebration. Imagine it, a seething, ongoing conflict reached its boiling point over seating arrangements at a feast, which is the commemoration of God's redemptive intervention of His Chosen People! Of course, I guess one setting is about a good as another if it's an argument you are determined to have. People have arguments on the way to church. People have arguments on the way home from church. People argue at church. Denominations argue. It is embarrassing. No event... no relationship... no ministry... no cause... is any more sacred than the attitude with which we approach it!

Read: Philippians 2: 12 - 18

Lord God, once again I am reminded it is not what I do which best reflects my relationship to you, it is what I am. I pray other people can see you more by way of my attitude.

Significant Crossroads

Not many miles from Fork Union, Virginia, there is a place known as Zion's Crossroads. That intersection is not only an important spot where two highways come together and continue on their separate ways, it serves as a symbol to my own memory. As a fourteen-year-old boy, I boarded a bus, after a long train ride from West Palm Beach, Florida, to Richmond and made my first journey to Fork Union Military Academy. Riding along on that bus, I had all the typical fears one would expect, being so far from home about to enter school in a strange place. I entertained thoughts of getting off the bus and going back home, but then I realized I didn't have the price of a ticket. That wasn't a real obstacle though for I thought about "thumbing" my way home. With those thoughts swirling about in my head, the bus paused for a stop at Zion's Crossroads. Just beyond the intersection, I saw the sign indicating that Fork Union was just a few miles ahead. I settled back in my seat for as I saw it, there was now no turning back. My four and a half years at the Academy proved to be a real crossroads in my life, the making of so much of what I would become. My ties with my "chosen" home state of Virginia and the opportunities of serving the Lord in this part of the world are ultimately traced to that day when, just a little beyond Zion's Crossroads, I stepped onto the campus of Fork Union Military Academy. I have come to realize that crossroads are more than highway intersections. They are sometimes significant moments in life from which God determines the rest of your life.

Read: Deuteronomy 30: 15 - 20

Father, you have given me the privilege of making choices but I need to realize what an enormous responsibility goes with that privilege. Help me see the crossroads which are involved in my choices.

A Missionary Mother

✤

Few people have the legacy I can claim. My mother came to know the Lord early in life. She learned "lady hood" from my grandmother, learned "county-seat Alabama-clay" values from my granddad and learned about God from the Bible she studiously read. Somewhere along the line, she learned a lot about love, because she wasn't afraid to love people, especially God's people. God was double good to Mother. He gave her a husband, my dad, who knew the Lord well and who went to be with Him early in life. Twenty years later, God brought a Christian widower into her life, my step dad, one of the most gentle men I ever knew. I really don't know how the Lord has arranged it all but there is no doubt that there has been a happy reunion in heaven. To remember my mother is to think of family. Earlier in life I did not know how to appreciate the loyalty and those virtues, which almost border on pride and protectiveness for family. I've lived long enough now to realize that Mother, her sisters and the rest of the Stewarts and Fullers were on to something too few today know how to value. Make no mistake; Mother had some unique turns in her personality. She could "flutter" a bit and she was more proud of her son than she should have been. I have vivid memories of my mother on her knees. I recall the sound of her voice in earnest intercession especially for unsaved people she loved. As long as I can remember she talked about her unfulfilled desire to be a missionary. Yet she was a missionary to me and to most anyone who ever really knew her.

Read: II Timothy 1: 2

It is good to realize that there is no mission field more crucial to the Kingdom than our own homes. Help me to fulfill my calling to that mission field before I travel to any other one.

Keeping Records

❧

As I understand it, the largest brass musical instrument in the world is a tuba, 71/2 feet tall. And the world's spaghetti eating record was set by 4 people who ate 100 yards of spaghetti in a minute and a half. A professional golfer has the lifetime record for holes-in-one at 35. These quick observations make us mindful that people are forever keeping records and keeping up with records. But we ought not to forget God is keeping records too. God knows who has invited His Son into their lives and who has not. The Bible calls God's record book the Lamb's Book of Life. Is your name written into God's record? It can be, if you will ask Jesus Christ into your life to stay. Once your name is written into the Book of Life it will never be erased and according to the Book of Revelation, the Lord Jesus will continue to verify your name before the Heavenly Father.

Read: Revelation 3: 5 – 6, 21: 22 - 27

Dear God, I realize you know everything which is the object of knowledge. You know me through and through. You know the record of my life, but I thank you for the forgiveness which has made way for my name to be written indelibly into the Lamb's Book of Life.

Overcomers Not Escapees

Some years ago, one of the more popular movie actors of the time facilitated his idea about "getting away from this present world". On a Tahitian island called Tetiaron, some 4,000 miles out into the South Pacific, he had built a "primitive" hotel where 30 to 40 people at a time could get away from it all for $70 a day. The actor explained that these modest accommodations on his private atoll would help to make it a place of primitive beauty to which select persons could fly in his private plane and escape what he called "the tribulations of this world". Our Lord has an altogether different plan. He said, "In me you may have peace." And the peace He offers requires absolutely no attempt to get away from this present world. To the contrary, His plan for peace is available while we are very much in this present world. "These things I have spoken unto you, that in me you might have peace. In the world ye shall have tribulation, but be of good cheer." (John 16:33) And how can our Lord offer the encouragement…"Be of good cheer" in a world of: Sin, Suffering, Sorrow, Spite and death? The answer is to be found in the last phrase of the same verse wherein He insisted good cheer was possible: "…I have overcome the world." In Christ we are overcomers not escapees.

Read: Philippians 4: 4 – 7, James 1: 2

To be truthful, Lord, I would rather not have to encounter difficulties in life but I know that is unrealistic. What is for real is your peace amid times of unrest. It is that peace I claim as I pray in the name of Him who gives it.

Above The Clouds

🎝

Perhaps you have had the experience of boarding a jet airliner under overcast skies and taking off to soar above the clouds. If so, you know the sensation of flying above the heavy clouds in the clear, clear air that is always bathed in sunshine. Flying at 30,000 feet, leaving the dismal weather below is not only an experience for today's jet traveler, it illustrates what can be done in rising above the storms of life. The Bible speaks about the opportunity for Christians to be "together in heavenly places in Christ Jesus". (Ephesians 2:6) That Bible verse is not talking about heaven after we die, it is talking about the here and now. If we will get our eyes off the foreboding woes of life and fasten them on the hopes Christ has to offer, we will find ourselves living above a lot of our dark and cloudy experiences.

Read: Psalm 30

Lord, I thank you for every day I have bathed in the sunshine of health and happiness. But I thank you also that you are the same amid days best described as dark and dreary. Weather changes and so does life, but my eyes are fixed on you, come what may!

The Wonder of Expectancy

๖๙

The rain poured down as I drove back home from an overnight retreat where I had been speaking. It was obvious the wet weather had set in for the weekend. It seemed the earth, trees, grass, mountainsides and flowers were alternating gulps of refreshment with outbursts of thanksgiving. We needed the rain. For weeks we had talked about our need for more rain. We had sympathized with the farmers. We had watered our lawns one day, hoping we would not have to do it the next. The rain seemed so timely. Then over my car radio came the snappy voice of the announcer who said, "The next song I'm going to play for you expresses our sentiments on this dreary afternoon." "Rain, rain, go away, come again some other day…" Oh, I realize the disc jockey was just trying to weave some cute remarks into the fabric of his show, but I could not avoid making an observation. We are so often… so hard to please. We think we know what we want, but when we get it, we dislike the form in which it comes. We even pray for something, but reserve the right to accept or reject the answer when it arrives. Maybe we moderns are so accustomed to creature comforts and controlled circumstances that we have lost the wonder of expectancy. At this point, we need a good dose of Philippians 4: 12 – 13 "… in any and every circumstance I have learned the secret of being filled and going hungry, both of having abundance and suffering need. I can do all things through Christ who strengthens me."

Read: Psalm 65

Your character, Oh God, is ever predictable, changeless and reliable. But the ways of your blessing and the how of your provisions are often surprising and filled with wonder. What a truth to live by! Increase my capacity for expectancy.

A friend of mine was a waist gunner on a B-29 during World War II. He tells of one mission he flew when bad weather required a considerable amount of flying in a holding pattern, thus consuming a great deal of precious fuel. So much fuel did they use, they could not make it to their home base, so they had to emergency land on an alternate field located on a small island which had been taken by marines after much sacrifice. When my friend stepped off the plane, he saw a hillside dotted with crosses, marking graves of marines who died taking the island. He realized that he owed his life to those who had given theirs. Then he remembered another hillside and the cross of Christ and realized he owed his eternal life to Jesus who made the supreme sacrifice. Christ died for you too, my friend. For that matter, He gave His life for every family member and friend of yours and mine. That thought ought to excite us over the possibility of sharing that news with them.

Read: Mark 15: 22 - 29

The whole idea of sacrifice is less and less extolled in our day and time. But, Lord, without your sacrifice we are without hope. Increase my gratitude for my salvation by am unfading mental picture of the hill called Calvary.

During certain times of the year we repeatedly hear of someone who has fallen victim to that plight called the flu. Schools are sometimes closed for a few days in an attempt to break the chain of contagion. Absentee rolls can reach enormous proportions at times. Of course, the hacking coughs, the fevered brows, the post-flu "washout"... and other accompanying problems will slowly disappear as the viruses spend themselves and recovery makes its welcome appearance. There is a lesson in it all, however. The effects of sin in a Christian's life are comparable to the decommissioning results of the flu. Though there are exceptions, the flu does not take one's life. It just makes life miserable. Sin is found in a Christian's life. True, it ought not to be there, but like John said in his First Epistle, "If we say we have no sin, we deceive ourselves and the truth is not in us." The eternal consequence of sin... of all sin... has been dealt with by the death and resurrection of our Lord, that is true, but the temporal consequences of sin we have to deal with here and now. No temptation, no sin, can take our salvation from us, but like flu, they can so inflict us with guilt and defeat that we cannot enjoy our salivation. The remedy? Daily inoculations of confession and prayer... and where possible, to avoid sin's unnecessary "exposure"!

Read: I John 5 - 10

Heavenly Father, I have to believe you grow weary of my repeated confessions of the same sins. Yet your Word assures me that your grace awaits my honest confession and repentance. Thank you for faithfulness in the face of my failures.

Looking through a magazine once, I saw a fascinating photograph, but I had no idea what it was about until I read the description beneath. It was the highly magnified photograph of a snail's tongue. Did you know the tongues of those little creatures have thousands of tiny teeth growing on them? That explains how they can rip through the leaves and stems they eat. To say the least, a snail's tongue is a wicked little instrument. But, for that matter so can a person's tongue be a wicked instrument. When the tongue is used to curse God, slander people and degrade a conversation, the Bible says it is "full of deadly poison". On the other hand, our tongues are a chief instrument by which we can bless God, encourage a broken heart and tell a world about Jesus. Let God use your tongue to bless the rest of your day. Remember, "Death and life are in the power of the tongue." (Proverbs 18:21)

Read: Colossians 3: 12 - 17

Dear Lord, I need a great awareness of my accountability in the use of my tongue. It's too easy to say whatever comes to mind. I want to submit my tongue to the mind of Christ. Then I will be free to speak my mind.

The symbols of the ordinance we call the Lord's Supper are really three in number. That the bread emblemizes Christ's body and the cup His blood is well know to most. However, the symbol of the table itself is little known even to those who have frequented the memorial meal through their years as Believers. The Passover Table symbolized the place of family acceptance, oneness and fellowship. To be included at the table was to evidence one's unique relationship to those gathered about it. Likewise, the Lord's Table symbolizes our unique relationship to one another through Christ and it should proclaim in silent eloquence a wholesome oneness in our spiritual family. The remembrances prompted by the memorial supper are actually two in number. That the bread and cup remind us of our Lord's sacrificial death is a familiar fact. That the cup and bread also are reminders of His bodily return to earth is the regrettable overlooked aspect of the ordinance. The self-examination, which accompanies the observance of the Lord's Supper, is also two-fold. Again, one phase of the memorial experience is well known while another phase is overshadowed. Not only are we to approach the Table of the Lord with updated confession regarding our sins against God; we are to purge our conscience of every bitterness and variance we have with other people.

Read: I Corinthians 11: 27 - 33

Thank you Jesus, for giving me the Memorial Meal, as a vivid reminder of what you have done for us, and what you will do. Don't let us forget that same meal is a reminder of our need to forgive others.

The Race

Jogging has become a staple these days among those who want to keep themselves fit and firm. There's no doubt about it, running and walking can go a long way toward conditioning the heart and improving our health. And God is pleased with us when we take care of our bodies. After all, the Bible says a Christian's body is the temple of God. The Bible also says the Christian life is a lot like running a race, but at the beginning and end of that race is a person; Jesus Christ. In other words, He starts us on the race, He runs it with us, and He is at the end to receive us. It is significant to note, however, the Lord does not run the race for us. We need to b

Reminded there are some things only the Lord can do, but there are some things the Lord will not do for us. The Lord provides the stamina, the encouragement and the reward for running life's race, but we are responsible to submit ourselves to the discipline that conditions us to run it.

Read: I Corinthians 9: 24 - 27

Like a well conditioned athlete, Lord, I want to live for you. To be lazy in my spiritual discipline will make me a loser not a winner.

He Speaks Your Language

A few years ago I was traveling in Europe and came to the city of Florence for a short stay. I suppose I wanted to appear to be the well-exposed world traveler, because I decided to use a few Italian words as I encountered some of the local citizens. I went to the hotel desk to get my messages and said to the desk clerk, in my best accent and rolling my r's, "Gratze". He smiled knowingly and said in perfectly good English, "And thank you!" The Bible tells us that God knows what we want to say, even though we say it poorly or even before we say it. It says, "The Holy Spirit makes intercession for us with yearnings which cannot be put into words." God knows your heart today. Don't worry about how to speak to Him. He speaks your language. He not only knows and speaks your language, He knows the emotion which lies behind your words. After all, He lived life as we live it, in the flesh, and He tasted life as we experience it. He knows weariness and pain. He knows desertion and the betrayal of a friend. He knows tears and enjoyment. He knows you and wants to hear from you.

Read: John 2: 23 – 25, Hebrews 4: 14 - 16

It is both comforting and exciting, Lord, to realize that you k now me and what my life is like. Help me to remember you not only hear me when I pray, you understand how I feel when I pray.

Free To Live

❧

Flying a kite makes for an interesting study. It is not the wind alone that causes a kite to fly nor is it only the structure of the kite itself. Actually, it is the kite string, which plays the most vital role in the life of a kite. The same string which permits the kite to soar high is the string which holds it under control. To release that kite string would not mean freedom for the kite, but would insure its aimlessness and destruction. Only as the kite is held under control is it free to fly. That is the way it is with people. Only as we are under God's control are we free to live gracefully and confidently. Paradox though it is, the inward control of God is the same thing which gives us liberty with safety. That's what Jesus meant when He said, "If the son of man makes you free you are free indeed". (John 8:36) Before sailing into the winds of change and opportunity, we need to be sure we are bound by the string of prayer and trust to the Hands of Divine Control.

Read: John 8: 31 - 38

The Enemy would have me believe that you want to control my life, Lord, and do it to restrict my freedom. What a lie! Dear God, I want the liberty you give so I hand over to you the controls of life. I want you to be Lord of my life!

Hope Beyond the Headlines

Reading the headlines in a daily newspaper can lead us to stories which are informative, puzzling, shocking, even frightening. But finding hope in those headlines is so often next to impossible. Strange zealots are building bombs in remote hideaways. Other zealots are bombing innocent people as some sort of "strategic" attack on the government. Endless news stories of child molestation, domestic murder and gruesome discoveries in shallow graves...Photographs of swollen tummies in far away places, yet not too far to prompt some agony of conscience. Recurring reports of ethnic wars, which apparently will never end... The drug and alcohol scene with its ugly achievements... Divorce rates in continuing assent...leave us all too little foundation for hope. Yet the Apostle Peter exhorts us: "be ready always to give an answer to every man that asketh you a reason of the hope that is in you". (I Peter 3:15) We do have hope for man and his planet, but it is a hope which exceeds the promise or problem of treaty, platform, truce, dissent or counter dissent. Our hope is in the rebirth of people, hence, world change in the process. Is that just a pipe dream? Not at all. Christ Himself is the reason for the hope. Because that is true we know there is hope beyond the headlines in any day's newspaper.

Read: I Peter 1: 3 - 21

Keep reminding me, Oh Lord, the world around me is in need of hope. Convict me of my failure when I am a merchant of discouragement. Help me to be a reason for my friends to believe you have the hope for which they hunger.

Malnutrition

Some time ago, a press release across the country told of a 71 year old widow who died of malnutrition. Malnutrition is a cause of death we think of in the underprivileged countries of the world, but this lady died for the lack of proper food right here in the United States…in Florida, in fact…my boyhood home. Even more baffling is the fact the lady was a wealthy woman. She died, leaving behind an estate of nearly a million dollars. The only explanation the courts had to offer for this senseless death was that the lady was incompetent due to senility. Think of it…. a woman worth $840,000 died of malnutrition! No less tragic is it though, for God to have made His heavenly, eternal riches available to all of us and so many refuse it. When you refuse Christ….His forgiveness….His plan for you…you starve your soul in the presence of abundance! That is malnutrition of the worst sort! Come to His table today and help yourself.

Read: Ephesians 1: 3 - 14

Father, it is a sobering thought that I can rob my Christian life of its nourishment. I realize I cannot provide the spiritual food I need, you do that, but I can avail myself of the table you spread before me. Before this day is over, Lord, I'll be back to your Word for a second helping!

October is the best of autumn's world. Crisp chilly nights...brisk, frosty mornings.... warm clear days.... combine to fulfill any weather forecaster's dream. I've often thought if the Lord put me in charge of the weather, the calendar would be made up of twelve Octobers. I would plan no February ice storms, no blistering July afternoons, no dismal, drizzling weeks of November, just October. But after a decade or so of such changeless days and seasons, it would get to be terribly monotonous. There would be no need for adjustments to life outdoors, no challenge, no seasons to get ready for, or to enjoy. There would be no need for sleds, or skis or hunting licenses. There would be no smell of rain, no daffodils, no Christmas holidays, just October. There would be no Final Four, no Super Bowl, and no Spring Training, just October. And if there were nothing but the rainless days of October, the earth would die of thirst and the imbalances of nature would eventually destroy every form of life there is. Its circumstances that I want to be attractive, conducive, uninterrupted and comfortable. God is not preoccupied with circumstances but with the ultimate results of those circumstances. God is interested in eternal outcomes: gratitude, not selfishness; faith, not predictability; endurance, not comfort; praise, not presumption; Christ-likeness, not a charmed life. Thank God, there is more to life than just October.

Read: II Corinthians 4: 13 – 18

Father, give me a vision for more than the immediate. Give me the Spirit of an overcomer. Help me find you in whatever my circumstances may be. Teach me to live with change.

Leaves, Leaves, Leaves

The fall of the year brings not only colorful mountainsides, it brings leaves, leaves and more leaves to be raked and bundled. Life is a lot like raking leaves. Regardless of how hard you work at it, if you do not get things securely tied together, some unexpected experience can blow things apart and scatter life into pieces! The Scriptures tell us that Jesus Christ is the One who ties life together and makes life make sense. Get your Bible and underline the sentence found in Colossians 1: 17, "Christ was before all else began and it is His power that holds everything together." Does your life make sense? If some stormy blast were to hit you from one of the blind sides of life, would you be able to hold together? You can be certain about it with Christ in your life. But even when Jesus is your Savior you must learn to trust Him on a daily basis to deal with the unexpected and unwanted earth side moments of life.

Read: Colossians 1: 1 – 23

Lord, I seek the perfect peace your Word tells me is available to all whose mind is fixed on you. I can't see my blind side, but with my eyes on you, I will not fall apart regardless what side adversity strikes.

Power in Waiting

One morning, as our family went through the paces of readying for a new weekday, I was impressed with our need for power. Without electricity, we would be virtually paralyzed. Awakened by an electric clock radio, our family turns the household bathrooms into veritable beehives of electronic activity. The exhaust fan buzzes above the shower which flows with hot water, while coffee perks in its electronic caldron and electricity turns the stove into a "breakfast machine". For all of our electronic equipment, however, there could be no progress without a reliable source of power to propel them. That of course, serves as an obvious illustration. But let us take a turn less often followed in the illustration. Power can exist without the means to put it to use; an inertia of a different sort. When a Christian is daily yielded to the overrule of the Holy Spirit, then he becomes a personified power plant. However, there are still appliances to be propelled, lest there be only power-in-waiting. Empowered prayer, empowered Bible study, empowered conversation, empowered witness, and empowered worship... head the list of appliances, which are ours to connect.

Read: Acts 1: 8, Hebrews 4: 12 – 13

You do not give us an assignment which you do not empower us to do. So, Lord, it doesn't make much sense for me to be empowered to do what I neglect or refuse to do. At this moment I want to change all that and connect my will to your power.

Choosing Sides

One of the darkest moments in a boy's life comes when his gang gets together for a baseball or basketball game…and "choose up sides". They pick two captains who in turn alternate choosing their team members. There is inner torment for a boy when he is last to be chosen and I am sure the same torment awaits a girl when she is unwanted and left out. Even adults get their feelings hurt in such a moment. The Lord Jesus Christ understands that experience. The Bible says, "He came to His own and His own received Him not." (John 1: 11) He came into the world He made. He came to the world He loved. He came to the world He sought to redeem, but for the most part, refused Him. Hopefully, you have received Him as your personal Savior, but do you leave Him out of your everyday life? It is just as much a choice to seek His will, or study His Word, to refuse a temptation, or to enthrone Him as Lord of all.

Read: Deuteronomy 30: 11 - 20

Thank you, dear Lord, for the power of choice. It is a powerful thing to choose you as Savior. Today I want to make the choice which will allow you to make the difference in my every day life.

Reflections of Light

If we are not contributing to the enlightening of our world, then it must be noted that we are contributing to its darkness. Jesus said to those who bear His name, "Ye are the Light of The World", but is not Christ "the Light of The World"? Why then this confusion? He is the original Light of God's resplendent revelation; we are redeemed reflections of that Light. Ours is not a light which we can generate, but His is that original Light. We reflect His light of gospel truth not that the response of those who believe will be toward us, for such would be usurping a claim that the light is our own. The choice of words in Jesus' statement challenges any misunderstanding: "Let your light so shine before me that they may see..." See what? "That they may see your good works", is His response. But the Scripture continues on its road to clarity, "... and (that they may) glorify..." Glorify whom? That they may... "Glorify your Father which is in Heaven", rebounds the answer. Such glorious light is not to be hidden especially when we realize that the hidden Gospel is hidden to them who are lost. But the message of the Light of Christ is not to be hidden. It must be shown and told. By whom? You and I have that answer.

Read: Luke 8: 16 - 21

It grieves me to consider how often I have hidden the light of Christ. By my timidity and by my chosen silence I have helped hide the Gospel. Lord, increase my boldness to intentionally place myself where I will reflect the Light of Christ even in the darkest places.

When news first reached England of Wellington's victory over Napoleon, there was some confusion about the report. The signal was sent by semaphore from a sailing vessel. The message was read slowly as the little flags spelled the message: "Wellington defeated..." As the message reached the conclusion of the word "defeated", a heavy fog slipped in and the rest of the message was hidden from view. For hours the news was that Wellington had been defeated. When the fog lifted though, the rest of the message came. It said, "Wellington defeated Napoleon!" Jesus was crucified on Friday, was in His tomb Saturday, and for hours it looked as if He was defeated. But when the Sunrise of Easter revealed and empty tomb, it was known, "Jesus defeated Satan!" That same Jesus wants to drive away every fog that darkens and confuses your Monday through Saturday world. Get the message, loud and clear, Jesus is your victory!

Read: Exodus 15: 1 - 13

Help me, Lord, to think victory not defeat. To do that I will need the reinforcement of your mind over my mind. I truly want to think like you do because you always think like the Victor you are.

The Old Suitcase

On a plane trip I made several years ago, my suitcase was damaged. The airline with which I traveled voluntarily assumed responsibility. They told me the suitcase world either be repaired or replaced with a new one. Several days later, the airline called to tell me they had purchased a new bag for me. When I went by to pick it up, the agent said, "Here's your new bag and here's the old one. You might as well take along the old one, too. If I were you, I would still use the old bag for plane trips and save the new one for special occasions." That was probably good advice for an air traveler, but it would be a poor principle to apply to Christian living. When we become Christians, the Scripture tells us: "…. old things are passed away, behold, all things become new." (II Corinthians 5:17) That is why Paul wrote to the Roman Christians: "knowing this, that our old man is crucified with him, that the body of sin might be destroyed, that henceforth we should not serve sin." (Romans 6: 6-7) Old and new suitcases may be used interchangeably. In the Christian life, however, the old "us" does not even exist. As far as God is concerned, just the new "us"…. in Christ…. exists. Simply stated then, practical Christianity is a matter of constantly taking the old "us" out of circulation.

Read: Romans 6: 12 - 19

God in heaven, why do I even have interest in the worn out temptations Satan darts before me? You have the way to abundant life, and I choose to live it!

Mansions and More

Sometime ago, when traveling through an area of the country that was new to me, I saw an interesting sign marking the entrance to a newly developed suburb. It was called "Sherwood Mansionettes". The mental pictures, which I had around the word "mansionettes", were intriguing. I remembered something Jesus once said, "In my Father's house are many mansions. If it were not so I would have told you. I go to prepare a place for you... that where I am there you may be also." (John 14: 2 – 3) Think of that! When we give our lives to Christ, He will start preparing a heavenly mansion for us. But there are no mansionettes in heaven...no replicas...no mere suggestions of grandeur...No! Where Christ is there we will be, not in "mansionettes" nor in "heavenette", but where His is and everything is full sized! That promise calls for a full sized commitment on our part to obey and serve the architect and builder of our future abode!

Read: II Corinthians 5; 1 - 9

It is hard to take in, Dear Lord, but I am thinking about what you have prepared for me in heaven. Then I realize you have glorious things for me to claim here on earth. I deserve none of it, but if I do not claim it, I am disobedient to you.

OCTOBER 12 *Better Seen Than Heard*

❧

Church windows occasionally provide me with an opportunity to "see" sermons being preached. One Sunday between services, I watched a group of little people, with their adult workers, playing on one of the pre-school playgrounds. Two little fellows clung to a favorite teacher, while other children clamored for her attention. It was all she could do, holding a child in one arm and trying to lift another with the other arm. Finally she sat down on the ground, Sunday dress and all, to become surrounded by children who obviously appreciated the fact that one of the "big" people had come down to visit their world, at their height! I thought; this dear Christian preschool worker is preaching the kind of sermon which makes God believable, and the church one of those good memories. Then as some arrived early for the next service, I saw a man taking a parking-lot stroll with his daughter. They walked along, hand-in-hand, enjoying a few precious minutes together.... sharing daughter-talk, putting in Daddy-time. I thought; there is a sermon being preached to a congregation of one, but few sermons are more important! No doubt about it, as God Word says, "It pleased God by the foolishness of preaching to save them that believe." But remember, there is a place for those other sermons, better seen than heard.

Read: Titus 2: 1 – 15

Heavenly Father, it would seem that there are church buildings in all directions and I am grateful. Remind me, however, that some of the most effective preaching is done by ordinary Christians, like me, whose pulpits are not found in churches.

Asking Forgiveness

༚ઇ

Have you ever stopped to think about the position a person is in when he needs forgiveness? He is never in a position to say to someone from whom he seeks forgiveness, "Say, I deserve to be forgiven"... or...."I demand that you forgive me!" No.... the person who needs forgiveness is only in position to sincerely ask, "Please forgive me." That is the way it is between God and men. We are not in a position to make any demands or any bargains with God. We are only in a position to realize that we need God's forgiveness and ask for it. But we really do not have to wonder what God's response is going to be, like we do when we ask forgiveness of unpredictable people. God is ready to forgive those who give Christ His rightful place in their lives. My friend, why carry that burden of guilt any longer? God will take it away, but you will have to.... ask. The truth still applies when a Christian sins. In His crucifixion and resurrection the Lord Jesus has dealt with the eternal consequence of our sin. But we must acknowledge our sins and ask for forgiveness to experience God's grace day by day.

Read: Micah 7: 18 – 19, Luke 18: 9 - 14

Dear God, you want us to live in the peace of forgiveness. But I realize that peace waits on my confession and repentance. That peace also waits on my willingness to forgive others. I come to you now in the spirit of confession, repentance and a willingness to forgive.

Not For The Fainthearted

❦

Among the memories I have of the tragic midair explosion of the space shuttle, Challenger, is the statement made by then President Ronald Reagan to the nation: "The future does not belong to the fainthearted." Mr. Reagan knew he had to be more than just empathetic on that occasion; he had to prime the nation's resilience. He was on target. There are many bewildering interruptions in life, but to pitch our tents at the scenes of sorrow, discouragement or fear is to terminate a future without allowing it to bless us! The future does not belong to those who are fainthearted about exploring space. Neither does it belong to those who fear the adventures of: the will of God ... the power of prayer ... the soul winner's attempt ... the tither's faith ... the risk of an apology ... the claims of Scripture ... the triumph over the unknown. The sudden, unexpected explosion of the shuttle ten miles above lift-off clearly underscored the frailty and brevity of life, even at its scientific best. For every Christian, the whole incident renewed the realization we have in the Gospel of Jesus, the most indispensable information ultimately needed by all of human kind. And, in the tragedy, we learned again: "The future does not belong to the fainthearted."

Read: Psalm 31: 1 – 5, 21 - 24

Our enemy, the Devil, will use any form of discouragement to break our spirit. But you, Lord, have the ultimate victory in all things. So be my resilience!

Marooned

A sailor once spent a long while marooned on a deserted island. He was overjoyed to see a ship drop its anchor one day near the island, sending a small boat to shore to rescue him. As the story goes, the first thing the officer aboard the small boat did was to hand the sailor a bunch of current newspapers. He said, "The captain suggests that you read these newspapers to find out what's going on in the world, then let us know if you want to be rescued." Of course the story is a spoof. We cannot really get away from life…its difficulties…its temptations…its challenges. But there is something we can do. We can invite Christ into our lives and deal with life by depending upon His resources and His wisdom. And that is a form of being rescued from this present world! Once Christ is in our lives we not only have His rescue, we are qualified to be rescuers, directing the despondent to Him.

Read: Revelation 21: 1 - 8

God in heaven, you know all about earth side life and you know the ultimate outcome. It's foolish for me to claim you as my God and to fret over unwanted moments in life. You are my God and I am secure!

Sharing The Recipe

❧

Not all hermits are withdrawn, antisocial, misfit, eccentrics. In fact, not all hermits are people. There is a version of a "hermit" which, in my opinion, is one of the best homemade cookies ever to grace an oven. I remember the hermits my late mother-in-law made from time to time and sent our way. I recall saying I thought the recipe for hermits probably went to heaven with her. No. "Big Mee-Maw's" recipe for hermits didn't go to heaven with her. Thankfully she and others passed on what had been passed on to them. That's not just a lesson in the legacy of cookie makers; it's a lesson in the legacy of soul winners. Those of us who have been given salvation's plan must not even entertain the idea of keeping it to ourselves and taking it to heaven with us! More than ever we need to be committed to personal soul winning. By no means am I suggesting that we neglect ministries of nurture and discipleship, but we must also hold ourselves accountable for the salvation of thousands who share our part of the world with us. Someone awaits your recipe for eternal life right now.

Read: I timothy 2: 1 - 7

Lord, sometimes we are told that religion is a private matter; that we are not to wear our religion on our sleeves. As I think it through, such advice is not found in the Bible at all. Increase my soul winning courage.

Imagining Things

❧

A doctor once decided to analyze his patients who were typical worriers. He found that 40 percent of them were apprehensive about things that never happened. 30 percent concerned themselves about the past over which they had no control. 12 percent were afraid of losing their health, though the illnesses they feared were really in their imagination. Others worried about family members and friends.... leaving less than 5 percent who had legitimate concerns. The Bible says, "Be anxious for nothing", (Philippians 4:6) meaning; Don't worry unnecessarily." It's like the bassoon player who once told Toscanini that his instrument would not sound the high E flat. Toscanini smiled and said, "Don't worry, there is no E flat in your music for tonight's concert." Cast all your care upon the Lord. He is quite able to handle it. In fact, He is able to handle the concerns we haven't had to face yet.

Read: Philippians 4: 4 - 14

To be sure, Father, imagination can be far more troubling than reality. I invite you to take charge of my thought life and keep me focused on the peace that passes all understanding.

With any war of global involvement and especially with outbreaks of war in the Middle East, those who study Biblical prophecy are compelled to explore the fascinating subject of end times. Make no question about it, the events that transpire in the Middle Eastern world are very significant in the Scripture's announcements of how history will progress in its conclusion. Anyone who overlooks, or rejects, the Bible's role in preparing us for our Lord's return and our world's end is assigning himself an unpreparedness of serious consequences. I question, however, that all Middle East conflict is a prelude to Armageddon. The geography is close enough and the makeup of involving nations is certainly possible. To read other passages though, makes one realize there are still other developments involved in the consummation of human history. We are reminded of some very important instructions which the Bible gives us. "Of the day and hour when Christ shall appear, no one knows, not even the angels." (Matthew 24:36) Remember, the Lord did not call upon us to be accurate in our predictions, but to be ready for the unpredictable.

Read: II Peter 3: 3 - 6

More than when it is to be, Lord, the exciting truth is the assurance you are coming again! Help me to live every day as if it is the day of your return. I want to be ready!

The Tip

A preoccupied Christian went into a restaurant to order a meal. The waitress was curt when she said, "Take our order?" The man absent-mindedly answered, "Yes ma'am." The waitress was irritated and asked, "You want the special?' ... "Yes ma'am."... "You want coffee?"..."Yes ma'am." The waitress sarcastically reacted, "Is yes ma'am all you can say?" "Yes ma'am", was the customer's answer. The waitress stamped away. At that, the Christian customer realized how difficult he probably had been to serve. Upon leaving the restaurant, he sacrificially left a large tip. Seeing the tip, the waitress apologized for her behavior and explained some of her problems, opening the opportunity for the customer to tell her about Jesus. I am not suggesting that you leave a large tip for every curt waitress you meet, but I am saying a kind word is the best response. Why not let every word from your mouth have the potential for still another and deeper conversation later.

Read: Colossians 4: 1 - 6

What an instrument you have given me in my tongue, Lord. It is in my power to degrade or encourage; to comfort or to disrupt; to worship you or to keep your praise to myself. My prayer is that you will take control of my tongue.

She stood behind a gate to the fenced-in playground and peered through the wire. Those upturned eyes of hers just disarmed me. She was one of those precious children entrusted to the Children's Daycare Center. As I greeted this little charmer, she responded by means of a quiet announcement: "We are cowboys in here." I chuckled and replied, "Oh, you are?" As I walked on I was thinking, "It is hard to be a cowboy on a Day Care Playground where there are no horses, no corral... not even a bunkhouse." Then I corrected myself; "To the contrary, it is not too difficult to be a cowboy in such surroundings... if you are only pretending." By that time the sermon-urge had just about overtaken me and I began preaching to myself. To be a bona fide cowboy, one has to at least get out of the ranch house and try to rope a steer or saddle a horse. By the same token, the true test of what we Christians are is not put to us in surroundings we carefully choose, but in those which are realistic and demanding. Little girls can pretend. It's fun. Christians can't afford to pretend. It's deceiving.

Read: Mark 12: 38 - 44

Lord, the best evidence of my relationship to you is not in the Sunday morning church world. Rather, the best tests of my Christianity are in the Monday through Saturday world which is anything but friendly. Strengthen me for the realities of that world.

The Unexplored Bible

❧

An elderly man, living in New Jersey, discovered several thousand dollars in a family Bible. The money had been systematically scattered throughout the pages of the Bible. At the turn of the century his Christian aunt had died and left him the Bible, as part of her will. The nephew had been reduced to near poverty and spent much of his life living on a very small pension. His misery could have been easily relieved had he only been aware of the treasure tucked away in the inherited Bible which he never read…not even once. Very late in his life, the man did open the bible to read and made the discovery of his fortune. But it was too late to be the good it could have been. An even greater and eternal treasure awaits anyone's discovery when reading and studying God's Word. Let the pages of your Bible be like God's deposit slips invested in you with great dividends to be claimed.

Read: Psalm 19

Dear God, I am so grateful that it is your nature to want us to know you. You have revealed yourself in nature and supremely you have unveiled yourself in Christ Jesus. The Bible is like your voice in black and white. Right now I renew my readiness to read my way in to a closer relationship to you.

God's Specialty

❦

"God specializes in things that seem impossible. He knows a thousand ways to make a way for you." Those are some of the words in a chorus which enjoyed popularity several years ago. When analyzing the entire song, you can discover some weak theology here and there, but the words, "God specializes in things which seem impossible", are as accurate as the Bible itself. This is part of the impact which belongs to a Christian's stewardship testimony. In the view of most people, no one can afford, except a few well-to-do folks, to give away ten…fifteen…. twenty per cent of their income. Such an idea falls into the realm of the impractical and "impossible". Oh to be sure, most "respectable" people feel an occasional contribution to charity is virtuous, but it need not be overly generous. However, to pledge one's self to a systematic, even sacrificial plan of giving is seen as impossible in the face of life's many other obligations. Such reasoning, though, does not allow for the multiplying work of God, who is the owner of all things anyway. So how is it done? God's people are faithful and God specializes in the impossible.

Read: Luke 18: 18 - 27

Father, I am so inclined to think of reasons I cannot do something that I simply don't undertake them. Please prompt my memory that your Word says, "Greater is He who is in you than he who is in the world."

The Open Door

A young woman, living in Scotland, had strayed badly from the godly example and teaching of her parents. She had left home and was leading a riotous life in Edinburgh. Eventually, she grew weary of her depraved life and decided to commit Suicide. Before she did so, however, she decided to secretly visit the home of her childhood one more time. Under cover of night, she slipped homeward. When she arrived at the old house, she was startled to find the front door open. Fearing something tragic had occurred, she rushed inside, only to awaken her widowed mother. The mother embraced her daughter and explained she left the door open every night since the girl left home. She said, "I prayed you would return and I wanted you to find an open door when you did." That story of a mother's compassion is hardly surpassed except by the one usually captioned, "The Parable of the Good Shepherd". Jesus describes Himself as the Shepherd who is the Door of the sheepfold: "If anyone enters through me, he will be saved." (John 10:7)

Read: John 10: 7 - 18

Lord Jesus, as the Door to life eternal and life abundant, you are my entry to God, my earthly protection and my eternal security. Thank you for inviting me to step through that door.

Jesus' descriptive statement to those who follow Him, "Ye are the salt of the earth", is replete with varying applications. Perhaps we are most conscious, if glibly, of the interpretation which depicts the Christian as a personal soul-winner offering the "seasoning" of Christ to otherwise spiritually "savorless" lives. There are still other dimensions to this saltiness principle, however. In an earthly society, what if anything makes us as Christians, distinctive? I suppose the matter simply reduces itself to the basic inquiry, what accent in our living wins the comment, "They are different"? Of what significance is our professed faith if we only contribute to the blandness of living? If our attitude is one perpetually sour, negative, critical and argumentative, how are we different from those unseasoned by salvation? The early Church shook the world, but how? While the world was flavored by spite and hatred of the early Christians, it was said, "See how they love one another." While aimless living sought to entertain itself by the massacre of human flesh, the Christians sang enroute to the arena. They were different... are we?

Read: Matthew 5: 13 – 20

Left to myself, Lord, I will settle for being too much like the world which surrounds me. It doesn't make sense to be a Christian and to think and act like an unbeliever. So I seek the wisdom and courage to be different for Jesus' sake.

The Beautiful Christian

❧

I once heard about a newspaper story, which bore the headline: "The Beautiful American". We have heard so much about the "ugly" American traveling in other countries and I wanted to know more. The news story was about a man named Downey who as a U.S. soldier had seen the need for an orphanage and hospital in Africa. Following his discharge from the service, after he had met with much success in business, Mr. Downey sparked the drive that led to the eventual erection of the needed orphanage and hospital. For this labor, the Governor General in that foreign country labeled Mr. Downey, "The Beautiful American". There is still a higher honor, though, and that would be for one to be known as "The Beautiful Christian". Do you see a need that you can meet today? Do it to the glory of God and let the world meet a "Beautiful Christian".

Read: I Peter 3: 1 - 12

Heavenly Father, you are altogether lovely but I can blight that beauty with my ugly behavior. Forgive me for the times I have been a distraction and help me allow the likeness of Jesus to be seen in me.

The study of languages can be a considerable task without the benefit of much real interest and fascination. On the other hand, a knowledge of word-meanings, or syntax, or grammar, can provide us some meaningful insights. Take for example, the Biblical passage known to us as the Great Commission: "Go ye therefore and teach all nations baptizing them..." The verse, as a whole, forms a command, but the first word is not a command, it is an assumption. The word "Go", if literally translated from its original text, appears "As you go..." You see, our Lord simply assumed we would be going, busily engaged in the Lord's work, and based upon that assumption, He gave some instructions about what to do as we "go". In our case, is the Lord assuming more than we have considered? Is His confidence in us misplaced? Based upon Christ's presentation of how to witness to a world, it is quite impossible to reach people lest we go to them. It is not adequate to say, "We provide a church building and an attractive program, now let those who want God come to us." If they are going to come to Jesus, we must go to them.

Read: II Corinthians 5: 17 - 21

As I think it through, Lord, the enemy doesn't try to get Christians to renounce or deny our faith, he just wants us to keep quiet about it. Increase my courage so that I will be part of your plan, not his.

Giving Thanks

The night Jesus was betrayed, He shared a very important meal with His disciples. It was the Jewish Passover Feast. We Christians call that the occasion of the Last Supper for it was precisely that, His last such formal dinner with His disciples. It was during the Last Supper that He instituted what we call the Lord's Supper. He took bread and His cup on the table and said, "Let these two things symbolize my body and blood which will be sacrificed on the cross." Before they ate that symbolic meal though, the Bible says, "Jesus gave thanks." Think of that! In the face of His ensuing death, He gave thanks. But that is in keeping with what He has taught us to do. We have been blessed so much…that no experience of life prevents our thanksgiving to God! To be sure, we cannot always be thankful for every experience in life, but we can be thankful in every experience.

Read: Psalm 107: 1 - 22

Father, in my prayer life I am much to short on giving praise and thanksgiving and much too long on asking for favors. Forgive me for that imbalance and increase my vision for seeing reasons for praise.

Choosing Sides

❦

I like the classic story of a Christian deaf-mute. Each Sunday, morning and night, as well as each Wednesday evening, the silent Christian was seen leaving his home for the church building a block away. With Bible under his arm, he walked toward his church with a cadence of expectancy. Across the street from this faithful saint there lived a self-styled skeptic who took peculiar delight in making ridicule of Christians. One day he decided to "entertain" himself at the expense of his Christian neighbor. Taking a note pad, the skeptic wrote the following question, designed to harass the deaf-mute: "You cannot hear nor speak. Why do you waste your time going to church so much?" The unruffled Christian read the message and wrote his answer on the pad, just below the question: "So people like you will know whose side I'm on." I like that... It says volumes... It prompts probing. Do people know whose side we are on? There are so many life situations, which divulge whose side we are on. Our Lord said, "He that is not with me is against me; and he that gathereth not with me scattereth." (Luke 11:23) It is time to pick sides... It is always that time.

Read: Mark 8: 34 - 38

Thank you, Lord Jesus, for identifying with me on the cross. You took my place and paid the penalty for my sin. I want to be identified with you now. I choose to be known as someone on your side.

The Follow Through

Whether it's swinging a baseball bat, a golf club or throwing a football, the secret is in the follow through. Golfers spend hours learning how to follow through with their swing. Punters kick a football over and over until the follow through is second nature. And what is a "follow through"? Simply stated, it's to continue your motion until it's complete. In other words, don't stop short of complete action. The Bible tells us we're to follow through with God. Jesus said, "No person, having put his hand to the plow and looking back is fit for the kingdom of God." (Luke 9:62) Maybe it was years ago that you believed in Christ... you were baptized... and joined a church. Are you still following through with all that? Actually, it is who we are in the long term that makes for the stronger witness.

Read: Romans 5: 1 - 5

I can always count on you, Lord, you are forever the same. It is that quality I would like to see in my life. Help me realize the experiences you send my way and ingredients for my maturity.

A Key To Prayer

❧

Victorious Christian living has never been experienced apart from an effective prayer life. No believer having laid possession of the secret to fervent prayer is often defeated by any siege of testing. Although unfounded ridicule has referred to prayer as psychological escape, the person who has lingered at the Throne of Grace would testify to far greater experiences than that. Readily though, it must be said that a hurried bit of petitioning mumbled in a weary moment while perched on a bed-side will seldom produce memories of Divine encounter. Such explains the lack of excitement on the part of too many professing "prayer-lifers" when the subject of prayer results enters the conversation. Prayer is not the repetitious bombarding of God's heavenly hideaway, it is the aligning of our will to His so that the blessing of His response may be consistent with His character and attributes. If there is any single key to prayer which has blessed my own life, it is the discovery that we ought not to attach our desires so much to the petitions we make, rather we should attach our affection to God through the petitions we make.

Read: John 16: 23 - 28

Dear God, analyzing prayer is not the best way to learn prayer. I know that prayer is its own best instructor. So my prayer today is that you would convict me of the need to spend more time with you day by day.

The Championship

The athletic teams who finally arrive at the top do not get there by last minute excellence. They work and win throughout the season of their sport. I well remember what our youngest son said when he was just seven and his sandlot football team lost the first game of the season. He said, "I don't care if we lose all our games so long as we win the championship." Needless to say, that would be hard to come by. But all too many people have that outlook on life and eternity. They hope that maybe somehow at the end of life, God will award them the championship of heaven. But God wants us to taste of spiritual victory now. With Christ in your life today you can enjoy daily victory now and heaven later. In fact, there is a passage in the Bible which is too often equated with the blessings of heaven, when in fact, it has to do with the victories for the here and now.......

Read: I Corinthians 2: 6 - 13

Lord, I have settled for many mediocre days in my Christian life. I need the reminder you did not save us for heaven alone, you saved us for the here and now. I want to claim some of those victories awaiting me today.

The responsibilities of Christian citizenship are not fulfilled when we cast our ballots and walk away from the voting precinct. Nor have we satisfied our citizenship accountability when we voice a conversational opinion about a political issue, or write a letter to the editor. Some Christians privately contribute to election campaigns, attend party conventions, and subscribe heartily to advancing the cause of their political posture. Such individual enthusiasm and involvement are commendable when balanced with a similar zeal for leading unsaved people to the greatest decision of life… the choice of a Savior. There is however, an assignment for Christian citizens, which exceeds others: we are to be found faithful in praying for the spiritual and moral well being of the nation. It is with that in mind that I offer "A Patriot's Prayer List". **Pray** that God's people will get a burden for the nation we love. **Pray** that God's people will learn to pray between national crises, not just when we confront them. **Pray** that God's people will keep patience and refuse to despair. **Pray** for public officials and especially pray for their salvation. **Pray** for the courage of Christians in public life to risk moral leadership. **Pray** for Divine intervention in changing outcomes beyond our control. Be faithful, fellow Christians, in the prayer closet as well as the voting booth.

Read: Daniel 9: 1 – 19

Heavenly Father, I love my country. There is so much about her legacy to honor. Yet there are enemies of this nation who intend to cause her collapse. I pray that you would protect us from such enemies, not because we deserve it, but because we need it!

Like many of you, I have vivid memories of a wedding day! It was a hot August evening in southeast Florida. A thunderstorm had struck late in the afternoon and by evening the air was cooler and more pleasant. Nervous as I was, I recall the beauty of the service... there was candlelight.... a large crowd of relatives and friends...and there was never a bride more lovely. It is no mere accident, nor is it insignificant, that the Bible describes the relationship between a Christian and Christ as that of the bride and the Bridegroom. Just as a couple being married give their lives to one another, so Christ has given His life for us and to us.... and we are to give our lives to Him and for Him. Having accepted God's love, and having made Jesus your personal Savior, the bible describes you as the Bride of Christ. From that illustration we are instructed about our own marriages. As the Bridegroom, Jesus laid down His life for the Bride, so should a husband be willing to die for his wife. And the wife, being so deeply loved, will truly defer to the husband.

Read: Ephesians 5: 22 - 33

It is beyond comprehension, Lord Jesus, but I accept your love and sacrifice for me. I defer to your leadership and will. It is a joy to take the name of the Bridegroom and to be known as a Christian.

❧

"Church is for little people"…so said one of the youngsters attending Vacation Bible School. The Bible schooler went on to say, "Church is not for big people. My Daddy says so. When I get big I'm not going to church either." Tragic, is it not, for a grown man to misinform his own child, giving him such a twisted concept of manhood? But the situation is another reminder that it is difficult for any spiritual influences to rise above those of the home. With that in mind, let me call your attention to a penetrating passage of Scripture, one which has often returned to mind since I read it in The Living Bible paraphrase: "About that time the disciples came to Jesus to ask which of them would be greatest in the Kingdom of Heaven. Jesus called a small child over to him and set the little fellow down among them and said, 'Unless you turn to God from your sins and become as little children, you will never get into the Kingdom of Heaven. Therefore anyone who humbles himself as this little child is the greatest in the Kingdom of Heaven. And any of you who welcome a little child like this because you are mine is welcoming me and caring for me. But if any of you cause one of these little ones who trusts in me to lose his faith, it would be better for you to have a rock tied to your neck and be thrown into the sea.'" (Matthew 18: 1 – 6, The Living Bible)

Read: Proverbs 6: 20 - 23

Dear God, it is good to remember that you intended for children to get their first and lasting impressions from the adults in their family life. Don't' let me forget what an honor it is to represent you to young, impressionable lives.

More Than A Sports Fan

Being a sports fan, I have often pondered the "hype", the mania, the wild enthusiasm captured by the world of championship sports. I have heard some, with disdain; compare this uninhibited excitement to the lack of it among "Church people". Upon closer scrutiny, I have come to realize a stadium-like excitement may be an inadequate and inappropriate reaction to matters of eternal importance. It's true! A touchdown, a winning basket, a home run, a service-ace, a 10-under-par tournament... all warrant a passing excitement. But, that's the point. The excitement is passing. True followers of Jesus develop a commitment that runs as deep as a sports fan's mania runs high. A personal relationship with Jesus Christ brings an enduring enthusiasm...a lasting investment...an abiding peace. To say that a game, a team, a win, is "life" is to make diversion a living. The apostle Paul puts a healthy perspective into words, "For me to live is Christ." (Philippians 1:21)

Read: Psalm 39: 4 - 8

Dear Lord, there are numerous things in life which excite me, sporting events being one of them. I realize that is not bad in itself, but when it exceeds my excitement over you and my relationship to you, it has to go. If I am to be a fanatic, I want it to be about you.

More Than Capability

God has provided human beings the capacity to think, to reason, to choose, hence, many assert that man is left to his God-given devices. One dare not deny that such reasoning contains the seed of truth, but no seed is ever the whole growth. God is ever revealing Himself to us, in order for us to know His desires for us and furthermore, know the attitude in which he would have us pursue those desires. God wants men to employ their own reason, logic and energy and personality, but not until those capacities are shaped by the hands of Christ-direction. Until then, we cannot trust the best of our logic or the fervor of our enthusiasm.

Read: Ephesians 6: 10 - 20

Father, whatever talents or abilities you have given me are not all that I need. In fact, there are times when I don't need your help, I need you. Give me the wisdom to know what I can do and what only you can do.

A New Religion

A skeptic once approached the famous Talleyrand and said boastfully, "I am going to found a new religion here and it will be greater than Christianity." Talleyrand said, "If you do, then there are two things you will certainly have to accomplish." The skeptic replied, "And what are they?" The statesman said, "You will have to be crucified and rise again from the dead." The boasting skeptic was silenced by that observation because he realized that no man could accomplish such things, only God could do that. Men can dream up moral codes, ethical teachings and even devise objects of worship but only the Son of God could be Virgin born, die for mankind, conquer the grave and live forever to love this earth until there is no earth to love.

The lyrics of a song put it well, "Give me that old time religion... It's good enough for me." To replace just one word would make the song more accurate, "Give me that all time religion... It's good enough for me."

Read: Galatians 6: 1 - 11

Over and over, Lord, I discover that the Gospel is Jesus Himself. The Bible articulates the Gospel in many ways but the centerpiece is Jesus. Help me to make Jesus the changeless centerpiece of my life.

❧

This may come as a rude awakening to some, but Jesus is Lord... whether one acknowledges it or not! God's Word is plain: "At the name of Jesus every knee should bow...and every tongue confess that Jesus is Lord, to the glory of God the Father." (Philippians 2:10) So whether He is your personal Lord and Savior or not, the day will come when every knee will bow to acknowledge Him as Lord. There is still more about His Lordship: "Christ Jesus, Who being in very nature, God, did not consider equality with God something to be grasped, but made Himself nothing, taking the very nature of a servant, being made in human likeness... He humbled Himself and became obedient to death – even death on a cross!" (Philippians 2: 5 – 8) The conclusion to all this is also part of the same passage: "For this reason also, God has highly exalted him and given Him a name which is above every name." (Philippians 2: 9) If indeed, God has exalted Him, how can we do less?

Read: Acts 2: 29 - 36

When I read in the Bible the ways God is exalted and Jesus is honored, I realize how deficient is my worship. Amid this moment of prayer, I want to give you my undivided attention and my whole hearted praise.

Child Of The King

A Christian grocery shopper discovered an excited checker at the cash register as she rolled her grocery cart up to the checker's stand. "Wouldn't you like to touch me?" said the excited checker. "I just shook hands with a movie star! He passed through my lane just a few minutes ago. Wouldn't you like to touch my hand?" The shopper saw her opportunity to be a Christian witness and replied, "No thank you, but would you like to touch me?" The checker asked, "Who did you shake hands with?" The Christian answered, "No one. But you see, I am a child of the King." She went on to explain that Christ is the King and every Christian is a child of the King. All too seldom do we think of what position we have as Believers in Christ. We are children of the King of Kings and Lord of Lords. Such a realization is not designed to make us proud and exclusive. Rather it gives us a humble spirit and a quiet authority.

Read: Romans 8: 12 - 17

Praise God! I thank you, Father, that you have chosen to make me a joint heir with your Son, Jesus. There are times I live my life and approach matters as if I were a homeless pauper. Not with arrogance but with your authority I will claim your victory and resist the Tempter.

Peace In This World

❧

One actor's idea to "get away from this present world" is on a Tahitian island called Tetiaron. There, some 4,000 miles out into the South Pacific, the actor had a "primitive" hotel constructed where thirty to forty people, at a time, can "get way from it all" for $50 to $75 a day. He explained that these modest accommodations on his private atoll helped to make it a place of primitive beauty to which select persons can fly in his private plane and escape the "tribulations of this world". Our Lord has an altogether different plan… He said, "In me you may have peace." And the peace He offers requires absolutely no attempt to get away from his present world. To the contrary, His plan for peace is available while we are very much in this present world. "These things I have spoken unto you, that in me ye might have peace. In the world ye shall have tribulation, but be of good cheer…" (John 16:33) And how can our Lord offer the encouragement…"Be of good cheer?" His answer follows, "I have overcome the world." (John 16:34)

Read: Psalm 19

Sometimes, Father, I take my cues from the world and I create my own fears. It's so unnecessary to one to do that. You are my endless peace and I claim it for this very day.

Way To Go

The word "way" has some interesting applications. For instance, if I said, "There is only one way to go", what would I mean? Would I mean there is only one route to take or would I mean there is only one kind of transportation…or, still again, would I mean there is only one style worth considering? I could mean any one or all of those things. The Bible records something Jesus once said, "I am the way, the truth, the life, no man comes to the father but by me." (John 14:6) Indeed, Jesus is the only route to heaven that God has provided. Furthermore, Jesus is the one whose life is the source of life and His kind of life is the only life style really worth living. Jesus is the way to God. He is also the only way we can point out to others for their eternal and abundant life. Any other way is to mislead and misguide.

Read: Matthew 7: 13 - 21

Some may call it too narrow, even intolerant, to believe that Jesus is the only way to God. I believe your Word, Lord, so I can only believe what it says. Double my courage to not only believe it, but to share it.

Disciples In Training

Walkers and joggers are everywhere these days. The early mornings in your neighborhood and mine would seem strange without the sounds of the huffing and puffing of joggers on our streets. And what would downtown be like now without the sight of all those office workers, wearing sneakers, walking instead of lunching, or walking off the results of lunching? But then there are walkers, and there are walkers. There are joggers and then there are joggers. The difference is in dedication. It is with such mental pictures that I better appreciate what the Apostle Paul was talking about when he wrote these lines to the Christians living in the city of old Corinth: "I therefore so run, not as uncertainty; so fight I not as one that beateth the air: But I keep under my body and bring it into subjection; lest that by any means, when I have preached to others, I myself should be a castaway." (I Corinthians. 9: 26 – 27) In the simplest of terms, Paul was saying something like this: "When all is said and done, I don't want it said of me, 'He did little more than talk a good game'..."

Read: I timothy 4: 6- 10

Father God, I don't want it to be said of me that I am into doing what I must to have a healthy body while neglecting the condition of my spirit. Be my trainer making demands of me, and I will be the spiritual specimen I want to be.

Treadmills

I once heard someone ask a friend, "How are you today?" The friend's answer was classic. He said "I a somewhere between miserable and disgusting." Do you ever feel that bad? Maybe, this very minute you feel life is stuck somewhere between miserable and disgusting. If you are, I have some good news for you. God is in the business of getting life unstuck from its emptiness and treadmills. God sent Jesus to this world, according to the Bible, so that we could "have life and have it more abundantly." With Christ in your life, you have a relationship to God that is like one between a child and a father. You have forgiveness for every evil in your life. You are free of phony goodness and reality is yours to claim. Then when asked "How are you?" you can honestly say, "I'm somewhere between God's mercy and God's goodness."

Read: Psalm 119: 153 – 160

Not every day is the happiest of days, Lord, but you are in the midst of every day I live. Keep your promises before me and give me a vision to see beyond the hard times.

A Disciplined Life

Discipline is hardest to come by when self-imposed. Not too long ago, there was a report on the physical well being of the nation's young people, which has helped to motivate the growing excitement over fitness and exercise in America. The report indicated that 40% of boys, 6 to 15 years of age, could not touch their toes without bending their knees. In the same age bracket, 40% could not manage more than one pull-up, and 25% could not do any. Fifty percent of the girls, 6 to 15 years of age, could not run a ten-minute mile, nor could thirty percent of the boys. When the measurements of a disciplined life move from the athletic to the Christian realm, the results are no less graphic. Christians ought to seek to be as healthy, agile and physically alert as possible. Walking, jogging, exercising Christians are good exhibits of the Spirit's temple. But an unread Bible, a prayerless day, a hidden verbal witness, a sporadic church attendance, a negative disposition, untithed income and an uncontrolled tongue yields the worst statistics and the most blatant evidence of an undisciplined Faith.

Read: I Timothy 4: 6 – 10

Dear God, forgive me for not doing the things I know I should do. You have given us all we need to grow and to be healthy Believers. My problem is that I don't follow the regimen. I want to correct that right now.

❦

In an attempt to curtail the skyjacking of commercial planes, there was a proposal some years ago by the Cuban government to seize all hijackers and to put them into a 4 ft. by 4 ft. box to live the rest of their lives! Think of that! To be sure, the threat of such a fate might help to dissuade hijackers. But the thought which I would prompt today is one taken from the prospect of life in a 4 ft. by 4 ft. box. One living in such confines could not stand up, nor could he ever stretch out to sleep. But...you know...many people lead a terribly confined sort of life outside of any 4 by 4 box. God's people can live in a far bigger world than most have allowed themselves to claim. Have you ever stopped to think what joys, what fulfillment, fellowship, purpose... are missing in your life when Jesus Christ is not there? Invite Christ into your life today and really start living. No less tragic is it for a Christian to have fullness and liberty in Christ but to choose to live in the confines of self centeredness, fear and distress. That is to rob yourself of what is rightfully yours.

Read: Ephesians 1: 15 - 23

It is increasingly obvious to me, Lord, that Satan is not attempting to make unbelievers of us, just to have us ignore God as if he had nothing to offer us. I resist the Devil and turn to you to be all in all.

The centerpiece of the Christian Faith is indeed, Christ himself. It is not the Church or the Christian ethic, or missions or charity... or prayer. Take Christ out of the Gospel and there is no Gospel. To be sure, the Word of God, the divinely inspired Bible, is our authentic and authoritative record of Christ. Without the infallible Voice of God in print, we would have no reliable account of who Jesus is and what He accomplished. Hence, the Bible must be trustworthy; else what we know of Christ cannot be validated. Make no question of it; the Bible is the foremost tangible tool of our faith. The centerpiece of our Faith, however, is Jesus Christ Himself... the Son of God.... God in human flesh.... virgin born.... sinless, though tempted as we.... crucified.... gloriously raised form the dead.... and literally coming again to this present world. But, of all the events of Jesus' life and ministry, which one is the most crucial to the Gospel? There can be little question; it is the Resurrection of Christ! That Jesus died could mean little more than He was an example or a martyr or an exhibit of unbelievable love. But that Jesus rose from the grave means He conquered sin, death, the grave, and every other consequence of evil has been ultimately overcome. What a centerpiece!

Read: I Corinthians 15: 1 - 11

Thank you, God, that you have made very clear the way of salvation through Jesus. He is indeed my hope, my assurance and my security. What a centerpiece!

Ten Strings

❧

An older Christian once prayed in a mid-week prayer meeting, "Oh Lord, we will praise you. We will praise you with an instrument of ten strings." The people in attendance were bewildered about what he meant until he continued his prayer. "We will praise you with our <u>two</u> eyes by looking unto you. We will praise you with our <u>two</u> ears by listening to your leadership. We will praise you with our <u>two</u> feet by walking according to your instruction. We will praise you with our <u>two</u> hands by working to glorify you in the world. We will praise you with our <u>one</u> tongue by clean speech. And we will praise you with our <u>one</u> heart by loving you with all of it. Keep all ten strings in harmony and in pitch...In Christ's Name, Amen." So remind me there is no orchestration of praise until, or unless, all the instruments are put to use.

Read: Luke 10: 25 – 28, Revelation 5: 1 - 14

Lord Jesus, too many times I have been less than wholehearted in my worship. It is so easy to get used to the patterns of worship that I can be less than focused on you. Forgive me for that and tune all of my strings for "hands on" praise!

❧

Some years ago, while on an international flight from Tel Aviv to Frankfort, I saw a man, sitting across the aisle, reading what I thought was a Bible. Momentarily, I engaged the man in a conversation, and asked, "Is that a Bible you are reading?" He answered, "You might say that." Bewildered by his answer, I asked, "Are you a Christian?" He replied, "Let's say I am a Believer." In short order, I found myself involved in a long exchange with an ardent devotee of the Bahai faith. Having invested about a half hour of polite attention, I then shared with my conversational partner the message of salvation as the Bible presents it. When I asked if he could accept Christ as his Savior he courteously declined. When our plane landed in Frankfort, I had three hours to wait before my flight connection. It seemed everywhere I went the Bahai disciple was following me. Frankly, his confrontations became irritating, but then it struck me, though his style was overbearing and counter-productive, his zeal could not be questioned. By no means should we take a chapter from this cultist's book on the art of witnessing, but we would do well to recognize how vital it is that our world know how serious we are about attempting to reach our world for Jesus Christ. The cultists cannot "out-truth" us, but no one should "out-zeal" us!

Read: Acts 18: 24 – 28

Lord, I must acknowledge that my zeal as a personal soul-winner is often very lacking. There are people who are stronger in spreading their heresy than I am in sharing the truth. Forgive me, Lord, and recharge my zeal.

More Than A Job

I am told that Noah Webster labored 36 year writing his dictionary. And John Milton rose at four every morning in order to have enough hours in his day to compose and rewrite his poetry. _Gibbon spent 26 years writing the classic book, The Decline and Fall of the Roman Empire. Bryant rewrote some of his poetic masterpieces 100 times before he released them for publication. I guess the lesson we learn from great people is clear. If you want to leave footprints in the sands of time be sure and wear "work shoes"! Or to understand that truth as the Bible states is, one would turn to Ecclesiastes 2:24, "There is nothing better for a man that he should make his soul enjoy.... his labor." Think about that when your workday starts dragging this afternoon, or when your next weekend is about to give way to that some-old, same-old job you have. There's more to the work you do than you may realize.

Read: Ecclesiastes 2: 24 - 26

Take from me, Oh Lord, the idea that the Christian life is always to be filled with pleasure, excitement and accomplishment. Give me a heart for the thing you desire most from me, obedience.

Stronger Than Gravity

The earth spins around…. at the breakneck speed of about a thousand miles an hour. How then does anything remain on its surface? It would seem, at that speed, everything would be thrown off the earth's surface out into endless space. That is precisely what would happen were it not for a magnetic phenomenon called the Law of Gravity. We move about on our planet, walking, driving, and flying with every anticipation that we will always be held to our earthly domain. To attribute the wonder of earthly magnetism only to the Law of Gravity though, is to overlook the real reason for its existence. Take the time to read this simple, but profound statement of scriptural fact: "He is before all things and by him all things hold together". (Colossians 1: 17) In the simplest of terms, terrestrial cohesion and cosmic order are not accidents to which we have given names, but they are results of a Divine omnipresence to whom all things ultimately give account. How can we face, endure and overcome life's unraveling experiences lest we hold on to Him who brings it back together? If Christ is the Cohesion of the universe, wouldn't it be sad for His people not to allow Him to be their Cohesion as well?

Read: Colossians 1: 13 – 20

Be my cohesion, Lord, for left to myself, I would live with frustration and erratic peace, knowing there is more to being a Christian than I have allowed.

The Fly

An ungodly man who loved music decided to attend one of John Wesley's revival meetings. He determined that He would listen to the music and when Wesley began to preach, he would cover his ears. But God has a way of getting to people. As Wesley began preaching, the man covered his ears as he had planned. Momentarily, a fly circled about his head and landed on his face. He uncovered one of his ears to brush away the fly with his hand. As he took his hand away from his ear, he heard Wesley reading the Scripture verse, "He who has ears to hear, let him hear ..." (Luke 8:8) Startled, the man listened and was later converted. There are other things which God wants us to hear, but obstructions need to be moved for it to happen. When we are captive to unrepented sin, we cannot hear the Lord clearly. When we are preoccupied wit anger or engaged in gossip, we do not have an ear for the Lord. To be living a lie dulls our hearing of the truth. The Lord readily communicates to anyone who will listen with ears for God.

Read: Psalm 29

You have given me the capacity to be obedient, Lord. I have ears to hear, eyes to see and a will to apply. At this moment, I want to remove every sin and obstacle which hinders my capacity to obey you.

Advising the Thessalonian Christians, Paul wrote, ".... study to be quiet and to do your own business and to work with your own hands.... that ye walk honestly toward them that are without and that ye may have lack of nothing." (I Thessalonians 4: 11 – 12) Notice the accent upon the little possessive pronoun, "own"? Here is a distinct assumption that a Christian is going to engage in honest work. The Christian is endowed with abilities unique to him and it is simply assumed that he will utilize those abilities. In the course of daily life, then the Christian is able to have inward peace in that he commits to God's control those things with which he is unable to deal and he works honestly at that which God as equipped him to do. As a practical result of this principle in living, the Christian has his testimony among those outside of Christ and he has, at the same time, the needs of his own sustenance met. This is a strong Scriptural appeal for honest Christian work and at the same time, a stern disapproval of laziness, indolence and dependency. The fact of the matter is that this principle applies also in the life, sustenance and influence of a church. Each of us is to "do his own business" and "to work with his own hands". I know that we are unresponsive to clichés, oversimplifications and hyper familiarities, but the fact remains that the timeworn statement is true, "Each has his part".

Read: II Corinthians 9: 6 – 15

God, your Word is plain about how your mission is to be accomplished. The Church is your instrument to accomplish the work of Christ. And you have given us spiritual gifts to do that work. Help me find and do my part.

Always Thanks

There are many times… traditionally… we give thanks. But the Bible says, "We ought to always give thanks to God." (I Thessalonians 1:2)

In another passage we read, "In every thing give thanks." (I Thessalonians 5:18) And yet another verse puts it like this: "Always give thanks for all things…" (Ephesians 5:20) "How!" you say, "is that possible?"

The answer comes in this verse: "Thanks be to God who gives us the victory through our Lord Jesus Christ." (I Corinthians 15:57) You see, when Jesus is Savior and Lord of your life, He will see you through every circumstance.

Through Isaiah, God speaks to His people like this: "When you pass through the waters, I will be with you; and through the rivers, they will not overflow you; When you walk through the fire, you will not be scorched." (Isaiah 25:3)

Yes, the child of God can always be thankful. In fact, the spirit of thanks is one of the character traits of a twice born child of God.

Read: Psalm 136

Lord, I truly want to have the spirit of thanksgiving. It is a way to give clear witness to a healthy relationship to you. It makes for a happier life and it wins daily victories over the Enemy.

Old And Thankful

Several years ago, I visited with an attractive, refreshing Christian lady who was 90 years of age. Her mind was extremely alert but she had lost almost all of her eyesight. As she thought back upon her life and talked about it, she smiled broadly and said, "I am so grateful to God for my life. Even now, though I cannot see, I am not bitter. I just have too much to be thankful for." As I listened to this dear Christian woman, her outlook and confidence reminded me of something one of the Bible writers once wrote. It was King David who said in the 37th Psalm, "I have been young, and now I am old; yet have I not seen the righteous forsaken, nor his seed begging bread." (Psalm 37:25) Such remarks, by people who have lived a lot of years, are a real encouragement to trust the Lord throughout all of life. Take a long look at your own outlook on life. Are you "collecting gratitude" so you can be a reason for others to take heart?

Read: Psalm 71: 1 - 18

Thank you, God, for the abundant memories of your care and provision in my life. Forgive me for allowing Satan even a split second of self pity. Send someone my way today that I can encourage to your glory.

Specific Thanks

༜

It is Thanksgiving time but I cannot but wonder how many outward expressions of gratitude will actually transpire among those of us who stride through all the benefits of the holiday. Maybe we are like the little girl who was admonished by her other to thank a favorite uncle for a gift. The child's reply was revealing even by way of its innocence ... "Oh, I've thanked Uncle Frank... I just haven't told him yet." Being genuinely grateful within is the heartbeat of Thanksgiving but expressing gratitude without is the point of it all. Like prayer, thanksgiving, which is general, broad and not specific, is not nearly as effective and fulfilling as it is meant to be. Be **specific** when thanking God, loved ones and friends. Be **personal** and **individual** in your approach of expressing gratitude. Be **open** and **warm** even though embarrassment and timidity seek to detour your desires. Be **sincere**, thus to know you have been appreciative, not just complimentary. Be **gracious** when you are the recipient of somebody else's gratitude. After all, both the thankful and the thanked are to be blessed by thanksgiving. Be **determined** that Thanksgiving is going to be more than a landslide of football games and an overstuffed weekend.

Read: Psalm 107: 1 - 15

Father, long before we Americans made a holiday out of thanksgiving, you gave us the capacity for thanks and the command to exercise it. To be sure, I will enjoy the holiday, but I pray you will enlarge my fulfillment in being one of your grateful children.

❧

We have an antique clock in our home, but it has not operated properly in years. Actually, it does not run at all now. The hands on the clock never move. They are stuck with the long hand pointing to twelve and the short hand to three. So the clock does not keep time, yet two times every twenty-four hours, it is correct. At three every afternoon and at three every morning, the old clock is right. Too often we are like that antique clock. We think because we are right every now and then and when compared to someone else, we are basically good. What we need to do is to see ourselves, not by an occasional standard or by carefully selected times to pass judgment, but to see ourselves by the flawless example of God. Then we realize that we are not righteous at all, but need forgiveness and cleansing…. And Jesus Christ does that forgiving around the clock for those who confess and repent of sins, trusting the blood of Jesus to cleanse from all unrighteousness.

Read: Joel 2: 11 - 13

As I think about it, Lord, I guess I've come to you, seeking forgiveness, just about every hour of the day, and a lot of hours of the night, It reminds me of my sinful nature but, praise God, it also reminds me of your amazing grace!

It is said the ten most essential words in a marriage are these: "I love you." "Thanks." "I was wrong." "Please forgive me." There is little to argue with in that statement. I would only go a step further and say the same ten words are indispensable in practically all human relationships. We can isolate any one of those four statements and amaze ourselves about the potential mileage built into them. Take the word "thanks", for instance. Wrapped up in that simple, six-letter word can be other words like: grace, appreciation, recognition, praise, fulfillment, pleasure and encouragement. To say "thanks" then, can mean more than meets the eye. Of course to say thanks is one thing, to express thanks is another. Sales clerks say "Thank you" as a common courtesy. Little children are taught to say "Thank you" before they know the meaning of the words. Total strangers say "Thanks" when a door is politely held open. It is the expression of thanks which calls for more than an appropriate word. It is the expression of thanks, which calls for: memory, sensitivity, reciprocation, creativity, warmth and sincerity. I am thankful for words like "thanks". I am glad for special occasions like Thanksgiving Day. But I am praying to learn more about how to express my thanks to God and my thanks to people.

Read: Psalm 33

Teach me more, Dear God, about expressing thanks with more substance. When I offer praise and gratitude to you, guide my mind to specifics. And when I say thanks to others, help me do it with feeling.

Giving Directions

There are two very distinct ways to give directions to someone who is traveling through town. One way is to say something like, "You go to the third traffic light and turn left. Then you go two blocks and turn right. Then you follow that road for about a half mile I guess. Then you will see a new development off to your left. Watch then for a fork in the road and follow the road to the right. Look for a service station on our left, turn left, right after that and the road will lead you right where you are going". The other way to give directions is to say, "I am going out that way myself. Follow me". There is a lot of difference between telling a person the way and showing him the way. Jesus is the way to God, the only way. He doesn't just tell us how to live. Furthermore, He makes the journey with us. He doesn't say figure it out for yourself. He says, "Follow me." (Mark 2 – 14)

Read: Matthew 4: 18 – 25

It has occurred to me, Lord Jesus, that my desire alone to follow you is not adequate. Thank you for not just pointing us in some sort of godly direction, but for being that direction. It is a blessing to know that you make the journey with us.

Forget Not

I read recently about a radio program, which was on the air in the past, called, "Job Center of the Air". The program's host said he had, by means of the broadcast, helped thousands of people find employment. Then his voice struck a tone of disappointment. He said of those thousands, he recalled only 9 or 10 who had called or written to express appreciation for his help. I guess we could say, "That's no surprise. That sounds like human nature." But it is a sad commentary. As you think back upon yesterday, or last week, do you recall some kindness provided you? Have you thanked them? And what about the favors of God? Have you thanked Him? It is like the Bible says. "Bless the Lord, Oh my soul...and <u>forget not</u> all His benefits." (Psalm 103:2) Do you notice the specific instructions the Psalmist gives us about thanking the Lord? We are not to forget all His benefits. That makes for quite a list of thank yous. The admonition is not to keep a meticulous list but to see His blessings every where we turn. Always Thankful.

Read: Luke 17: 11 - 19

Father, like a child I so often take your gifts and blessings for granted. Your goodness just goes along with who you are. That's the point, Lord; it is who you are that matters most. And that's where my thanksgiving begins. Thank you for being who and all you are.

The Egg

A chicken is not an extremely intelligent creature. Such is evidenced by the hen that was found setting on a white porcelain doorknob that she had mistaken for an egg. The farmer who made the discovery decided he would watch to see how long this would go on. Day after day he would find the hen squatting on the doorknob hoping to hatch it! Feeling sorry for the hen, the farmer finally removed the doorknob so she would give herself to more profitable things. We laugh about that. But wait. People are almost as foolish trying to hatch life out of unpromising temptations and vain living. The Bible says, "What shall it profit a man if he gain the world and lose his own soul?" (Mark 8:36) Living in God's will and purpose keeps us from fooling ourselves about the dividends of sin.

Read: Psalm 119: 1 - 8

Increase my perception, Oh God, so that I can recognize the false promises of Satan. He has some temptations which look so reasonable and harmless. Help me realize one of the wages of sin is a waste of time.

The Mirror

There is a humorous story about a woman who was getting ready for church. She dashed into the front hallway of her home and gazed into the large mirror there. She said, "I look terrible in the mirror in the bedroom so I thought I'd try this one!" Mirrors seldom do more than reflect exactly what we place before them, regardless what room they are in. The Bible describes itself like a mirror. Listen to a few verses from the New Testament book of James: "But be ye doers of the word, and not hearers only, deceiving you own selves. For if any be a hearer of the word and not a doer, he is like unto a man beholding his natural face in a glass. For he beholdeth himself and goeth his way and straightway forgetteth what manner of man he was. But whoso looketh into the perfect law of liberty and continueth therein, he being not a forgetful hearer, but a doer of the work, this man shall be blessed in his deed. (James 1: 22 – 25)

Read: Psalm 15

Heavenly Father, you have taught me that hypocrisy is more than intentional misrepresentation or designed deceit. It is also the art of denying the truth. Help me to honestly receive your Word and do what it says.

It was our son's last day of his rotation in a juvenile psychiatric hospital. The next leg in his medical school journey was a stint in obstetrics. He was telling his patients good-bye and came upon one young man whose life had been greatly damaged by child abuse. "This is your last day here?' the young patient asked. "You go to deliver babies now?" he continued. A long pause ensued. "Don't hurt those babies. Don't squeeze them", was the young man's plea. Knowing this patient's history, the medical student understood the pain behind the plea. That's one of those moments when an understandable lump lodges in the throat of a fledgling doctor. Hurting people are everywhere. They are on the other side of the world and they are down the street. They sleep under bridges and they spend their nights in mansions. Hurts are everywhere. And who is to say who hurts more than another? One observation is hardly debatable; regardless who the hurting soul may be, what hurts most is that no one seems to care. That brings us precisely to the point of Christmas. That God cared is the message of Christmas. That he cared enough not just to send a message but also to send His Own Son is what Christmas is about.

Read: Ephesians 2: 4 - 10

Heavenly Father, unless we are careful we will settle for inadequate definitions of Christmas. True, Christmas is about giving, the virgin birth, celebrating God's love, but help me to understand what lies behind it all, we matter to God.

❧

I saw a sequence of railroad boxcars sometime ago. Just beneath the large loading doors on each boxcar I saw some print, which had been scribbled in chalk. The print conveyed this notation: "Clean, 3/27/08…" then there was a set of initials. That chalked-on report was the verification by a foreman or railroad worker that the boxcars had been duly cleaned on a certain date and had passed inspection. If you please, a similar message was written across my life some years ago. In effect the message was: "Clean, November 20, 1948, signed by Jesus Christ." That was the day I invited Christ into my life…. and He cleaned up my life, making it fit and acceptable to God. I could never have done it, but He did, so His signature is the only one duly authorized. The Bible says, "If we confess our sins, Christ is faithful and just to forgive our sins and to cleanse us from all unrighteousness." (I John 1:9)

Read: Hebrews 9: 11 - 14

Lord, I want your signature all over my life. I seek to know you and to follow you so there can be no doubt I belong to you. I want you to be the center of my will and purpose, so I seek your cleansing to that end.

"Infidel"…is a word, according to Webster, which describes "Unbelievers, disbelievers, those in contempt of holy writ…. those who refuse to believe in the inspiration of and origin of holy writing". According to the late Saddam Hussein, those of us who constitute the western world of Christian influence are the "infidels" in what he described as a holy war. But my purpose is not to feature how an Iraqi dictator described us. I am not too sure how responsible the man was anyway. My primary purpose in bringing up the accusation of our "infidelity" is to prompt a heart searching among us who call ourselves "Believers" and others, "unbelievers". The zeal of the Moslem world is increasingly apparent as we are witnessing the spread of its missionary efforts even in the United States. The prayer life of the Islamic people may be mechanical, rote and coercive, but Moslems pray and pray a lot. But we are the Believers. Those of us who know Jesus Christ personally are the "faithful". What zeal do we evidence as we seek to evangelize a world for the only true Savior of humankind? We call the one and only living God, Abba, "Father", but how much do we commune with Him in daily prayer? Do we Christians "out believe" those we call the "unbelievers"?

Read: Acts 16: 22 – 24

Dear Lord, I want to be a Believer in more ways than a name. It is an honor to be called a Believer in Christ, but I want the word to describe me and to define my commitment to you.

When I was a boy, I remember one of the popular soft drinks was a brand of orange soda called Nehi. One of my favorite things to do was to hold a bottle of Nehi beside my leg and say, "This drink isn't 'knee-high.' It is not even close!" Often a precise standard makes a claim for something woefully inadequate. The Ten Commandments in the Bible were not given to show us how well we measure up to God's perfection, but they were given to show us how unrighteous we are and how impossible it is for us to produce holiness. Like the Scriptures tell us, "The law of God was our school master to bring us to Christ that we might be justified by faith." (Galatians 3:20) We cannot measure up to be good enough to go to heaven but we can give ourselves to Christ and go to heaven by His goodness. Furthermore, just as we are saved by God's grace, we live like we are saved by His grace.

Read: Galatians 3: 23 - 29

There is no doubt in my mind, dear Lord; you are my Savior, my only Savior. Just as I could not accomplish my salvation by self effort, I know I cannot live the Christian life on my own. So I ask you to live out your righteousness in me.

There is an old Spanish proverb...."El pez por suboca muere" (The fish dies because of its mouth). Of course, the proverb addresses itself to the self-destruction, which results from compulsive gossip. And the proverb is as right as rain. Let me mention another type of gossip, which is not to be avoided, but rather, is to be sought. In fact, the result of failing to gossip in this instance can mean a tragic fate for someone else. Evangelism is a common word in the vocabulary of evangelical Christians. "Evangelism" is an English word which has its roots in a descriptive word in the Greek New Testament...."evangelize". A pure translation of that word is a bit difficult, but a close proximity would be, "to gossip the good news". That's truly a great way to describe personal witnessing, "to gossip the good news." As conversations about spiritual matters arise, don't forfeit your chance to put in a positive word about your Lord...your confidence in Him and His readiness to love us all, sinners though we be. Give new meaning to a word in need of a greatly improved reputation..."holy" gossip!

Read: Psalm 40: 1 - 10

Lord Jesus, you have told us that we are to be your witnesses in our Jerusalems, our Judeas and to our worlds. I want to do what you have commanded. Build in me the incentive to be a holy gossip!

It took awhile, but I finally had to admit that I needed reading glasses. I had prided myself in my excellent eyesight but there came the day when the print in the telephone book was, at best, a blur and my arms were just too short to help my eyes focus properly. So now I wear glasses and I am delighted to do so...After all, I like to see what I'm looking at. In the same way, we do not have eyes to see the truths of God until or unless we are given spiritual sight. Like the Bible says "Hear now this, Oh foolish people and without understanding; which have eyes and see not; which have ears and hear not". (Jeremiah 5:21) When a person invites Christ into his life to be Lord and Savior he is given spiritual vision. That is what the bible is talking about when it says "...But a natural man does not accept the things of the Spirit of God, for they are foolishness to him; and he cannot understand them, because they are spiritually apprised." (I Corinthians 2:14)

Read: I Corinthians 2: 1 - 13

It astounds me, Father, to know I have the Mind of Christ. So often I settle for my ideas and my opinions when I can do better. Right now I want to place my mind under the rule of your Mind and think like Jesus.

✤

Many years have passed since the shocking announcement came that our country was at war with the Empire of Japan because Pearl Harbor had been attacked on December 7, 1941. It was not until four long years had passed that the war ended and during those years we underwent all of the agonies that go with war. Since then our nation has been involved with still other wars. Men and nations at their best have despised war, written treaties to avoid war, yet have continued to make war. The Bible tells us there is but one way to insure peace among people and that is for God to settle the spiritual warfare inside them, which makes them restless, ruthless and destructive. When a man is at peace with God, he has a capacity for peace with people. Christ's presence in our lives should give the world just that much more of an idea of what real peace is like.

Read: Psalm 46

It would seem, Lord, that peace on the international scene is basically the absence of war. I'm grateful for any time there is the absence of war but I seek to know and share the lasting peace which comes only through the indwelling Christ.

The Family = Bible Version

❧

"Family values" have become a topic of keen interest in recent years. But family values are more than items to latch onto for political expedience; they are essential ingredients for our national survival! But I am not oblivious to the legitimate claim to family by those whose households are not of the so-called nuclear configuration. Some of the finest parenting I have seen has been done by divorced, single mothers. Circumstances have put children into the hands of grandparents to raise, and in those homes can be found many of the greatest virtues of family life. I can think of some situations where widowed or divorced fathers have provided wonderful homes for their children. There are those who ridicule traditional family values by giving them straw-man definitions and then, tearing them down. The issue of family values is not about how much our households resemble those of the western frontier of the 1920's or the postwar '50's. What is at stake is the defense and preservation of those qualities without which our nation's future is in unquestionable jeopardy! Old fashioned? Yes, even older than black and white television. As old as God's word, in black and white.

Read: Deuteronomy 6: 1 – 9

The family is your creation, Dear God, and yours to preserve. I thank you for the place of family in my life and I rejoice in knowing I am in the family of God. Indeed, I want to be a champion of the family as you define it.

DECEMBER 9 — *A New Nature*

Things are not always what then appear to be. Years ago, our then eight-year-old got ready for a sandlot football game he was to play on a Saturday morning. He was fully attired in soccer shoes, stirrup socks, shoulder pads, helmet, mouthpiece and all, but his mother and I were not quite ready to take him to the game field. So he had a few minutes to pass. He turned on the television set to watch cartoons. There he sat, geared and clad for gridiron warfare, watching "Bugs Bunny"! You see, football equipment notwithstanding, he was still an eight-year-old on the inside and naturally liked cartoons. The lesson is obvious. It is not what is on the outside which counts in life as much as what is our nature within. The Bible says we have a sinful nature until we let Christ put a new nature in us. With a new nature there is the capacity to think and live differently. Only when there is a new nature within can Christ likeness be a reality.

Read: Colossians 3: 1 - 11

Lord Jesus, I could never explain it, but when I asked you to be my Savior, you placed a new nature in me. I don't have to live by the impulses of my old nature any longer. Keep before me the potential I have for a newness of life.

No Substitute For Rain

❧

The illustration is not original with me for I've heard others use it, but it has special significance, seeing it has actually happened to me. During the dry spells of midsummer, we often resort to running sprinklers on our lawns to prevent a total parching of the grass. A few summers back, during just such a time, I set a sprinkler at one end of the front yard. Unbeknown to me, some clouds were gathering on the west side of the neighborhood, about to provide a clap or two of thunder and then a downpour. After a rumble of thunder, I felt the first drops of what quickly became welcome rain. For a few moments, before turning off the faucet, I stood at the door and "watched" a sermon illustration unfold. While refreshing mineral-laden rain fell from the skies, there the sprinkler was, doing the best it knew how, but there was no comparison as far as the results were concerned. God's program for refreshing and growing a Christian's life has no substitutes. Sunday churchgoing without daily prayer and Bible study is like turning on a sprinkler for an hour or two rather than being blessed by a daily rain. Why settle for only the presence of the Holy Spirit instead of His fullness? There's no reason to settle to be satisfied with a sprinkling of our souls when there's a 100% promise of a Divine rain!

Read: Isaiah 44: 1 5

Years ago, Father, I remember we sang, "Showers of blessing, showers of blessing we need, mercy drops round us are falling, but for the showers we plead." I pray for a refreshing down pouring of the Holy Spirit.

Loss For Words

When you try to talk to God, are you ever at a loss for words? I know I am. Sometimes we just don't know how to say what is on our minds or we are dumb-founded over a problem. There are times we are guilt ridden, ashamed and embarrassed before God. About all we can do is cry out. "Oh, God, help me!" But did you know the Bible tells us that God has made a way for those moments to be some of the most powerful ones we spend in prayer? Take the time to <u>underline</u> a verse in your Bible. It's found in Romans 8:26, "Likewise the Spirit also helps our infirmities, for we know not what we should pray for as we ought: but the Spirit Himself makes intercession for us with <u>groanings</u> which cannot be uttered." Think of that! We can pray even when we do not know what to say...if we would only entrust our "feelings" to God. He then translates our feelings into the language of prayer, calms our frustration and ministers to our groaning. In the final analysis, prayer is not a language of words but a language of the heart.

Read: Psalm 116: 1 - 19

Praise be to you, Father, for your listening ear. When I realize that just hearing our prayer is an act of your grace, I am overwhelmed with the realization you help us pray as well. Help me grow into the comfort zone of a conversational relationship with you.

Power With A Purpose

❧

Paul, the Apostle, said he wanted to know more about what he called "the power of the resurrection". (Philippians 3:10) In our day, we hear Christians talk about living in "resurrected power" or leading a "resurrected life". Unquestionably, there is available to us a share of "resurrection power" through the risen Christ who lives in us but the issue is, what is to be done with the "power of the resurrection"? Are we simply to accumulate this power so as to display our potential for all to envy? Of course not. To what then does "resurrection power" apply?

- Resurrection power gives us the authority to invade a world in the name of Jesus. (Romans 1:8)

- Resurrection power eliminates questions regarding the ability of the Gospel to transform any life. (Romans 1:16)

- Resurrection power gives impact to a ministry of impressions and influence upon nearby lives. (Acts 8:13)

- Resurrection power breeds a confidence which glorifies the God who gave it. (I Peter 4:11)

- Let us not only talk of Christ's power in the Resurrection, let us appropriate that power in our own life, seeing that we have been raised up with Him to newness of life!

Read: Ephesians 1: 15 – 23

Spirit of God, you dwell in me and I want you to live out all that you desire and do it in me and through me. I do not want to display your power, I want to serve your power.

A senior pilot for one of the major national airlines once said something to me I will never forget. I was on a cross-country charter flight when the captain left his cabin and the controls with the flight crew so he could visit with the passengers. While we talked, the captain spoke about some of the facets of landing a passenger jet. He commented about the needed length of a runway and about the importance of landing so as to have use of the entire runway available. Then he said, "You know, you cannot use what you fly by." I have recalled that statement often and thought how it illustrates a great spiritual truth. God has prepared a place in heaven for us and a way through Christ to get there. He has also prepared a life, earth side, for us to experience which defies description. But we will never have what we ignore or refuse to claim. In the language of the airline pilot, "Don't fly by what God has prepared for you!"

Read: Matthew 5: 25 - 33

You have made it clear, Father, just how I am to go about aligning my life with your blessing and provision. Seek first that which relates to your kingdom and righteous living and then, whatever follows is all that I need.

The Ultimate Best

It was early Monday morning... very early. I had a plane to catch in a short while. I could hear the rain pelting down outside and the wind gusting. It sounded good, for we had needed the rain. If course, at this time of year and in our part of the country, a winter rain can mean slippery streets, travelers advisories and cancelled flights. So I realized I might not be going anywhere after all. All of which reminds me of how subject our plans are to those things over which we have no control. That is a good reminder, for we easily and soon forget such things when life is relatively free of interruptions and obstructions. Then we can become terribly impressed with our goals, plans and mastery of life. Too quickly even we Christians can forget that God is Sovereign and the eventual shape of history is formed by His hands. This is no call for fatalism. Neither is it a license for laziness. The exercise of our will does enter into the picture of God's Sovereignty. We have a God-given mind to be used in planning, forethought and in demanding the most of ourselves to make the most out of life. While we lay our plans, however, let us keep submitted to the over-rule of God, for what he has in mind is always what is ultimately best.

Read: Psalm 139

Because you have the final word I want to be in step with you, Lord. You have given to me a mind of my own and the will to use it. That is the point, Lord, I want to be in your will so I can trust how I think.

Peaceable As Possible

❦

Some years ago, my study telephone rang and upon answering, I found a fellow pastor was calling. He began his conversation in a strange way. He asked, "Anybody mad with you today?" I answered, "Well…. not that I know of." I thought he might know something I didn't know. My preacher friend responded, "You are not serving the Lord unless someone is mad with you." Now I know that our Lord once said, "You shall be hated of all men for my name's sake", (Mark 13:13) but I hardly think He meant "all men" without exception. I am sure He meant "all men" without distinction. Unfortunately some Christians do not place as much value upon being pleasant and thoughtful as they should. To be sure, we will upset some people when we do things God's way. That is to be expected. But the Bible says we should live peaceably with all men…as much as lies in us, or…in so far as possible. (Romans 12:18)

Read: I Peter 4: 12 - 19

To be identified with you, Lord Jesus, is an honor. To experience rejection because of my Christian convictions is just part of the territory. But help me, Lord never to misrepresent you by suffering at the hands of my own poor judgment and misbehavior.

This Grace Also

Tunnel vision can be a problem in anyone's outlook. When we have our minds made up about a given mater we find it difficult to see anything other than what we expect to see. In fact that was essentially the problem with the ancient church in Corinth. Their minds were made up... they were a gifted fellowship... They were a church made up of spiritual excellence... They could not see that they were in need of improvement. For all their emphasis upon spiritual gifts however, they were woefully weak at the point of their attitude about giving. That explains such sentences as this one in Paul's letter to that congregation: "Therefore, as ye abound in every thing, in faith and utterance, and knowledge, and in all diligence, and in your love to us, see that ye abound in this grace also." (II Corinthians 8:7) Paul said, "... See that you abound in this grace also." What grace was that? It was the grace of giving. The apostle was attempting to break the stare of their "tunnel vision". They needed to see that being a good steward of one's material possessions is no less important than being a good steward of one's spiritual gifts.

Read: Matthew 6: 17 - 24

Dear God, thank you for showing me that ownership is the real issue when it comes to giving. You won everything. I get to manage what actually is yours. I truly want to handle what is yours with grace and gratitude.

Fresh Bread

I once saw a school bus parked outside a local bakery. As I drove by the bus, I could see little heads peeing above the windows. I knew then that a group of small children had made a tour of the bakery that day so they could see, firsthand, how bread was made. Doubtless each child was given a sample of fresh bread to eat and each child will have the lingering memory of the distinctive odor of bread in the making. There is nothing quite like the taste of freshly baked bread, is there? Jesus once said, "I am the living bread that came down out of heaven; if anyone eats of this bread he will live forever." (John 6:51) As far as the deeper hungers are concerned, there is nothing that will satisfy as will Christ in someone's life. He Himself is bread for the soul and spirit. Little wonder there are spiritual hunger pangs in any life until Christ enters that life. And with the Spirit of Christ within us we can feast on God's Word like it is fresh bread.

Read: Psalm 19: 7 - 14

I stand amazed, Lord, at the ways you have chosen to reveal yourself. You are to be found in nature. You are supremely revealed in Jesus. Then there is your written Word. Thank you for making yourself as available as you are in the Bible. Increase my appetite to devour its pages.

Is a servant ever greater than his Lord? Notice how Jesus sought the mountain when He prayed. Aside from the fact that He sought a solace in the mountains, there is symbolism therein. Mountain views transfigure our outlook. There we can distinguish between the apparently great and the truly great. There we see the relative size of things like we could not down below. If we spent more time on the mount of prayer, we could get a God's-eye view of things, have false outlooks corrected, and then we could serve Him more readily and zealously. We need to examine our "urge" to do something from time to time, making certain that it is not simply a "front" for our failure to pray. I am the first to recognize the plausibility of the statement "God gave us a mind of our own and we are supposed to use it", but too often such a remark is only the bluff for not really knowing, nor perhaps not caring what the Will of God is in the matter. Prayer is a glorious task, let us take it on.

Read: Psalm 42

What a privilege you have given me, Oh Lord. You have made it possible for me to actually enter into your presence in the name of Jesus. Why do I not pray more? Why is prayer such a weak aspect of my walk with you? Forgive my failures at prayer, Lord, and hear my intent to enlarge my prayer life more than ever.

Someone has said, "Worry is fear's extravagance. It is paying interest on trouble which may never come." A wise and seasoned woman admitted, "I have had a lot of trouble in my life, most of which never happened!" In other words, she had fretted over things she was afraid would come, only to find they never arrived. It was an unknown poet who wrote, "I heard a voice at evening say, 'Bear not thy yesterdays on tomorrow, nor load this week with last week's load of sorrow. Lift all thy burdens as they come, nor try to weigh the present with the by and by. One step and then another, take thy way...live day by day'!" Jesus said, "Take no thought for the morrow, for the morrow will take thought for the things of itself." (Matthew 7:34) Since our God is sovereign the future is in His hands. It's best that we leave it that way and work on what <u>is</u> in our hands.

Read: Psalm 111

God, one of the hardest things for me to do is to discern what you would have me to do as opposed to what you alone should undertake. I want to be found faithful doing what you expect of me and I do not want to be foolish undertaking what you alone can do.

Amplified Evangelism

A funny thing happened to me on the way to a baptismal service. In an attempt to experiment with the use of a new cordless microphone, the committee responsible rigged the apparatus about my neck and neatly hid it from view under my baptismal robe. All went well until the moment before I stepped into the baptistry, when the microphone slipped from my neck and began its slow, detached descent inside my chest high rubber boots, all the way to the inside arch of my right foot. There was no time for retrieving the microphone. It just had to stay in its peculiar place until the baptismal service was over. All the electronic experts doubtless would tell me I had nothing to fear and besides, what little jolt there might come from an electronic shock would be of little consequence. But you know the place for a microphone is not deep inside the foot of a hip high rubber boot. If a microphone is of any use it must be close enough to one's mouth to amplify what is being said. Like so, the place for a Christian's personal testimony is not deep within, so well hidden that it remains a secret to others. The Lord intended that we openly share our knowledge of Christ whenever the door of opportunity swings open to us.

Read: Matthew 5: 14 – 16

Embolden me, Lord, so that I will be heard from when it is time to witness. I know that salvation is personal but it is not private. Give me a holy mixture of courage and common sense as I speak up for you.

In the gospel of John we read, "In the beginning was the Word... And the Word was God... The Word became flesh and dwelt among us." (John 1: 1, 14) You see, God Himself, came to us... came to live in our midst. He took a body... was born as a baby... His name is Jesus. He came to show us what God is like and to provide a way for us to have a relationship with Almighty God. The apostle John also writes of Jesus: "... to all who received Him, to those who believed in His name, He gave the right to become children of God – children born not of natural descent, nor of human decision or a husband's will, but born of God." (John 1: 12 – 13) If you have not yet received Jesus or believed in His name, I encourage you... do it! In Jesus, you'll be a child of God. And if you have made Jesus your Savior, celebrate Christmas like the child of God you are.

Read: John 14: 6 - 14

Lord Jesus, my best understanding of what God is like is when I take a long look at you. You are one and the same with God the Father. What a mystery! What an explanation of Christmas!

Manger Scene

᭶

A little girl carefully made a manger scene in a shoebox as an art project in school. She laid the box over on its side so as to give her makeshift scene a roof, a back and two sides. The day school was out for the Christmas holidays, she took her manger scene home and proudly placed it at the foot of the family tree. Then she anxiously awaited her father's arrival from work to show him her masterpiece. When her Dad arrived, he was immediately led into the living room and told to look at the manger. Almost with a preoccupied tone, he said, "Oh yes, I see it's very nice." His little girl said, "Daddy, you can't really see it standing up. If you want to see Jesus in the manger, you have to get down on your knees!" That is a parable, to say the least. There are many ways to celebrate during the holidays, but if you want to celebrate Jesus you must fasten your eyes on Him and bend the knees of your heart.

Read: Luke 2: 25 - 32

Lord Jesus, even the humble surroundings of your birth could not overshadow the worship and adoration which belongs to you. I pray that the distractions of Christmas will not divert me from offering praise and thanksgiving for my Savior.

Encouragement is one of those things today's Christian can say is "just what I need" for Christmas. If Christmas means anything, it means some things are definite! It verifies that God cares. It does matter to Him that man is in need of being re-created. And whatever man may do to himself through unbelief or ignorance, God is unalterably committed to giving him newness of life. If Christmas means anything else, it assures us that God believes man is worthwhile. God has gone to both extremes and details to redeem our sinful but valuable world. Furthermore, Christmas means that God keeps His Word. He promised for Old Testament centuries that He would send a Savior. That Savior came and God's greatest promise was kept. When He speaks of His love now, His presence now, and His comfort now, we cannot question His integrity for He is eternally honest. Christmas is a timely gift of the encouragement it signifies. We rejoice over all that Christmas is to the "household of faith"...especially celebrating the encouragement it brings.

Read: Isaiah 9: 1 - 7

Lord Jesus, I celebrate you at Christmas, but even more specifically, I celebrate the grace of God which designed your coming before the foundation of the world.

Hope Of The Centuries

❦

Though a complete understanding of His Messianic purpose was not grasped by the world of Jesus' day, that world waited hungrily for His entry into human affairs. And He came. If the first Christmas means anything, it means mankind's expectations were, or could be, fulfilled. Doubtless, this Christmas could mean more to us if we possessed some of the expectancy, which belonged to the first Christmas. We believe in Christ. We accept the validity of His promises. Hence we should be looking for His arrival... His second advent. Have we so lost touch with the truth of His second coming that we think it peculiar to look for Him this Christmas? Would an arrival on His part be an interruption in our Christmas plans? The wonder and glory of the first Christmas was that Deity put on mortality and equally as glorious will be His immanent return. If Christmas means anything, let it be a splendorous reminder that the Christ of Divine Intervention in the first century will be the needed Divine Intervention when He returns. The Christ of Christmas then, remains the hope of all centuries.

Read: Titus 2: 11 – 15

Lord Jesus, thank you for your promised second coming. The anticipation of your return just makes Christmas all the more meaningful. You cared for us enough to come as our Savior and you care enough to come again as our King.

✣

I am glad God thought of Christmas!   ...Not that annual rehearsal of madness with which we all are too familiar, but God's Christmas. There is such peace, real peace, in God's Christmas, far more than gifts and giving, more than hymns and holly. It is Heaven's message that God cares for every sin-stricken, heart lonely man and woman the world around. It tells that He cared enough to come to Bethlehem while stars and shepherds stood watch... enough to work in a carpenter's shop so busy men might see God with a hammer and saw. Then His care walked sandal-shod, lifting, healing and helping humanity back to hope and Heaven. His care caused "Thy will be done" to be said for us in Gethsemane... His care bled into Calvary a love so deep and pure, only the Father's heart could comprehend its measure. All this and more... for there was the Resurrection! I am glad God thought of Christmas! We need it desperately. Men need to see Christ's star and believe the message of the miracle in a manger. That kind of Christmas is a difference maker!

Read: Luke 2: 21 - 38

I praise you, Heavenly Father, for your plan to send Jesus to this world even before it existed. That thought makes me realize what an earth shaking, eternity making event Christmas is! Thank you again for God's Christmas.

The Wrappings

❦

Following the festivities at our house on Christmas Day, it became important to quickly gather up all the discarded wrapping paper, boxes and ribbons to be stowed in plastic trash bags and put street-side for the following day's garbage pickup. There is a real study to be found in that pile of trash bags in front of our house. Call it the "lesson of the wrappings", if you will. Boxes, packages, paper and ribbon take up more space than the gifts they contain, but when all is said and done, it's the boxes, packages, paper and ribbons which wind up in trash bags waiting for the garbage truck. It's the unwrapped gift which remains and matters most. The lesson of it all is obvious. We would do well to spend less time trying to make what we are and what we do for the Lord to look better than it is. When God gets through unwrapping all our offerings and efforts, guess what remains? Not the wrappings, but the sacrifice, loyalty and obedience are what make Him know we love Him deeply and dearly. Let's major on giving the Lord gifts, not wrappings.

Read: Matthew 2: 1 – 12

Lord, if I understand properly, the Wise men brought expensive gifts to the Christ Child. But their gifts also represented time, worship, thoughtfulness and care. That's what I want my life to be, a genuine offering to the Lord Jesus.

In order for Christmas to take on its deepest meaning we must certainly consider the mystery of Christmas. The astounding mystery of Christmas is that the chasm between heaven and earth was bridged by the coming of Jesus Christ – God with us. Isaiah wrote, "For my thoughts are not your thoughts, neither are your ways my ways, saith Jehovah. For as the heavens are higher than the earth are my thoughts than your thoughts." This prophetic statement addresses itself to our inability to explain how this marvel took place, when the sovereign Son of God became a Jewish baby. Why God chose this mysterious injection of Himself into human affairs is not so difficult to ascertain. He completely identified Himself with humanity, experienced life as mortals know it, and was victor over those mortal enemies, sin and death. You and I then, have a Savior. We trust in one who came "down" to help us who were helpless. He does not require that we "grapple" for heaven. He came to us. This is the mystery of Christmas, our source of amazement and rightful joy!

Read: I Timothy 3: 14 – 16

During the Christmas season, Lord, it has been a joy to hear the singing of familiar carols. It has been an encouragement to again be reminded that you so loved us, Jesus came to us. But the mystery of Christmas continues to take my breath away!

Packing The Manger

❧

When you took down Christmas decorations and packed away the manger scene, I hope you didn't pack Jesus away as well. True.... He came at a certain time in history, but the Bible says Jesus was with God in the beginning and was sent before the world was even created. Today, Jesus still lives. God's Word says, "There is His incomparable great power for us who believe. That power is like the working of His mighty strength, which He exerted in Christ when He raise Him from the dead and seated Him at his right hand in the heavenly realms." (Eph, 1: 19 – 20) Then too, Jesus has sent His Holy Spirit to live, today, in every twice-born child of God. And the future...is He a part of that too? Indeed His is! The Bible emphatically teaches Jesus will come to earth again. As you celebrate the first coming of Christ, remember He lives today within the lives of all who receive Him as Savior. And, with excitement remember that same Jesus is coming back.

Read: John 14: 1 – 6

Until you return, Lord, your kingdom is within the hearts of Believers. I need to be as excited about your reign in that kingdom as the one to come when you return. Remind me, Lord Jesus, the kingdom is wherever the king is.

Little children pretentiously "playing house" can no more truly nurture a growing family than juvenile=church-men, vainly playing the part of The Bride, can foster a thriving spiritual family. It is Christ who performs the act of redemption, and we at our consecrated best, cannot save. Nevertheless, it has pleased God to use the tongues and lives of men to urge other men to Christ who WILL save. "Infantile" voices occasionally uttering pious words mingled with pouting, tattling and gossip, betray an immaturity undeserving of an audience with the spiritually unborn! While many REFUSE to believe, perhaps others CANNOT believe for they cannot believe in us who do believe. Hardly can we over exaggerate the utter necessity of regenerate eyes focusing upon "the stature of the fullness of Christ", until we abandon our "cribs" in pursuit of Christ-likeness, the Bridegroom must patiently succor His Child-bride, while His heart breaks for those yet unborn in the Faith! May God help us to mature and may we allow Him to do it.

Read: Colossians 1: 3 – 12

Christmas reminds me, Lord Jesus, that you were born so that we might be reborn. And we are reborn to show others how they may be reborn and to nurture them in the Faith. Forgive my immaturity and help me settle for nothing short of the stature of the fullness of Christ.

Faithful

One of the moving stories to come out of the Korean War in the 1950's involved a young sergeant in the battle of Heartbreak Hill. When the shooting was over, a rescue team entered the area to assist the wounded. The sergeant was found dead, but the circumstances of his death were quite unusual. With his hands having been paralyzed, he clenched between his teeth the two ends of a communication line which had been broken. In his death, he directed his energies toward the needs of others by keeping the messages going through. To use an expression of the Bible, the sergeant was "faithful unto death". In the same but greater way, Jesus Christ was faithful to us. He directed His efforts, while He died on the cross to get this message across to us: "God - 14did not send His Son into the world to condemn the world but that the world through Him might be saved." (John 3:17)

Read: I John 3: 7 – 14

Lord Jesus, I best learn faithfulness from studying your commitment to us. The thought is overwhelming, you love us even while we are yet sinners, and you came to this world for the express purpose of dealing with the consequences of our sin. Your faithfulness to me is unquestionable, but I want to prove my faithfulness to you.

Satisfying Your Appetite

It has been reported that two college students on the west coast ate dog food for a couple of weeks to save money. After they had saved their money for a while, they took their savings to a restaurant and bought a full-scale steak dinner with all the trimmings. I suppose their experience bears out the truth that once you have tasted the good life, it is difficult to be satisfied with less. When God conceived us, He placed in us a spiritual image like His own. So we were made for fellowship with God. Nothing less than a right relationship with the Lord, will satisfy the natural hungers of our inner nature. We may try to satisfy our spiritual hungers with substitutes, but nothing less than the life Christ can supply will ever fulfill that appetite. To receive Jesus as Savior is only the beginning of the life he has to give and multiples to the extent we allow Him to live out His life in us.

Read: John 10: 7 – 10

Dear Lord, increase my hunger and thirst for the life you have in mind for me. Create a holy unrest in me when I settle for less than the abundant life you have promised.